CHANGING CONCEPTS IN PSYCHOANALYSIS

CHANGING CONCEPTS IN PSYCHOANALYSIS

Edited by

SHEILA KLEBANOW, M.D.
New York Medical College

With a Foreword by
SILVANO ARIETI, M.D.
for Society of Medical Psychoanalysts
New York

GARDNER PRESS, INC.
New York

Library of Congress Cataloging in Publication Data
Main entry under title:

Changing concepts in psychoanalysis.

Bibliography: p.
Includes index.
1. Psychoanalysis. I. Klebanow, Sheila. [DNLM:
1. Psychoanalysis—Trends. 2. Women—Psychology.
WM 460 C456]
RC504.C47   616.89'17   81–1542
ISBN 0–89876–008–9   AACR2

Gardner Press, Inc.
19 Union Square West
New York 10003

Printed in the United States of America

CONTENTS

FOREWORD

At a time when so many people are directed to believe that psychoanalysis has remained static in the original positions and that the best way to search and attain psychiatric progress is by focusing exclusively on biological research, the present book is a very useful, cogent and persuasive antidote. This volume, which Dr. Sheila Klebanow has edited with so much care and fine discrimination, will reaffirm that psychoanalysis is continuing its march toward a deeper understanding of human nature and human growth, of the intricacy of the human conflict and predicament, and toward more rapid and more effective therapeutic procedures.

This book deals with various subjects, but it has a hidden theme: the changes which have occurred and are still occurring in psychoanalysis. The various chapters enlarge the reader's horizons in many directions. Some are general in character. For instance, Irving Beiber gives an accurate account of how much psychoanalysis has changed in the last four decades, during which time he himself has been responsible for some of these important changes. Leopold Bellak once more discloses his ability to synthesize his encyclopedic erudition by stressing the need for new conceptualizations, and Earl Witenberg singles out what is myth and what is reality in psychoanalytic practice. Whole parts of the book are devoted to areas where outstanding new developments have recently taken place: the borderline patient, attachment and detachment in early childhood and, especially, various aspects of psychology of women, discussed both from a theoretical and a practical point of view.

Approximately two-thirds of the chapters are written by the members of the faculty of the Psychoanalytic Division of New York Medical College and reveal the pluralistic approach of that school. The other third consists of valuable articles by people trained according to different schools of thought.

For most professionals, it has become increasingly difficult to keep track of worthwhile contributions not ordinarily or not quickly enough presented in the psychoanalytic mainstream. The conscientious clinician who does not want to be caught by surprise by what has escaped his reach, the theoretician who seeks new dimensions and directions, the therapist who wishes to be up to date with the latest progress in the established forms of psychoanalytic therapy, will find in this book a medium which, to a considerable extent, will fulfill these requirements.

SILVANO ARIETI, M.D.
New York

PREFACE

In 1978, the Society of Medical Psychoanalysts celebrated its 30th anniversary by holding a symposium on changing concepts in psychoanalysis. This volume is a compilation of the papers that were presented. In organizing the program, we chose to examine the many contributions that psychoanalysis as therapy has to make in an increasingly complicated world.

Several themes were developed and explored. Psychoanalysis historically has been defined in terms of technique. As psychoanalytic treatment has evolved to encompass many patients who do not fit into the category of those who develop a classical transference neurosis, a gap has emerged. An endeavor has been made in this volume to bridge the gap between standard definitions of technique and of process. Thus many of the contributions underscore the evolution of psychoanalytic hypotheses by tracing them from Freud to current amplifications, modifications, and revisions. The chapters focus upon the unique therapeutic value of psychoanalytic techniques as they are devoted to the aims of developmental change and the alleviation of neurotic suffering.

Five major topics were selected for exploration: psychoanalysis as therapy: myth and reality; evolving theories and clinical applications; psychoanalysis of the borderline patient; childhood; and women.

In Part One, Leopold Bellak and Earl G. Witenberg examine myth and reality in psychoanalysis as therapy. Bellak, in a pithy and incisive chapter, views the therapeutic process as one of learning, unlearning, and relearning. He exposes the myth that there is only one psychoanalytic technique and that this technique can be delimited clearly from psychotherapy.

Witenberg distinguishes between mythical and actual therapeutic goals. Although myths and beliefs have always existed in practice, certain of them are antitherapeutic because they interfere with an individual's efforts to find his or her unique psyche beyond biological, socio-cultural, and interpersonal referents. Witenberg stresses the importance of analysts' knowing when they are uncertain and of their ability to communicate this to patients, so as to enable their patients to know what is knowable and what is unknowable.

xi

Irving Bieber, Paul R. Dince, and Joseph Barnett offer contributions on evolving theories and clinical applications. Bieber gives a personal overview of his clinical and theoretical position over a 40-year period. He sees transference as involving the irrational components of replicated reactions rather than the totality of a patient's psychopathology. In a position similar to that of Bellak, Bieber does not distinguish between psychoanalysis and psychoanalytically oriented psychotherapy. He regards as psychoanalysis any therapy that is oriented toward delineating neurotic fears and irrational beliefs about injury and that explores both the genesis of such beliefs and the defenses relating to the fears, so as to resolve them.

Dince, in a seminal chapter, underscores that borderline pathology and treatment cannot be understood by means of traditional psychoanalytic concepts, including the assumption that only through analysis and resolution of the regressive transference neurosis via interpretation can genuine characterological and structural changes be made. Work with borderline patients emphasizes the crucial role of damage in object relations sustained in the earliest years. During treatment, progression through the developmental stages takes place within the context of a dyadic, analytic relationship that is both real and transferential. Given the experience with the borderline patient, a positive therapeutic outcome results not from the working through of a regressive transference neurosis but from the interpretation within the context of that crucial object relationship evolved by patient and analyst.

Barnett introduces a cognitive approach. He views character as a behavioral and cognitive reflection of the organization of experience in a person's life. The task of analysis is the task of character analysis. The central task of psychoanalytic therapy is cognitive repair—that is, the correction of the distortions and imbalances of the person's systems of knowing and meaning and the repair of those dysfunctional or nonfunctioning mental processes and operations that prevent integration of meaning with experience and action.

Contributions by Michael H. Stone, Sherman Feinstein, and Frank Crewdson on the borderline patient appear in Part Three. In a major chapter, Stone postulates that for otherwise similar patients at the psychotic or borderline level, the more nearly the symptom picture reflects affective disorders, the better the prognosis. The more the symptom picture inclines toward "pure" schizophrenia, the worse the prognosis, at least in regard to the likelihood of benefit from psychotherapy. The most favorable therapeutic outcomes would be gained in patients who are predominantly depressive rather than manic or schizophrenic, who are borderline rather than psychotic in psychostructural level, and who are depressive rather than cyclothymic or schizoid. Characterologically, obsessive, hysteric, and infantile patients fare better than do antisocial or severely narcissistic patients.

Feinstein makes an analogy between the study of adolescent process and that of borderline states. Both studies have experienced delayed growth and development on account of ambivalence about giving up old and comfortable conceptualizations. He believes that careful use of developmental and structural concepts can clarify whether an adolescent is moving in a normal, albeit stormy, pathway through adolescence or is at a neurotic, schizophrenic, or borderline state.

Crewdson delineates transformations of internal object fantasies during the psychoanalysis of a borderline patient. He demonstrates structural changes that are possible within the analytic process by tracing the transformation of fantasied object relations from the patient's actual relationships to outside figures and then as expressed in the transference.

David E. Schecter and Clarice J. Kestenbaum have contributed to the section on childhood. In his study of attachment and detachment, Schecter notes that deficits in ego and in interpersonal development stem largely from an early failure to achieve constancy of relationship. It is a lifelong developmental task to retain and to modify constancy amid the vicissitudes of separation-individuation and of ambivalent feelings. He describes the intrapsychic detachment defense as becoming available to the child during the separation-individuation phases in childhood and in later stages. In his work with adults, Schecter, like Dince and Crewdson, focuses on the need to build a stable constancy of relatedness with the analyst and on the importance of the real as well as transferential relationship of the analyst to the patient.

Kestenbaum addresses herself to the issues of those factors that produce symptom removal and structural change in child analysis and to the nature of the therapeutic relationship that promotes this change. She stresses the importance of the real and the transferential relationship of the analyst to the child in the generating of structural change.

Part Five focuses on women and contains chapters by Marvin Drellich, Jean Miller and her co-workers, Doreen E. Schecter, and Esther Greenbaum.

Drellich reminds us that revision of psychoanalytic theories of feminine psychology is an ongoing process. He describes two dynamically different versions of the female castration complex. The feminine component is a response to a perceived or real threat to the sexual organs in the context of normal development in which the little girl strives to be effectively feminine. The phallic component, or penis envy, is always a dependent variable related to specific developmental pathology. Drellich underscores the importance of the role of both father and mother for both normal and pathological feminine development.

Miller et al. examine aggression in women. They postulate that early in life women, for a variety of psychocultural factors, become convinced that their own healthy, self-directed, and self-generated aggression is intolerable. Since aggression poses a threat to the woman's self-esteem, it is suppressed or can be used only in the service of others rather than in the service of one's self.

Both Schecter and Greenbaum address the issues of masochism and fear of success in women. Schecter focuses on masochism as a pathological defense mechanism that stems from the fear of success and ultimately to the fear of retaliation and abandonment by the pre-Oedipal mother. The wish to succeed becomes unconsciously equated with guilt over the intended, murderous aggression toward the mother deriving from the rapprochment crisis of the separation-individuation phase and thus is renounced.

Greenbaum also underscores the stage of separation-individuation as contributing to the establishment of autonomy necessary in the pursuit of success but notes that she has seen patients unable to attain success on account of Oedipal as well as pre-Oedipal conflicts and societal interdictions. The therapy of women with success phobias often is facilitated by identification with the female analyst, who serves as a model of a successful, autonomous woman.

Finally, I wish to express my appreciation for the collaboration and support of the many colleagues and friends who assisted in organizing the symposium and this book. Drs. Edward T. Adelson, Irving Bieber, Gloria Clare, Paul R. Dince, Esther Greenbaum, and Henry Greenbaum served with me on the program committee and all provided invaluable input. Dr. Martin Wayne together with his wife, Loretta Wayne, M.S.W. ably and unstintingly handled the arrangements. Dr. John P. Briggs graciously acted as consultant on public information. My special thanks go to Mrs. Dorothy Harte, secretary to the Society of Medical Psychoanalysts, and to my personal secretary, Mrs. Ella Pinsker, both of whom worked unsparingly and good-humoredly on their myriad tasks.

SHEILA KLEBANOW, M.D.

CONTRIBUTORS

Joseph Barnett, M.D., Faculty, Division of Psychoanalytic Training, New York Medical College; Training and Supervising Analyst, William Alanson White Institute; and Training and Supervising Analyst, Postdoctoral Program in Psychoanalysis and Psychotherapy, New York University, New York, New York

Leopold Bellak, M.D., Clinical Professor of Psychiatry, Albert Einstein College of Medicine, Bronx, New York; and Clinical Professor of Psychology, Postdoctoral Program in Psychotherapy, New York University, New York, New York

Irving Bieber, M.D., Faculty, Division of Psychoanalytic Training, and Clinical Professor of Psychiatry, New York Medical College, New York, New York

Frank Crewdson, M.D., Training and Supervising Analyst, Division of Psychoanalytic Training, New York Medical College, New York, New York

Paul R. Dince, M.D., Faculty, Division of Psychoanalytic Training, and Clinical Associate Professor of Psychiatry, New York Medical College, New York, New York

Marvin G. Drellich, M.D., Faculty, Division of Psychoanalytic Training and Associate Clinical Professor of Psychiatry, New York Medical College, New York, New York

Sherman C. Feinstein, M.D., Director, Child Psychiatry Research, Michael Reese Hospital and Medical Center Chicago, Illinois; and Clinical Professor of Child Psychiatry, Pritzker School of Medicine, University of Chicago

Esther Greenbaum, M.D., Faculty, Division of Psychoanalytic Training, and Assistant Clinical Professor of Psychiatry, New York Medical College, New York New York; and Associate Clinical Professor of Psychiatry, New York University School of Medicine, New York, New York

Clarice J. Kestenbaum, M.D., Director, Division of Child and Adolescent Psychiatry, St. Luke's–Roosevelt Hospital Center, New York, New York; and Associate Clinical Professor of Psychiatry, Columbia University, New York, New York

Sheila Klebanow, M.D., Faculty, Division of Psychoanalytic Training and Assistant Clinical Professor of Psychiatry, New York Medical College, New York, New York

Jean Baker Miller, M.D., Associate Clinical Professor of Psychiatry, Boston University School of Medicine, Boston, Massachusetts

Carol C. Nadelson, M.D., Associate Professor of Psychiatry, Harvard Medical School, Boston, Massachusetts

Malkah T. Notman, M.D., Associate Clinical Professor of Psychiatry, Harvard Medical School, Boston, Massachusetts

David E. Schecter, M.D., Training and Supervision Analyst, William Alanson White Institute, New York, New York; and Associate Clinical Professor of Psychiatry, Albert Einstein College of Medicine, Bronx, New York

Doreen E. Schecter, M.D., Assistant Clinical Professor of Psychiatry, Albert Einstein College of Medicine, Bronx, New York

Michael H. Stone, M.D., Associate Clinical Professor of Psychiatry, Department of Psychiatry, Westchester Division, Cornell University Medical College, White Plains, New York

Earl G. Witenberg, M.D., Director, William Alanson White Institute of Psychiatry, Psychoanalysis and Psychology, New York, New York; and Associate Clinical Professor of Psychiatry, Albert Einstein College of Medicine, Bronx, New York

Joan Zilbach, M.D., Associate Clinical Professor of Psychiatry, Tufts Medical School, Boston, Massachusetts

Part One

PSYCHOANALYSIS AS THERAPY: MYTH AND REALITY

1

PSYCHOANALYSIS AS THERAPY: THE NEED FOR NEW CONCEPTUALIZATIONS

Leopold Bellak, M.D.
*Albert Einstein College of Medicine, New York, and
New York University*

One of the major myths regarding the practice of psychoanalysis is that one should consider clinical psychoanalysis as anything other than a form of therapy, the task of which is to attain optimal results in the shortest possible time with the largest variety of people and the broadest range of problems. That postulate should hardly sound revolutionary or novel, and yet to many it will. There does not appear to be much analytic literature that addresses itself precisely to this problem and how to attain these goals, especially in the shortest possible time, nor does there seem to have been any preoccupation with making analysis shorter since Ferenczi and Stekel, unless it were Alexander.

The failure to address analysis as a process from which one wants the best results in the shortest possible time for the broadest range of people and problems has cost psychoanalysis dearly, both in practice and in theory. This has been the case in theory because such an attempt would have had to have led to the sharpening of concepts and to more intensive investigations of the therapeutic process than have been done, and in practice, because psychoanalysis has lost much support from the public. This failure has its roots in some covert myth of various nature as well as in the fear of offending dogma and the fear of being considered a reductionist. One root of this problem lies in the notion that because the unconscious is timeless in the sense of not sequencing, the analytic attitude should be passively expectant, almost with a sense of timelessness. This unrealistic attitude can be unkindly equated with "it will all come out in the wash in due time."

THE MYTH OF PASSIVITY

A part of this particular attitude was the misunderstanding of the process of free association. Most of the time the process of communication in psychoanalysis involves neither associations nor freedom. (1). It has been suggested that the well-working analytic patient usually has a clear preconscious mental set or framework about what should be discussed. This mental set is determined by what ails him and by the rules and silent expectations operant in the analytic situation. The myth that one need not keep a therapeutic goal in mind and attempt to reach it as soon as possible was embedded further in the myth of the passive analyst as a mirror or as a tabula rasa. This was originally based on a lack of awareness of the subtlety of the two-way street in the dyadic relationship. Passivity as the only attitude is certainly a harmful myth. It is likely to be more responsible than any other single factor for many therapeutic failures or "stalemates," as Glover (2) called them, or interruptions. Many people have to learn a long time before they can tolerate a relatively silent analyst. They need feedback, approval, and guidance until they either are better off or have learned the process. Very often it is simply poor psychoanalytic technique to be too silent and passive and to permit resistance to interfere and is, ultimately, a failure to live up to the therapeutic alliance on the analyst's part.

This kind of technique of passivity and rare communication was an inheritance of psychoanalysis as a method of treatment with only a very narrow scope in its so-called classical technique. Psychoanalysis dealt only with the classical neurosis of a socioeconomically and geographically stable group of people. As many have remarked, this was more a matter of insisting that the patient fit the therapy rather than ensuring that the therapy be made suitable for the patient. As was once said of a certain doctor: "He is a doctor for the healthy. God help the sick."

THE WIDENED SCOPE OF PSYCHOANALYSIS

Awareness of this particular problem led at the Arden House Conference to the reluctant admission of parameters in treatment and to what since has been called the "widened scope of psychoanalysis," namely, that the technique should adapt itself to the patient and to his or her particular problems.[3,4] Reality, in that instance, forced a change in dogma, if not in myth. This viewpoint, however, came under scrutiny again, by Anna Freud and Leo Rangell, at the International Psychoanalytic Congress in London in 1975, in response to Andre Green's proposal for extensive modification of analytic technique.[5,6] It was Anna Freud's and Leo

Rangell's belief that analysis might best stick to what it can do best, namely, to deal with the classical neurosis and not to expect that analytic understanding be matched by analytic effectiveness. It is an understandable viewpoint, but one that cannot be shared by some analysts. The therapeutic process is one of learning, unlearning, and relearning. The different disturbances simply may need different learning, unlearning, and relearning methods, and that is a matter of searching and researching rather than of accepting limitations.

One of the most damaging myths is that there is only one psychoanalytic technique and that its rigid observance is the mark of a good analyst. There are almost as many psychoanalytic techniques as there are personal styles, but many analysts have some preconscious image of how this or that great ancient analyst would behave under certain circumstances, and they feel guilty if they "deviate," for instance, by being more active than merely offering an occasional interpretation. Nobody has stated it more eloquently than Leo Stone in his classical book, *The Psychoanalytic Situation*—that humanity and responsiveness are more important than technical correctness. The idea that there is only one psychoanalytic technique and that it can clearly be delimited from psychotherapy came most obviously to grief in the repeated failure of many panels and round tables at the American Psychoanalytic Association meetings and of others who tried to define the difference between psychoanalysis and psychoanalytic psychotherapy.

In reality, it makes sense to see relatively "pure" psychoanalysis as only one point on a continuum of dynamic psychotherapies. The relative degree of technical neutrality is probably the most decisive criterion for measuring the "purity" of the psychoanalytic process; that is, the more technical neutrality analysts can maintain, the closer they are to the model of a classical psychoanalysis, and the less technical neutrality, the further away they are. The optimal technical neutrality is the greatest technical neutrality that a particular patient at a particular time can utilize. This definition is as consistent with scientific methodology as it is with clinical pragmatism.

PSYCHOANALYSIS AS THERAPY

It hardly needs mentioning anymore that even technical neutrality in its extreme hardly permits the myth of the absence of values and value judgments in psychoanalysis-as-therapy. The whole concept of mental health involves a value judgment—different people and different concepts of it—and such concepts as the attainment of genitality and "object constancy" also involve value judgments. In turn, the changing values of society have profoundly affected all aspects of psychoanalytic practice, including the types of patients, the types of disorders, and the types of superegos. One of the realities that psychoanalysis-as-therapy has to deal with is the fact of social changes in the population. One of the most vexing of these, incidentally, is the great mobility of the population that comes to analysis. The chance of having a corporate executive in treatment for four years is small, simply because the chance of his being moved to another position in another state or country is great.

Nothing is as realistic or as practical as a good theory. Therefore, psychoanalysis as therapy must be closely predicated upon psychoanalysis as a theory of personality and as a theory of psychopathology. There are variations in the theory—for instance, object relations viewpoints, structural viewpoints, and others and combinations thereof. All that is necessary is that one's theory of therapy be clearly conceptually related to whatever model of a theory of personality and a theory of psychopathology one subscribes to for use with a given patient. Therapy without a close relationship to theory can hardly be considered a rational process. Of all the analytic propositions, continuity—namely between childhood and adulthood, between normality and pathology, and between waking and dreaming—is the most basic. Psychoanalytic treatment must be based on the optimal understanding of these continuities.

Personality is a gestalt, or a configuration of the biological matrix and learning. Therapy, then, consists of the optimal techniques of learning, unlearning, and relearning toward an optimal mode of adaptation. As Strupp has recently suggested, there are at least three aspects of a desirable therapeutic attainment to be kept in mind: the patient's own feelings about how he or she is doing, the criteria of our society, and the criteria of our theory.[7] Certain quick-help fads, for instance, stress mostly "Do your own thing," with little regard for social interaction. This sort of gives permission for narcissism and acting out or for simple direct gratifications. As another example, a hypomanic person may feel perfectly well subjectively but not appear so in the eyes of society. Some repressive therapies might make a hallucinated and deluded person socially acceptable but far from happy. "Flight into health" might satisfy both the patient's and society's criteria, but not those of our theoretical postulates. In this sense, psychoanalysis is the most demanding of all therapies. Most nonanalytic psychotherapies do not have enough of an underpinning in the form of a theory of personality or a theory of psychopathology to have any internal criteria that must be met.[8]

The learning process in psychoanalysis takes place in the transference and by insight, identification-introjection, and conditioning, which is what takes place in "working through." Working through is the applying of previously learned common denominators to new situations in and out of the analysis and learning by trial and error gradually. One also learns in analysis by direct instruction and by the interaction with the real person of the analyst. This gives a clear basis for the importance of who an analyst is—that is, that he or she not be just a technician. The realistic task of the psychoanalyst is to provide for optimal and fastest learning by whatever parameter may be necessary to achieve it, as long as one never uses more parameters and variations in technique than are absolutely necessary and that can be appropriately conceptualized. Again, the optimal degree of analytic neutrality is the maximum of neutrality that is useful and tolerable in a given patient at a given time.

Among the parameters that are especially useful are conjoint interviews, for instance, with spouses; episodic use of drugs, even in anxiety neurosis; and group psychotherapy combined with individual psychoanalysis. Although the introduction of these and other factors into an analysis needs to be analyzed, they not only are consistent with a good analysis but are often essential to attaining the optimal results. One of the dangerous myths is that the dyadic relationship is either necessary or optimal for all therapeutic results. Experience with psychoanalysis moves one closer to the position that the dyadic relationship of the analytic situation is rarely enough to reproduce optimal results in the shortest possible time. Similarly, drug therapy is found to have a definite place in the armamentarium. An excess of anxiety may indeed inhibit progress in the form of an approach avoidance, which can be decreased by tranquilizing drugs, if they are used judiciously and not in such a way that they interfere with motivation.[9] To the contrary, they can increase motivation by decreasing paralyzing anxiety.

THE ANALYST'S TASK

Comprehensively, the task of the analyst is to create optimal conditions for fastest learning in every way possible. For that purpose, a careful, extensive history should be done, as well as a careful assessment such as was discussed in an article on ego function assessment of analyzability.[10] To have the analytic process proceed optimally, one should be clearly aware of the assets and the liabilities of the patient and of potential dangers, such as acting out, psychotic transference, liability for panic, depersonalization, or excessive dissociation and insufficient synthetic function to utilize the analytic process.

Psychoanalysts have a difficult and unique task to perform, especially if they want to be as economical and as efficient as possible. An analysis can and needs to be a very orderly process. Surgeons need to make very careful diagnoses and to create conditions that will enable patients to survive their operations and to benefit from them. This may include preoperative blood transfusions or increased insulin for some patients and a variety of other measures for other patients. In our field, this may mean exploring the life situation and its suitability for analysis or spending some preparatory time in helping patients to establish the sort of life situation that will enable them to utilize analysis. This may involve having the patient see one person as a therapist who helps him or her with enabling conditions, such as guidance and support, while seeing another one for the analytic process, either consecutively or concomitantly, as the situation may be.

Surgeons must also do a good deal of planning, and this must include some clear-cut notions of the specific area of intervention, the method of intervention,[11] and the sequence of areas of intervention, based on a solid knowledge of anatomy, physiology, and pathology. When patients are on the table, surgeons have to exercise judgment, a judgment that they are entitled to use because the patients have selected them for their competence to make decisions as they are necessary. This means that in their interventions, surgeons follow a fairly well-defined, generally acceptable technique, while being ready to engage in such variations as seem to be indicated by specific situations.

The psychoanalytic process must be very much like surgical intervention. An extensive anamnesis is essential before one starts therapy. This should cover not only personal life history but also family history, as well as extensive medical history. Very often, the diagnosis should be arrived at with the help of such an auxiliary measure as psychological testing, both of a psychodynamic and a neuropsychological nature.

Before beginning the analytic operation, an analyst should also formulate some clear-cut plans and preferably write them down. These should include plans of *area* of intervention, *method* of intervention, and *sequence* of area and method of intervention. The analyst also should have some reasonable notion of the likely therapeutic goal, given the patient's pathology and life situation. To "analyze away" without regard to the life situation too often results in a situation analogous to what the Viennese called "operation successful, patient dead," or to the already mentioned term of Glover, namely "therapeutic stalemate."

Pragmatic Considerations

One of the misconceptions of the role of the analyst has been that psychoanalysis can be a research tool. Although psychoanalysis certainly can and must be a research tool, and although the psychoanalytic theories of personality, psychopathology, and therapy need a great deal more controlled research, the individual therapy of a patient is not a research project but an applied science technique with a therapeutic contract to do all possible as effectively as possible to help the patient. Pragmatic considerations must play a main role. One of the problems of the analytic technique, of course, is that as a dyadic process, it is likely to *permit* individual distortion, or lack of distance, by the analyst as well as by the patient.

Therefore, it is advocated that psychoanalysts review their patients at stated intervals with at least one colleague, and, among other things, keep the efficiency of the process very much in focus at such reviews. Small groups in psychoanalytic institutes and societies could do much better in serving for review and in sharing daily clinical experiences than in serving primarily for the reading of rather stale papers. It is a regrettable part of mythology that occasional sound taping, or even videotaping, is considered by some to be an unanalyzable parameter. Such a technique permits much closer scrutiny of the process and the patient by a colleague, with the written and explicit permission of the patient, of course, in every instance.

It may be possible to guide the analytic process by constantly reviewing what the relationship of the communication is to what ails the patient and to what caused the maladaptation and to relate one's interpretations back to relevant areas. This may indeed help shorten the therapy. It is a simple matter of keeping an eye on the analytic ball. Also, if a patient engages extensively in an "external travelogue"—namely, spending much of this time giving an account of actual events in his or her life—it is important to interpret this probably as a defense and a form of resistance and to help the patient to learn to engage in an optimal mixture of an account of real events just enough to be a platform for the "internal travelogue," or the thoughts, feelings, and conflicts that accompanied the real events. In that case, we have arranged for optimal communication that permits the finding of common denominators between the past and the present and the transference for interpretations and restructuring.

There are many such devices essential for maintaining the therapeutic process as a carefully modulated, and indeed, controlled, interaction. It is important that the analyst regulate anxiety and motivation generally and that he or she have a nearly standard set of techniques for dealing with various special problems and emergencies that might come up in the course of analysis. There is the increasing signal awareness for those patients who are likely to act out, and there is prediction in order to avoid the actual event and six or seven other points for acting out alone. There is cathartic interpretation to relieve disorganizing panics. "Mediate interpretation" can be used if a direct interpretation might be too unsettling—for instance, permitting oneself such a statement as "Well, if this would happen to somebody else, they would feel angry" in response to a patient who has to deny his anger and where it might be dangerous to interpret it directly. One might even, to take some more onus off, say, "In such a case, I would feel angry." These are subtleties of technique, however, which is the subject of another book.

A final comment on the many problems of psychoanalysis as therapy and on its myths and realities is that one should know what the limits of reversibility are. It is better to stop at what seems the optimal point attainable, at least at that particular time, with the proviso that one will start treatment again at some future point when intervening learning might have taken place continuously or the life situation might have changed to allow further changing rather than to persist in the myth that the longest analysis is the best analysis. There is a good deal to be said quite to the contrary, including substituting it for real relationships, undue passivity, excessive transference, and possibly excessive dissociation or compulsive analyzing as a substitute for other symptoms. As in many other endeavors, it is only realistic to know one's own and one's patients' limitations.

REFERENCES

1. Bellak, Leopold, "Free Association: Conceptual and Clinical Aspects," *International Journal of Psychoanalysis*, 42:9–20, 1961.

2. Glover, Edward, *The Technique of Psychoanalysis*, International Universities Press, Inc., New York, 1955.

3. Stone, Leo, "The Widening Scope of Indications for Psychoanalysis," *Journal of American Psychoanalytic Association*, Vol. 2, No.4:567–594, 1954.

4. Freud, Anna, "The Widening Scope of Indications for Psychoanalysis: Discussion," *Journal of American Psychoanalytic Association*, Vol. 2, No. 4:607–620, 1954.

5. Freud, Anna, "Changes in Psychoanalytic Practice and Experience," *International Journal of Psychoanalysis*, Vol. 57, Part III, pp. 257–260, 1975.

6. Rangell, Leo, "Psychoanalysis and the Process of Change," *International Journal of Psychoanalysis*, Vol. 56, pp. 87–98, 1975.

7. Strupp, Hans and Hadley, Suzanne, "A Tripartite Model of Mental Health and Therapeutic Outcome," *American Psychologist*, pp. 187–196, March 1977.

8. Bellak, Leopold, "Once Over: What Is Psychotherapy?" *Journal of Nervous and Mental Disease*, Vol. 165, No. 5:295–299, November 1977.

9. Bellak, Leopold, "Kombinierte Psycho-und Pharmakotherapie unter besonderer Berucksichtigung von Kurz-und Notfalltherapie," *Psychiatria Clinica*, 10:102–113, 1977.

10. Bellak, Leopold and Meyers, Barnett, "Ego Function Assessment and Analysability," *The International Review of Psychoanalysis*, Vol. 2, Part 4, pp. 413–427, 1975.

11. Bellak, Leopold and Small, Leonard, *Brief Psychotherapy and Emergency Psychotherapy*, Second Edition, Grune & Stratton and C.P.S., Inc., New York, 1978.

2

MYTH AND REALITY IN PSYCHOANALYTIC PRACTICE

Earl G. Witenberg, M.D.
William Alanson White Institute of Psychiatry New York, and Albert Einstein College of Medicine, New York

What is myth in psychoanalytic practice? What is reality in this impossible profession? Before comment is made on the myths and on the realities, the terms should be defined.

Myths are "unproved collective beliefs that are accepted uncritically and used to justify a social institution, as the belief in the biological inferiority of the slaves used in support of slave societies" (*Random House Dictionary*). Another vivid example of a myth is the term *Aryan* as used in Nazi Germany. Reality, on the other hand, will be regarded as the state or quality of being true, not merely apparent, ostensible, or nominal. The difference, then, is between what we believe and what we know. There are both myth and reality, belief and knowledge, in our daily practice. The danger that arises from this condition is our confusing myth with reality and thereby not facing the inevitable uncertainty (Witenberg 1978). This leads to inculcating our patients in our beliefs in lieu of searching for what is real or of admitting that we do not know but do believe.

The reality in psychoanalytic practice is not the objective reality of, say, the law. William Silverberg (1952), founder of this society, pointed this out eloquently in his book *Childhood Experience and Personal Destiny*. Psychoanalysts deal in subjective reality that is verbalized, so that they may arrive at consensual validation—namely, a sharing in the syntactic mode between the patient and the analyst (Sullivan 1953). At this point of consensual validation one may say that reality enters into the practice of psychoanalysis.

The most general myth about psychoanalysis as treatment is its goal— namely, that it affords patients a second chance at living their lives; that by learning about themselves, they will be able to refrain from being or

11

behaving in ways that had caused them and/or others harm or distress in the past; that they will be able to become what they might have been if such and such had not happened to them in their lives; that they and their dissociated systems will become as well known to them as they are to their analysts; and that they will be able to love and work productively. This is the psychoanalysts' myth, their belief. It may be viewed as a mythical goal. No one has achieved this goal completely. In psychoanalytic practice, goals are set with the patient—verbalized and shared goals, it is hoped. The actual goals however, take into account many factors, both external and internal; they are in flux as well. Analysts consider the life situation of patients—for example, their professional mobility and how many children they have in relationship to their financial standing. Among the internal factors considered are their motivation; their attitude toward themselves and their presenting difficulties—how despairing, how passive they feel toward their complaints, how much of "a freak" they feel, for example; their life histories—close relationships they have had, for example; and their "psychological-mindedness," or how they observe themselves.

GUIDING MYTHS HISTORICALLY IN FLUX

That the guiding myths or beliefs as to what is important in psychoanalytic practice have always been in flux is evident. The indications for psychoanalytic treatment change; the nature of the persons who present themselves for treatment is also changing. The way analysts talk about their work has changed remarkably; new vistas are offered on the basis of constructs from related fields—child development, psychology, social sciences, physical sciences, linguistics, and philosophy (namely structuralism). The social climate and the way people think—the paradigms they use—influence what they do and what they say they do. All these factors change with time. Technique ususally changes before theory.

Until 1919 Sigmund Freud dominated the field in the area of technique. From 1893–98 he advocated the cathartic procedure. From 1898–1910 he made some basic discoveries calling for changes in technique. Free association was substituted for the "pressure" method; the actual sexual seduction of children was dismissed as cause; and the formulation of the Oedipus complex was done in this period. The *Interpretation of Dreams* and *Three Essays on Theory of Sexuality* were the important volumes of the period. Making the unconscious conscious was considered, at this juncture, the important goal of technique.

From 1910–19 Freud consolidated his thinking about technique. The concepts of the "mirror analyst," the repetition-compulsion, abstinence, and the importance of the transference neurosis were elaborated on and stressed. There were the case histories and the papers on technique. His unbridled enthusiasm about the therapeutic implications of the transference neurosis reverberates to this day in the literature. Some share the unqualified belief in the efficacy of the transference neurosis; others tend to disparage its utility.

After 1919 Freud was joined by other innovators. Ferenczi and Rank are names associated with this period. Until 1926 the issues related to practice that dominated the scene were the negative therapeutic reaction, the post–World War I pessimism, the structural theory, and the dual instinct theories. The therapeutic importance of the superego became evident. The dawn of the era of ego psychology was 1926. With it the importance of guilt and sadistic symptoms was stressed. In the mid–1920s the analyst with the most damaged couch was considered the best analyst. In this period Melanie Klein developed her id psychology, and Wilhelm Reich dramatically showed how analysis of the resistance is necessary before the analysis of content.

In the 1930s, 1940s, and 1950s Hitler and World War II influenced analysis. Pari passu with the ego psychologists came the culturalists Horney, Fromm, and Thompson, with their emphasis on the influence of socio-economic forces on the formation of personality of the individual through the family. In this country, Sullivan, influenced by Meyer, Freud, and Whitehead as well as operationalism, focused on the interaction between people as the true inquiry in treatment. Fairbairn and Winnicott developed object-relations theory independently in Great Britain. Schultz–Henke did the same in Germany. The importance of communication and communication processes were stressed. The environmentalists' perspective on the internal structure of psychoanalysis as a body of clinical knowledge represents a break with connection of interpretive metapsychology and the psychology of unconscious experience. Examples of this change are as follows:

- Fromm–Reichmann's theme of experience instead of interpretation as therapeutic agent

- Sullivan's intensive study of parataxic distortion

- Thompson's understanding of the problems of women as derived from cultural processes

- Principle of ego's autonomous function; Hartmann, Kris, Lowenstein, and Rappaport, without the requirement of any inherent connection between such ego functions and the original function

Thus experience, the contextual nature of treatment, and methods of experiencing came to the fore.

CURRENT MYTHS AND BELIEFS

With the increasing openness in society, the attitudes and values of the analyst have come in for discussion. The emotional response of the analyst—transmitted verbally or not has become a matter for observation and study. New therapeutic realities face us. The treatment of narcissistic people has been going on successfully since the 1930s by analysts not troubled by the bifurcation of transference neuroses and narcissistic neuroses. Kernberg and others have compromised the libido theory in addressing this issue.

At the present time there are efforts to synthesize meaning and experience as essential both to cure and change. When an interpretation is made, the analyst is participating with the patient; thus there is an experience along with the content. Merely learning one's theory does not help the patient. Merely having an encounter does not help either. The combination, however, does, and it achieves it through language. That is why Lacan's use of DeSaussure's linguistics, Schafer's use of Ryle's linguistics, or Edelson's use of Chomsky's linguistics are so important as the next step in the evolution of theory. Practice has already shown the way by the verbal expressions used, by the use of focused inquiry.

Analysts enter into the experience of psychoanalysis with certain beliefs that are based on their own experiences. One is the belief that knowledge is better than ignorance. No facts seem to be against this belief. Another belief, namely, the value of conscious choice over unconscious compulsion, is impossible to contravene. An ideal, that insight into experience and outlook onto behavior penetrates transference and countertransference distortions, is both myth and reality in analytic practice. The latter enables both the analyst and the patient to enhance their lives; it also allows each to discover that he or she has a unique psyche.

There are a number of myths or beliefs in practice, however, that are not invariably accompanied by confirmation from reality. One is that conscious symptoms will disappear only from a knowledge of their unconscious determinants. This is true sometimes, but there are times when symptoms disappear without a knowledge of their unconscious determinants and other times when symptoms do not disappear even though the unconscious determinants are known. Another belief is that transference is related one-to-one with early childhood experience; in reality, life is so complicated that there are way stations between early childhood and adulthood where distortions take place and make the relationship more complicated. Another belief is that troublesome behavior will cease if one understands the meaning of this behavior on a genetic basis. This is obviously not sufficient—the dimension that has to be added is the quality of the experience in the analytic inquiry. There have to be a proper psychological set in the patient and an intense working relationship with the analyst. The patient who consciously feels helpless, despairing, and the passive victim of external forces cannot utilize the meaning and will not have the experience of enhanced awareness. There is the belief that personality is fixed by the age of six years; this is contradicted by reality.

The myth that the analyst is anonymous to his or her patient is contradicted by reality. Some of us would say that it is not possible for the analyst to be anonymous. There is a belief that there is no indoctrination in analysis, but the patient is taught the method of inquiry. What is hoped is that there is no indoctrination of content. There is a belief that analysis is one process; if it is, it assumes different forms.

There is also a belief that analysis reduplicates the parent–child relationship. This is limited by the reality of practice—patients are not children, and analysts are not parents and usually do not have the same feelings toward patients as they do toward their children. The analyst, for example, usually considers what he or she will say before anything is said to the patient. It is very difficult to imagine a parent invariably second-thinking.

Another belief is that the rule of abstinence applies to the patient; more probably the analyst abstains (which aids patients' abstaining) during the analysis. There is the myth of biography, that the patient recapitulates his actual childhood. The reality is that the past is reconstructed by the adult; its relationship to the actual past is not at stake, but it is a mythology shared with the analyst.

Other common myths are that analysis is one process—"if you have seen one, you have seen them all"; that the analyst is the same with all patients—that the patient necessarily has to regress in order to get at childhood memories; that intense feelings for or against the analyst are merely a repetition of the past; that the transference neurosis is essential to cure; and that the Oedipus complex is the root of all neuroses.

The most common belief is that interpretations are curative. Those analysts who have asked patients what was meaningful in the "good" session frequently find that the patients have gained self-esteem in ways that had not been intended.

SUMMARY

In summary, there have always been, there always are, and there always will be myths and beliefs in practice. They are an essential part of any endeavor where one is seeking knowledge, or facts. The beliefs assuage the anxiety of uncertainty. Certain myths or beliefs are antitherapeutic because they hamper individuals' finding their unique psyches beyond biological, socio-cultural, and interpersonal referents. The importance of analysts' knowing when they are uncertain and communicating it is that it will facilitate their patients' knowing what is knowable and what is unknowable.

REFERENCES

Random House Dictionary of the English Language. Unabridged ed., S.V. "myth."
Silverberg, W. *Childhood Experience and Personal Destiny.* Springer, N.Y., 1952.
Sullivan, H. S., *The Psychiatric Interview.* Norton, N.Y., 1953.
Witenberg, E. G., The inevitability of uncertainty. *Journal of the American Academy of Psychoanalysis*, Vol. 6, p. 275, 1978.

Part Two

EVOLVING THEORIES AND CLINICAL APPLICATIONS

3

PSYCHOANALYSIS, 1938-78:
A VIEW FROM THE CHAIR

Irving Bieber, M.D.
New York Medical College

As the title of this chapter suggests, my discussion is in the nature of a personal history in psychoanalysis. It is an account of the emergence of my clinical and theoretical position and will suggest and reflect in some measure, certain of the reconstructions that have transpired in psychoanalysis over four decades, as well as aspects of our discipline that, among classical analysts, have remained unchanged.

In 1938, I was completing the second year of a three-year personal analysis with Abram Kardiner at the New York Psychoanalytic Institute and was doing my 50-hour control with Sandor Rado. I was a second-year student and the presenter in a continuous case seminar conducted by Sarah Bonnet. My wife and I had married the preceding summer, during my training analysis. Up to that time, marriage during a candidate's analysis had been forbidden. Like the cadets at West Point, if one married, expulsion followed. We were the first at the institute to negotiate successfully this daring act, and shortly thereafter, several other candidates also married. Each was an analysand of Kardiner, who supported the romantic revolution.

My schedule was very demanding. In the full-time practice of neurology, psychiatry, and psychoanalysis, I spent six mornings a week at Mt. Sinai Hospital as an adjunct attending in neurology. I was on the neurological attending staff at Montefiore Hospital and on the neuropsychiatric attending staff at Queens General Hospital. My office practice was almost entirely psychoanalytic. I saw each patient five times a week, all on the couch. By 1938, my analytic fees had been raised to three dollars, having begun in 1936 at two dollars a session. I saw Dr. Kardiner five times a week at a fee of $7.50 and paid Dr. Rado $10.00 for control sessions.

Before World War II, many psychiatric patients were referred to a neurologist. They wanted to see a "nerve" specialist because they felt nervous. I had to spend considerable time convincing such patients that their problems were psychological, not organic. These patients were usually seen three times a week rather than five, but they all used the couch.

In 1938, Kardiner was completing the manuscript of his book, *The Individual and His Society (1939)*, a contribution that emerged from his collaboration with anthropologists, especially Ralph Linton, professor and chairman of the Department of Anthropology at Columbia University. Kardiner had already discarded the instinctual theory, the entire metapsychology, and even the Oedipus complex. His major emphasis was on human dependency and on problems in attaining maturity and independence. The concepts are essentially the same as those more recently presented by Margaret Mahler under the heading "separation and individuation." Kardiner, a conceptual radical, was, however, traditional in his technique. Rado was also a conceptual radical. Like Kardiner, he had discarded the metapsychology but continued to place major emphasis on sexuality, including the Oedipus complex. Rado focused on the problem of fear, on its inhibiting effects on sexuality, and, in particular, on human adaptation to threat and fear, which he termed *emergency control.* These ideas had an important influence on the development of my own concepts of psychopathology and psychodynamics, which will be elaborated on subsequently.

Neither Kardiner nor Rado stressed the analysis of the analytic transference. Neither ever proposed to me that a transference neurosis was necessary or desirable. I had the impression that Rado was a more active therapist than Kardiner, yet he, too, saw his patients five times a week on the couch. Both conducted their analyses as if Freudian theory, which they had in large part abandoned, had no fundamental connection with Freudian technique, that is, the use of the couch and frequency of visits.

Freud first described the use of the couch in his early publication *Psychotherapy of Hysteria (1893-95)*. Convinced that the neurotic symptom was linked to a memory of an antecedent, relevant, and traumatic event, Freud had the patient lie down and would insist that the patient remember the scene. When this did not turn out to be particularly successful, he would apply manual pressure to the patient's forehead, which, he wrote, "invariably worked." In his paper on the beginning of treatment, Freud (1913, p. 133) stated:

> Before I wind up these remarks on beginning analytic treatment, I must say a word about a certain ceremonial which concerns the position in which the treatment is carried out. I hold to the plan of getting the patient to lie on a sofa while I sit behind him out of his sight. This arrangement has a historical basis. It is the remnant of the hypnotic method out of which psychoanalysis evolved. But it deserves to be maintained for many reasons. The first is a personal motive but one

which others may share with me. I cannot put up with being stared at by other people for eight hours a day or more. Since, while I am listening to the patient, I, too, give myself over to the current of my unconscious thoughts. I do not wish my expressions of face to give the patient material for interpretations or to influence me in what he tells me. I insist on this procedure, however, for its purpose and result are to prevent the transference from mingling with the patient's associations imperceptibly, to isolate the transference, and to allow it to come forward in true course sharply defined as a resistance.

THE RELATIONSHIP BETWEEN THEORY AND TECHNIQUE

Four basic concepts constitute the theoretical underpinnings for the use of the couch: transference, transference neuroses, regression, and free association. The assumptions underlying each of these concepts will be discussed, especially as they relate to analytic technique.

Transference and Transference Neuroses

Freud's first mention of transference appears in the *Psychotherapy of Hysteria*, published between 1893 and 1895. In it, Freud talked of a young lady who had experienced a wish for a certain man to "boldly take her in his arms and give her a kiss." The wish appeared in a therapeutic session and was directed to Freud who interpreted it as a transference from the antecedent situation. He did not propose an alternate hypothesis—that this sexually frustrated woman, who was too inhibited to assert her own sexual wishes, entertained a modified rape fantasy that was evoked by men she found attractive, in this situation, her analyst.

Transference next appears in *The Interpretation of Dreams (1900)*, where it has a somewhat different connotation, yet exposes and reveals the basic assumptions underlying transference and transference neurosis. According to Freud, unconscious, unfulfilled instinctual wishes, like animals trapped in a cage, are constantly seeking a way out. The way out for an instinct is to connect itself to a conscious idea that has access to the motor apparatus, so that the wishes can become gratified through action. Thus, as a wood tick lying in wait for an unsuspecting victim, these unconscious impulses find a suitable conscious idea to attach to and then transfer or cathect the idea with instinctual energy. The idea may then seek expression in a neurotic act or symptom. One can infer from Freud's writings on transference that somewhere along the way, he came to believe that the analytic situation was an ideal hook for the latching on of unconscious and instinctual wishes as to object, the analyst, and the various aims deriving from the libidinal stages and phases that are described in the analysis itself.

In his paper on transference, Freud (1917, p. 444) stated:

> When ... the treatment has obtained mastery over the patient, what happens is that the whole of his illness is concentrated upon a single point—his relationship to the doctor. ... When the transference has risen to this significance, work upon the patient's memories retreats far into the background. Thereafter, it is not incorrect to say that we are no longer concerned with the patient's earlier illness but with a newly created and transformed neurosis which has taken the former's place. We have followed this new edition of the old disorder from its start. We have observed its origin and growth and we are especially well able to find our way about it, since, as its object, we are situated at its very center. All the patient's symptoms have abandoned their original meaning and have taken on a new sense which lies in relationship to the transference where only such symptoms have persisted as are capable of undergoing such transformation. But the mastery of this new artificial neurosis coincides with getting rid of the illness which was originally brought to the treatment with the accomplishment of our therapeutic task. A person who has become normal and free from the operation of a repressed instinctual impulse in his relationship to the doctor will remain so in his own life after the doctor has once more withdrawn from it.

Shortly thereafter, Freud (1922, p. 347) wrote:

> This *transference*, alike in its positive and negative form, is used as a weapon by the resistance; but in the hands of the physician, it becomes the most powerful therapeutic instrument and it plays a part scarcely to be over-estimated in the dynamics of the process of cure.

Clearly, if an old illness could, in fact, be transformed into a new one in which the analyst is the central object, then analysis of the transference and encouragement of transference neurosis would and did logically become the central technique of classical therapy. The couch is deemed essential in this undertaking because the analyst must remain impersonal and unseen. He has to be a "blank screen" onto which transference objects as experienced in childhood can be projected—mother, father, sister, brother, and so forth. Further, the analysis must be conducted in an atmosphere of relative privation since satisfaction of an instinctual wish removes the motive force for therapy.

All this appears to be organized and systematic, but it does not work as theorized. If transference is defined as a replication of aspects of an antecedent relationship, then transference to the analyst always occurs. If, however, analytic transference is restricted to the irrational components of replicated reactions, then transference may also include spouse, children, employer, friends, and so forth. The totality of a patient's psychopathology, or a major part of it, is not transferable to the analyst; that it can transmigrate and become a new illness is hypothetical rather than real, and it is a phenomenon that I have never observed. Each analyst evokes different transference reactions. One who expresses warmth may evoke anxiety about intimacy in certain patients. A more impersonal attitude may evoke anxiety about rejection. Male and female patients respond differently to male and female analysts.

In 1964, Lilly Ottenheimer and I presented a paper, *Transference and the Sex of the Analyst*, at a meeting celebrating the 20th anniversary of the founding of the Psychoanalytic Institute at New York Medical College, now the Division of Psychoanalytic Training of its Department of Psychiatry. We reported on two women, each of whom we both had treated. Both patients came to me initially and, after five or six years with me, completed their analyses with Dr. Ottenheimer. Each patient had a father transference to me; in one it was intensely erotic. Each had a mother transference to Dr. Ottenheimer.

Subsequent to the presentation of our paper, Dr. Ottenheimer and I treated a male patient concurrently. He, too, had a father transference to me but never showed evidence of a mother transference; he had a mother transference to Dr. Ottenheimer. The dreams that he brought to her were different in content and affect from those that he brought to me. Freud was well aware of this phenomenon and said so in *On Transference Love* (1915, p. 154) and in *Dynamics of Transference* (1917, p. 443). In *On Transference Love*, Freud spoke of the erotic transference of the female patient to a male analyst—that is, her "falling in love with him"—and said, "This phenomenon occurs without fail which as we know is one of the foundations of psychoanalytic theory."

In the 40 or more years in which I have been practicing psychoanalysis, many women patients have developed some sort of sexual feelings toward me, but these feelings did not constitute a "falling in love" or a transferential problem. Only a handful of women developed a significant erotic transference, and, with one exception, all of these patients have either been borderline or schizophrenic. When generalizations are made, they must rest upon the vast majority of cases, not upon exceptions. Freud also postulated that the positive transference of a male patient to a male analyst was basically erotic, although he did not use the phrase "falling in love." He stressed the hostile transference of the male patient to the male analyst, recognizing the Oedipal basis for the differences.

As to technique, I interpret transference to me only when I am clearly and convincingly the object either in dreams, attitudes, fantasies, or behavior. I do not assume that I am present in every dream or that I am the central concern of every session, though I am always aware of the presence of transference and interpret negative transference as soon as it is discerned or when it constitutes a resistance. A patient's distortions and irrational beliefs will be expressed and acted out vis-á-vis the many persons encountered in everyday life. I use the realities of individuals and situations as the bases for analyzing transferences. Distortions and irrationalities may be identified as they occur and thus, I focus on that, instead of concentrating on transference to me. This technique has important advantages. First, it considers what the patient is talking about and what he or she can readily understand. When a patient is talking about parents, spouse, lover, employer, or friend, he or she is talking about *them* and not the analyst. In this way, good contact is maintained, and it is maintained in the context of the productions; the patient is spared being presented with an obscure, speculative connection with the analyst, which may be submissively accepted but not understood. Second, the therapeutic alliance is not disturbed. An emotionally uncluttered working atmosphere facilitates the exploration of irrational transferences as they are acted out in the patient's real life, without obfuscation by unnecessary examination of the analyst-patient relationship.

An illustration of the importance of working out primary irrational beliefs before they appear as analytic resistances was demonstrated in a patient who was treated by a student some years ago. The student was analyzing a woman approximately his own age. The patient had a brother who was clearly the mother's favorite. The patient's relationship to her brother was characteristic of that of a nonpreferred to a preferred child and, in this case, also included a corrosive hostility. The student had failed to work out this aspect of the patient's psychopathology in the early phases of treatment. When it appeared in the analytic transference, needless to say, it was accompanied by highly negative resistance punctuated by an alienating hostility. Her hostility interfered with the cognitive clarity necessary to resolve the irrational aspects of her reaction, and it prevented her from accepting any analytic interpretations. With this impasse, the patient terminated treatment.

Thus, the analyst not only must be aware of transference but must consider what the transference is likely to involve. If the analyst is a male significantly older than the patient, a father transference is likely to be evoked; if the analyst is a female significantly older than the patient, a mother transference is likely. If the analyst is about the same age as the patient, a sibling or peer transference may be evoked, and if the patient is significantly older than the analyst, a son or daughter transference will likely be evoked.

I trust that I have not conveyed the idea that I consider the interpretation of the analytic transference as of minor consequence. For some patients, the concrete experience of analytic transference and its continued interpretation is absolutely necessary in order to work through fears of the parents, older siblings, and so forth. Each of the two women who started her analysis with me and continued it with Dr. Ottenheimer required a concrete experience with an analyst who could be a transferential mother; yet, neither of these patients would have accepted treatment from a woman to begin with—that would have been much too threatening. It took years of analysis with a man before their fears could be sufficiently attenuated to permit analysis with a woman. Dr. Ottenheimer and I stated in our paper that this type of patient would do well to have analysts of each sex, starting with one of the opposite sex.

As has already been indicated, it is usually the more disturbed patients who develop prolonged, intense transferences. When meaningful and intense transferences do develop—be they erotic or hostile—they occur just as readily with the patient sitting up as lying down. I also have found that negative transferences are more rapidly resolved when patient and analyst are face-to-face. My work on the analytic transference varies from patient to patient and with the same patient from time to time. Yet if the amount of time spent in transference analysis is any criterion, then transference analysis occupies a relatively small portion of my work with most patients. To emphasize in repetition: I do not hold with Freud that an old neurosis can be converted into a new one, that it is located in the transference, and that it can be resolved by analysis of an artificially constructed transference neurosis.

Regression

The term *regression* has come to have several connotations, such as relapse in mental health, a falling back to attitudes and behavior that were appropriate at an earlier stage but no longer are, and the appearance of disturbed or bizarre behavior—so-called primitive thinking. Freud, however, had a very specific construct in mind. The libido developed in stages; each had its phases with specific aims and objects. In the oral-acceptive phase, the object was the mother and the aim was oral gratification through sucking her breast or through participating in other oral activity related to the mother, such as eating, or its affectional equivalent, love. In the oral-active or cannibalistic phase, the aim was to exercise oral mastery on objects. After 1920 and the formulation of the death instinct, the active phase of libidinal development was identified partly with the aggressive instinct and partly with ego mastery functions. Al-

though never explicitly stated, the father was the object of the anal phase, particularly in boys. Freud postulated that the psychic representation of every libidinal phase remained intact, as if once-used stage sets of various plays were lodged in one big theater with all the players in place, each unit capable of being relit and reanimated by the proper triggering device, namely, regressive tendencies. Anachronistic phases could be recathected by regression, which took place when an instinctual impulse in a more advanced libidinal phase, such as the genital, was blocked or frustrated. The impulse would then seek gratification by returning to an earlier libidinal phase where it had once been successfully gratified. Regression could also occur when there was a fixation at a libidinal phase caused by frustration or, conversely, by overindulgence at that phase.

In my view, behaviors that are generally interpreted to be regressive are attempts to reinstate a previously adaptive technique. An adult who breaks a leg and crawls to a telephone is using the same crawl behavior as in early childhood and is now reinstating an earlier adaptive behavioral mode. An example more readily thought of as regressive is that of a five-year-old who reverts to the bottle and to baby talk upon the birth of a sibling. The earlier behavior is being reinstated but in a new and different context and for a different purpose. In infancy, the child nursed a bottle and talked baby talk because it was consonant with an appropriate level of neurophysiological development. Now the child is reverting to this behavior as a defense against the threat of loss of parental support, interest, and love. If a single component in a complex behavioral constellation is extrapolated from its meaning and context, comprehension of the total behavior integration is lost. The use of a component—that is, baby talk and bottle nursing—as evidence that a five-year-old has regressed to an early level of personality organization with a return of infantile aims and objects assigns fictitious and erroneous meaning to behavior whose realistic meaning in a realistic context is already known. A very young child who talks baby talk and takes a bottle is not the developmental or psychological equivalent of a five-year-old who is reinstituting such behavior defensively. Each subsequent stage of organization, though deriving from its antecedent, alters that antecedent irreversibly; though there may be identifiable components that remain, the early state as such is gone. One cannot retrieve the acorn from the oak. I once watched a colleague who is both an analyst and a hypnotist regress an adult under hypnosis to the preverbal period and then bring him back by *verbal* instruction. The analyst saw no contradiction in this procedure.

The concept of regression may also lead to false conclusions. A student interpreted a particular patient's behavior as regressive because when he had become angry, he shook his arms in rage as a child would. The student concluded that the reasons for the patient's rage were therefore childish and immature. When the situation was described more fully, the reasons for the rage were understandable, appropriate, and reflected nothing childish or immature. My analytic vocabulary for adults does not include such words as infantile, childish, adolescent, and immature. Such descriptions are inaccurate and analogically incorrect, and their intent is almost always pejorative.

Regression is also thought to occur when an individual in a state of helplessness becomes pathologically dependent on one or more others, giving the impression of a return to a child-parent type of relationship. Actually, pathological dependency is associated with an inflation of the image of the one who is helping and with magical expectations of protection and assistance. Such a posture is a reinstatement of an adaptational coping maneuver, that is, dependency in the face of helplessness. The pathology and the problem are concerned with the factors that created the state of helplessness, not with the secondary adaptational dependency, though the latter may contribute to the psychopathology. If regression and dependency are viewed as the primary sources of psychopathology, the emphasis is misplaced on the supporting crutch when concern should be focused upon the fractured limb that created the helplessness.

Free Association

Free association replaced Breuer's cathartic method as a technique for tapping unconscious material. The golden rule was for the patient to say whatever came to mind. Any break in the flow of free association was assumed to be a resistance; there was no considering other reasons for a break, such as fatigue or a pause when a newly remembered idea came into consciousness. Even if breaks in free association were resistances, however, they were not necessarily what Freud later interpreted them to be. As he further developed his ideas on transference, he came to the conclusion that a break in free association always heralded the beginning of transference resistance. He assumed that the patient had come across material that he or she did not want to reveal to the analyst and that the concealed idea contained an instinctual wish, either libidinal or aggressive, that was being directed toward the analyst. Also excluded was the possibility that the patient might be fearful of opening up a situation that he or she was not ready to face, either with the analyst or alone. I recently encountered a severe resistance in a patient who found it difficult to face his intense hostility to one of his sons and the destructive paternal behavior consequent to this hostility. The patient's resistance had nothing to do with me.

Free association has two connotations. If it refers to a patient's verbalizing uninterruptedly so that the analyst can follow themes within an organized train of thought, then it is not only valuable but an indispensable part of the analytic process. On the other hand, I have never found free association that consists of a series of verbalized disconnected thoughts to be of value in illuminating unconscious psychodynamics. Generally, each session has at least one major theme; some have several. If patients are not interrupted, this theme will be established in the first 5 or 10 minutes of the session. As in a dream, a reality situation usually determines the theme. If the theme is one of rejection, the likelihood is that the patient has experienced or believes that he or she has experienced a recent rejection and will give an account of it. If I think that the patient's inferences are unreasonable, or the reaction maladaptive, he or she is encouraged to remember a similar circumstance. Such associations are oriented toward establishing the psychogenetic bases for the patient's beliefs about rejection. Productions of this kind are just as easily obtained with patients sitting up.

I direct patients to associate to their dreams and lead them to those parts of the manifest content most likely to be productive. This type of dream association also does not depend on the recumbent position. If the patient becomes blocked or runs out of material, I do not say that he or she is resisting, nor do I assume that this is transference resistance. Silent periods, where the patient sweats it out uncomfortably, also are avoided. I do not favor the technique where the analyst says nothing or at regular intervals asks "What are you thinking about?" If the patient cannot talk, I do. I ask relevant questions about the theme of the session, elicit additional past history, or, if necessary, talk about something that interests the patient, thus stimulating verbalization. This avoids the torturous experiences many patients have with silent periods, and it avoids the secondary iatrogenic resistances engrafted upon the ones that interefere with analytic verbalizations in the first place.

Dreams are my major access to the patient's irrational belief systems, conscious and unconscious. I agree with Freud that dreams are the royal road to unconscious processes and, believing so, see no reason to place major reliance on secondary roads. Patients are encouraged to write down all dreams and to date and keep them after presenting them in session. If there is any question about how often patients omit significant aspects of a dream that was remembered upon awakening, one has only to ask them to relate the dream, first from memory, and then to read what had been written. As expected, what is left out is often the most telling part. When patients are not urged to write down dreams as part of the therapeutic program, the analyst may be unwittingly collaborating in a patient's resistance. Patients are advised against discarding written-down dreams; by keeping them, patients are able to retain a good record of their analysis. When a particular subject arises that deserves scrupulous attention, the patient is reminded to survey old dreams dealing with that subject. In one case, the patient dreamed of teeth from time to time. I requested that all previous dreams in which teeth appeared be brought into the next session. This review illuminated the meaning of the old dreams as well as the new. Before terminating, most patients are able to analyze their own dreams. It becomes an important aspect of the continuing analytic work that should follow formal termination of sessions. Some patients, though few in number, do not bring in many dreams. The analysis of such individuals is still possible, though it is more difficult and presents a greater challenge to one's therapeutic creativity.

From this discussion on the relationship between theory and technique I shall move on to the development of my ideas about psychopathology and psychoanalysis.

CONCEPTS OF PSYCHOPATHOLOGY AND PSYCHOANALYSIS

In 1953, Sandor Rado addressed the Society of Medical Psychoanalysts on the subject of emergency behavior. As the designated discussant of this address, I made the follwoing remarks:

> Dr. Rado has made profound contributions to a theory of psychoanalysis and, as my teacher, he has played a determining role in the development of my own psychoanalytic thinking. The concept that injury or the perception of threat of injury is a cardinal point in the understanding of the psychopathology of neurosis has been advanced by him for many years. As a consequence of this contribution, he then became interested in the somatic and psychological defensive adaptations to injury or threatened injury which he had grouped together under the title "emergency control." Dr. Rado has developed his ideas of emergency control to the point where he believes that "failures of emergency adjustment" are of paramount importance and that they are the basic factors in the etiological psychodynamics of all forms of disordered behavior.

Rado viewed parental and authoritative indoctrination and prohibitions as the source of the fears underlying emergency control. The child's relationship to power and authority formed the conceptual model on which he elaborated his ideas on adaptational modes—submission, defiance, and guilt. He tended, however, to underemphasize other important sources of pathology within the child-parent relationship: affectional deprivation, inadequate contact and stimulation, and defective communication. The roles of sibling and peer relations were similarly underemphasized. In explicating psychopathology, Rado's central ideas moved to "emergency control," mine to "irrational belief systems." In further response to Rado's address, I said the following:

> The neuroses arise from distortions and injuries in interpersonal relations, not only in early life, but throughout life. Irrational beliefs and belief systems become established consequent to the distortions and injuries that ensue from basic relationships that are destructive. The irrationalities are unrealistically projected to new situations so that the perpetuation of neuroses is based on the perpetuation of erroneous convictions. Psychoanalytic therapy rests upon the correction of irrational convictions toward the end that ideas and idea systems become consonant with reality. I believe that the continuity of irrational convictions has the effect of chronically tripping false danger signals that set emergency control into operation. Emergency control continues to respond to false signals until unrealistic perceptions of danger arising out of false convictions are abolished.

This quotation contains my basic concepts of psychopathology. These concepts were further elaborated on in two papers: in 1960, *A Concept of Psychopathology* and in 1977, *Irrational Belief Systems—the Primary Elements of Psychopathology.* I view psychopathology as the consequence of adverse interpersonal experiences, beginning with defective and disturbed parent-child relationships, sibling relationships, and pathogenic extrafamilial relationships.

Adverse experiences and idiosyncratic adaptations to adverse experiences are represented in the adult by fears, symptoms, disturbances in functioning, defenses, and mechanisms of repair. Fear is another way of saying that one believes that one will be hurt. Thus, fear of flying indicates that there is a belief that injury will result from going aloft. I define injury as any event or interaction that is perceived to be inimical to one's best interests, such as rejection, humiliation, physical injury, and so forth. In sum, psychopathology consists basically of irrational expectations of injury—expectations that become integrated with defenses and mechanisms of repair. These concepts have nothing to do with regression to infantile states or repressed instinctual impulses wanting out. Such ideas, in my opinion, have seriously confused psychiatry and psychoanalysis.

Any type of therapy that is oriented toward delineating neurotic fears or irrational beliefs about injury and that tracks down the genesis of such beliefs and delineates the defenses and reparative mechanisms relating to the fears in order to resolve them *is* psychoanalysis. These delineations make up its *strategy.* The ways in which these goals are accomplished are the *techniques* of psychoanalysis. The use of a couch or the frequency of visits is technical, not strategic. An emphasis on transference, transference neurosis, and so forth is also a technical aspect. I do not differentiate between psychoanalysis and psychoanalytically oriented psychotherapy. The differences are merely technical, not strategic. In psychoanalytically oriented psychotherapy, the patient does not use the couch. This supposedly alters the nature of analytic transference and the possibility of developing a transference neurosis. I have already detailed why I believe that such assumptions are not valid.

The face-to-face technique has many advantages over the use of the couch. It allows the analyst to be more active and tends to encourage more activity on the part of the patient. The couch tends to assign to the patient major responsibility for conducting the therapy. Face-to-face sessions require fewer weekly visits to achieve progress than do the classical four and preferably five sessions a week on the couch. My own quota is generally two or three sessions a week, depending on the patient's ability to use these frequencies productively. Once a week is acceptable and perfectly compatible with a successful analytic outcome. Therapeutic success or failure in the analysis does not depend on frequency of sessions. This is a very important consideration in view of the financial limitations of so many for whom a reconstructive type of therapy is indicated.

It is high time that we got over the idea that psychoanalytically oriented psychotherapy is a kind of second-best or poor man's psychoanalysis. Many years ago, the late Sidney Tarachow, a classical analyst, told me, with some bewilderment, that his results in psychotherapy were often better than those achieved in psychoanalysis. I think that for most patients what we call psychoanalytic psychotherapy is superior to classical psychoanalysis. I have no objections to the use of whatever techniques an analyst believes are optimal for attaining therapeutic objectives, including the use of the couch which I, too, use when it is deemed to be an advantage. What I object to are those analysts who confuse analytic goals with analytic techniques and who insist that a therapy is not analytic unless it includes the use of the couch, primary emphasis on analysis of transference to the analyst, four or five sessions a week, and so forth.

CONCLUSION

In 1938 I was a man without a theory. By good fortune, I chose an analyst and a control analyst who at that early date had already discarded metapsychology. The absence of a theoretical replacement was, however, very uncomfortable. I and my colleague, Meyer Maskin, would kid each other that our ideas were subject to change without notice and that we should put up such a sign in our waiting room. Yet, we were much better off in having struggled to find our conceptual way than to have been entrapped in the illogic of metapsychology so early in our careers. Today I have a theory, one that I find useful and effective, along with a reliable repertoire of techniques that make psychoanalysis available to the many without, in any way, alloying the gold of Freud's great contribution.

REFERENCES

Bieber, I. A Concept of Psychopathology. In *Current Aprroaches to Psychopathology* (Hoch, P., & Zubin, J., Eds.). New York: Grune & Stratton, 1960.

Bieber, I. The Concept of Irrational Belief Systems as Primary Elements of Psychopathology. *J. Amer. Acad. Psychoanalysis*, 1974, Vol. 2, 91–100.

Bieber, I. and Ottenheimer, L. *Transference and the Sex of the Psychoanalyst*. Paper presented in celebration of 20th Anniversary of Founding of Analytic Institute at New York Medical College, 1964.

Freud, S. Psychotherapy of Hysteria, 1893–95. In *Standard Edition*, Vol. 2 (Strachey, J., & Strachey, A., Eds.). London: Hogarth Press, 1955.

Freud, S. The Interpretation of Dreams, 1900. In *Standard Edition*, Vols. 4 & 5 (Strachey, J., & Strachey, A., Eds.). London: Hogarth Press, 1955.

Freud, S. On Beginning Treatment, 1913. In *Standard Edition*, Vol. 12 (Strachey, J., & Strachey, A., Eds.). London: Hogarth Press, 1957.

Freud, S. On Transference Love, 1915. In *Standard Edition*, Vol. 12 (Strachey, J., & Strachey, A., Eds.). London: Hogarth Press, 1957.

Freud, S. Dynamics of Transference, 1917. In *Standard Edition*, Vol. 16 (Strachey, J., & Strachey, A., Eds.). London: Hogarth Press, 1958.

Freud, S. Psychoanalysis, 1922. In *Standard Edition*, Vol. 18 (Strachey, J., & Strachey, A., Eds.). London: Hogarth Press, 1958.

Kardiner, A. *The Individual and His Society* New York: Columbia University Press, 1939.

4

IMPLICATIONS OF THE TREATMENT OF BORDERLINE PATIENTS FOR PSYCHOANALYTIC TECHNIQUE

Paul R. Dince, M.D.
New York Medical College

The clinical concept of the borderline syndrome has assumed a dominant position in psychiatry within the past decade. Increasing recognition has been given to that which has always been true, that is, that the majority of patients encountered in the office practice of psychiatry do not conform diagnostically to the criteria of the "analyzable" transference neuroses from which the theory and practice of psychoanalytic treatment have been derived. The expanding literature concerning the varying modes of treatment of patients who fall within the borderline category has supported several conclusions. Patients with severe, nonpsychotic psychopathology involving serious impairment of basic ego functions can achieve significant therapeutic results with analytic therapy. However, when that which has been defined as standard psychoanalytic technique is applied to the borderline patient, endless treatment with no improvement or worsening of the patient's disturbance is the likely result. It is further evident that supportive therapies do not ameliorate the pathology of the borderline patient (Kernberg 1967).

Beyond these empirical technical conclusions, various efforts have been directed toward the reexamination of previously held etiological concepts and developmental theory. Given the fact that the pathology and treatment of the borderline disorders cannot be understood by means of traditional psychoanalytic concepts, attempts have been made to fuse elements of object-relations theory to the tripartite and topographic formulations. The need to preserve the boundary between that which has been defined as standard psychoanalytic technique and that which has been defined as psychoanalytic psychotherapy has assumed a new urgency. Within these efforts, an historical polarity between psychoanalysis as process and psychoanalysis as therapy has resurfaced.

The premises upon which this chapter is based are twofold: (1) that the judicious and skillful use of psychoanalytic techniques are of unique therapeutic value when applied toward the goals of developmental change and relief of neurotic suffering in motivated patients and (2) that a confusing superstructure of mythological assumptions involving the concept of the transference neurosis overshadows the field of psychoanalytic treatment. The purpose of the chapter is to examine some of the findings derived from the treatment of borderline patients in order to distinguish unwarranted assumptions from the realities that make psychoanalysis an effective and unique form of treatment.

STANDARD PSYCHOANALYTIC TECHNIQUE

Many contributors have addressed themselves to the subject of psychoanalysis as a psychotherapeutic technique, as did Knight (1954) in the following:

> Psychoanalysis is one set of techniques subsumed under the generic term individual psychotherapy . . . it requires of the patient a rather high degree of sound ego functioning, and the more damaged the patient's total ego functioning is, the less suitable he is for the *standard psychoanalytic technique.* In the traditional psychoanalytic mode, gratification is at a minimum . . . the appointment length is strictly set, the patient does not face the therapist, extra-analytic comments before and after the session are minimal, physical contact is ruled out, communication is primarily verbal . . . extra appointments are rare (p. 116).

These stipulations provide for the therapeutic setting, which "permits the development of a full-fledged regressive transference neurosis, and the resolution of this transference neurosis by means of interpretation, carried out by the analyst from a position of technical neutrality" (Gill 1954). There has been no change in this overall definition of the standard psychoanalytic technique in the ensuing quarter of a century.

When studies have been carried out in order to determine what were the actual practices of psychoanalysts in their work with their patients, the precision and clarity of the preceding definition disappears. One such study was carried out by Glover in 1938 (Glover 1955):

> Full replies were obtained from twenty-four members, from the examination of which it transpired that on only six out of the sixty-three points raised was there complete agreement. Only one of these six

points could be regarded as fundamental, the necessity of analyzing the transference; the others concerned such lesser matters as the inadvisability of accepting presents, avoidance of the use of technical terms during the analysis, avoidance of social contacts, abstention from answering questions, and, interestingly enough, payment for all non-attendances, a ruling which, I am glad to know, is nevertheless honored by many in the breach (p. 376).

At another point, the same author stated:

In this connection ... it is easier to say what is not psychoanalysis than what is psychoanalysis ... in the old days, it was sufficient to say that whoever based his therapy on his belief in the unconscious, in infantile neurosis, in repression, in conflict, and in transference could call himself a psychoanalyst. And in spite of our most ambitious training schemes, this standard is still not wide of the mark (p. 384)

The literature concerned with the definition of the standard psychoanalytic technique replicates the inconsistencies and ambiguities characteristic of the Glover study. However, as in that study, it is the concept of the full-fledged transference neurosis which is regressive, induced in the patient, analyzed by means of interpretation, and worked through and resolved which is central to the definition of standard psychoanalysis as a process and therapeutic technique. The assumption is made that only through the analysis and resolution of the regressive transference neurosis by means of interpretation can genuine characterological, structural change be brought about. The stated goals of standard psychoanalytic technique are most ambitious as opposed to other therapeutic modalites which either willingly or necessarily settle for only symptomatic changes or only changes in overt behavioral patterns in terms of observable, external (i.e. superficial) criteria. Traditional psychoanalysis claims as its goals changes, which are variously described as "underlying changes, deep changes, structural changes in the ego, total characterological changes, etc." (Wallerstein 1965, p. 750). In the same paper, the author states that "though the most ambitious of therapies in its overall outcome goals, in practice (standard) analysis often achieves no more than other less ambitious therapeutic approaches" (p. 752).

There has not been a significant number of studies that test the foregoing assumptions and claims regarding the transference neurosis. Pfeffer (1961), in a series of follow-up studies of analyses judged to have been *satisfactorily* completed, discerned the existence of old (preanalytic) conflicts, which had lost their poignancy and had found new solutions. The old conflicts were, however, clearly discernible which throws considerable doubt on the concept of permanent resolution of intrapsychic conflict.

Balint (1950), after defining and discussing his goal of the "rebirth experience" in analysis, stated that in only two out of ten *satisfactorily* completed analyses did patients attain this so-called universal experience.

In previous papers (Dince 1977, 1978), problems of engagement presented by the borderline patient have been cited and described, along with an overall treatment approach that has proven effective. This chapter will concentrate upon factors that appear to be critical to a positive therapeutic outcome in the borderline patient and that may illuminate one vector that accounts for genuine improvement when it occurs in the psychoanalytic treatment of the neurotic patient.

TREATMENT OF BORDERLINE PATIENTS

The pathologic function and defensive operations of the borderline patient may be understood as representing efforts to ward off the experience of mortal terror, which accompanies the expectation of psychic dissolution, that is, psychic death.

> The borderline patient knows what it is to have been out of control, to have experiences that he defines as crazy, e.g. fugue-like states, eruptions of violent, blind raging or self-destructive behavior during which the individual felt as if he were someone else, periods of panic which have rendered reason unavailable to him for significant periods of time, episodes of unreality and the like. (Dince 1977, p. 341).

By means of massive denial and of projection, projective identification, omnipotent defenses, and vengeful behavior, patients desperately strive to protect against that which will evoke the mortal terror associated with feared abandonment and psychic death. The anticipation of change, of the modification of the core schizoid defense, also evokes the spector of that terror. In addition, patients have the conviction that they will have to face terror alone, as they had to face significant biotraumatic experiences in childhood in solitary fashion.

The analytic treatment of borderline patients will inevitably confront the terror or its anticipation. In patients with acute or chronic panic, it is confronted at the outset of treatment. In patients whose presenting symptoms are those of depression, impulsivity, or severe character pathology, it will be confronted as the analysis approaches the core of the illness later in treatment. Patients with panic symptoms adopt a clinging, yet help-rejecting, relatedness to the analyst, which belies the underlying schizoid defense of the borderline disturbance. In either event, sooner or later, and at moments of affective readiness on the part of patients, analysts need to make clear to patients that they need not face the terror by themselves and that they have an effective ally who will share the experience with them, hearing and responding to their signals of distress if they will but allow them to be made.

The borderline patient, in contrast to the psychoneurotic patient, needs to have that message communicated in concrete, as opposed to implicit, fashion. Words and actions must coincide in a consistent demonstration of the analyst's capacity and willingness to perform this auxiliary function. In times of genuine distress, availability by telephone between sessions, extra sessions, and interdiction of self-destructive acting out are required complements to the interpretation and working through of the unconscious belief that in the face of terror, the patient will be abandoned. When judiciously applied, this approach can bring about over a period of time the internalization of the analyst as a figure who will be there when the patient reaches out in genuine need. Anxiety dreams, which have previously been characterized by aloneness, drowning, suffocating, and being devoured, begin to be replaced by dreams that contain references to the presence of another person with whom the patient is able to make reassuring contact. The change in the nature of the dream content is accompanied by changes in the patient's functioning, in the direction of more assertive, autonomous, appropriate behavior in his or her real life. It is as if the patient were dramatizing the concept "I can face that of which I have been previously afraid because I am connected to a reliable person who is sharing the uncertainties and dangers and to whom I can turn for help or comfort if I must."

The choreographic and cognitive characteristics of this process bear remarkable resemblance to the process of individuation described by Mahler (1975), especially those patterns observed in the rapprochement phase. After a period of time, which varies in individual instances, gradual weaning from this kind of availability should be begun, in order to shift the burden of coping with stress increasingly to the patient. However, the potential need for such availability is never completely eliminated as a therapeutic consideration; one simply reduces the frequency as the patient makes better use of other relationships.

The patient's recognition that he or she is not alone and the gradual internalization of the representation of the analyst in the mode of the symbiotic object enable the patient to face the nightmarish experiences of childhood that have contributed to the genesis of the disorder. Incapacitating physical illness, anesthesia, surgery, hospitalizations, and other prolonged separations from parents constitute one category of experience. Memories associated with covert or overt parental hatred, the perceptions of which have been previously dissociated secondary to massive denial, represent a second category. The psychobiological integrity of the young child is dependent upon the belief in the existence of the good parent; to allow conscious awareness of the parental wish to be rid of the child is to face mortal terror (the prospect of total aloneness). The younger the child, the greater the terror and the greater the need for pathogenic alloplastic and autoplastic defensive operations. Subsequent modification of parental attitudes may never overcome the effects of early, fear-inspiring parental introjects.

Repetitive Themes in Borderline Patients

Childhood experiences in which the patient perceived and experienced an overwhelming (for him or her) reality in isolation, as well as events in which overwhelming anxiety was engendered by overt and covertly communicated parental hatred, constitute repetitive themes. One male and one female patient described prolonged periods of asthmatic disturbance in early childhood during which they covered their mouths with pillows lest the sounds of their wheezing and coughing be audible. They both described their gasping for breath and the painful efforts at expiration, accompanied by the fear of dying by suffocation. That fear was compounded by the guilt and terror experienced in anticipation of parental vilification for being ill.

Many patients who were raised by sadistic hired help felt unable to appeal to their parents, based upon the probably accurate belief that the parents preferred not to know. A male patient, whose younger brother died in his crib under somewhat mysterious circumstances when the patient was four years of age, was unable to deal with this event until the fourth year of his analysis. He reported a dream in which a woman detective was supposed to investigate a murder but was unable to act. The patient ran from the house—identified as the house in which the death occurred—having been told to find a policeman. His associations to the dream clearly reflected his unconscious view that his mother was not competent to protect her children from death. For the first time, he recalled that his father, who had been summoned from his office when the tragedy occurred, arrived at their apartment and fainted. For this patient, the analysis represented a protection against death, a guarantee of immortality. An important component of the transference was his need to see the analyst as a magical figure who could guarantee that immortality.

Another male patient was three years of age when his one-year-old sister contracted a severe case of polio, an event which resulted in his being sent to live with his grandmother for six months. His parents devoted themselves primarily to his sister, who required an enormous quantity of attention and medical care. His memories of the initial period of her illness are restricted to his room at his grandmother's house: "It was small, dark . . . I can't think of that room as having another person in it . . . it's as if I spent long periods of time there by myself. I thought my sister was going to die . . . I wondered if I would get polio and die."

It is possible to present countless histories of patients who have recalled or have been told of having been isolated—totally alone—in times of physical or experiential distress during their early years, of patients with parents who terrified them with threats of bodily harm or actively visited physical abuse upon them, and of patients whose parents verbalized death wishes. Parenthetically, whenever it has been possible to test the accuracy of these memories by interviewing parents of patients or having the patient consult with others present at the times in question, the memories have been authenticated in substance, if not in detail.

The most primitive fear to which man is subject, comparable in intensity only to that of somatic death, is perceived or psychic isolation, sometimes experienced as total emptiness. It is the terror of nothingness within a state of intrapsychic objectlessness which is equivalent to psychic death. For the infant, it is the symbiotic tie to the mother which serves as protection against trauma and death. To be abandoned means to the infant, and later to the neurotic and to those whom we have come to call borderline, annihilation or psychic death (Stern 1968). It is these patients who have not achieved the developmental level of object constancy—possessed of a brittle core, without a good internalized object and with a high degree of ambivalence to the primary object (Weil 1953)—who develop serious neurotic symptoms or psychotic disorganization with the anticipation or reality of loss of the primary object. The patient with a less severe neurosis is more effectively defended against the reexperiencing of total objectlessness and its accompanying mortal terror than is the borderline patient; more stable object relations characterized by a lesser degree of ambivalence provide adaptive, and therefore protective, support systems. The borderline patient requires the internalization of the new object (the analyst) in order to proceed further. Neurotic patients with significant disturbance in the sphere of object relations have a comparably fragile attachment to the primary object and thus pose similar problems in analysis.

The case study that follows contains data from a patient with a neurosis. It is presented in order to illustrate analytic process in a setting different from the usual analytic setting and to illustrate the relationship of internalization and clinical improvement.

CASE STUDY

The patient is a thirty-year-old male who began treatment two years ago for symptoms of impotence, which had its onset several months before he consulted me and at the time he and his wife commenced efforts to have a child. As a result of his sexual dysfunction, he was precipitated into a depression accompanied by feelings of worthlessness, self-recriminatory obsessional thoughts, and difficulties in concentration. There was no history of prior psychiatric disturbance, no vegetative signs, and no evidence, upon examination, of psychotic or borderline pathology.

Treatment was initiated on a two-session-per-week basis, with the patient sitting rather than using the couch. The initial phase of analysis of resistance was followed by clarification of his difficulty with assertiveness, which was most pronounced in his relationship with his wife, whose love he was terrified to lose. As the work continued, a new theme—his inability to perform upon demand—emerged. This is a very painful, practical problem for a male who is expected to perform sexually according to the dictates of a daily temperature chart.

Primarily through his work with dreams and through continuing analysis of his mechanisms of denial and avoidance, he recalled memories of his toilet training experience. The memories were clearly remembered and dated by the patient at the age of two years. His mother expected excretory performance on schedule, refusing to allow departure from their home until he eliminated to her satisfaction. She enforced her regimen with the aid of a leather belt, which she held at the ready, administering blows to his buttocks when she became exasperated and enraged with him.

> I used to hold back my feces . . . I enjoyed the feeling of the stool reaching my anus and forcing it back. Sometimes the stool got very hard and I would get constipated. I can remember my mother standing over while I was on the pot. She would hit me with the belt . . . once . . . so hard that the buckle broke off. She would sit there, snapping the belt so that it made a cracking sound to scare me. I feel scared talking about it.

In addition, she repeatedly humiliated him by complaining to relatives and neighbors, in the patient's presence, about his "spitefulness" in refusing to cooperate. A period of working through of his pattern of fearful defiance of having to perform sexually upon demand and deliver his sexual products at designated times resulted in a diminution of the symptom of impotence to the status of an occasional occurrence.

At the beginning of the second year of the treatment, he began to deal with his preadolescent relationship with his mother. Because of the divisiveness in the parental relationship, the mother made the patient her confidant, telling him of her pain and sadness and complaining to him about the "unsympathetic" father. The patient recalled many days in which he went off to school feeling miserable, confused, and fearful that he was unable to help his mother to resolve her problem. The implications of this experience—his feeling that he had to share a woman's depression in order to demonstrate his love—and the implications for his Oedipal struggle with his father, whom he loved then and loves to this day, have constituted the substance of the more recent analytic work.

In the 20th month of treatment, the patient reported a dream, which was divided into two segments:

I am in a room with a number of other people whom I do not recognize. A burglar has broken into the room and is taking everyone's money. I look for a place to hide so that he won't find me . . . I don't remember whether I succeeded or not.

Then I am talking with you, only it's you with my father's face. I am telling you that I don't have to be scared or depressed because there is nothing in the present that I can't handle; the problem comes from what I used to be afraid of as a child.

Upon awakening from the dream, the patient found himself thinking about the two women whose pregnancies he had learned about the previous day. (The patient's original problem of impotence has been supplanted by an infertility problem. Once each month within the past two years, he and his wife have had to face the disappointment that supervenes upon the appearance of her menstrual flow.) His unconscious belief that his father and other men strive to steal from him his masculinity was revealed by his associations as he continued to struggle with his feeling of sexual inadequacy, a feeling that had remained in spite of clinical evidence that the infertility problem was not explainable by any anatomical or physiological deficit.

Toward the end of the session, he made a comment which, at the time, seemed apropos of nothing specific:

You know, it was interesting how the day of the dream and day after went. Usually my wife's period coming and being told that someone else had conceived would drop me right into a lousy depression. I had the feeling this time that I didn't have to do that; that it didn't mean that I was letting my mother down.

Discussion of Case

This case is presented to illustrate several considerations. The first concerns the evidence within the dream and the associations to the dream of an internalization of the analyst as a therapeutic introject; the identification is with the therapeutic function of the analyst, who helps the patient to distinguish current reality from the intrusions upon the present of the irrationalities of the past. The dream portrays the intrapsychic representation of the analyst, which combines the reality of his therapeutic function with the representation of his significance as the transferential father. In the months following the session in which this dream had been reported, the patient's proneness to depressive reactions diminished to a considerable degree, and a new level of confident discourse with his world became increasingly apparent. The evolving process which fosters the intrapsychic incorporation of the collaborative dyadic relationship (combining real with transferential elements) is pivotal to the clinical improvement. In terms of process, it corresponds to the internalization of the analytic therapist by the borderline patient, associated with the insight that two people working together can successfully accomplish a formidable, even frightening, task.

The case demonstrates further that analytic process involving analysis of resistance, transference, dreams, and unconscious mental functioning can be carried out successfully with a motivated psychoneurotic patient in the face-to-face position on a twice-weekly basis. The changes that have occurred in the patient's overall functioning, the diminution of the intensity of his symptoms, and the developmental changes corresponding to his acceptance of himself as a professional adult and as prospective father differ in no discernible ways from the progress observed in patients who have employed the couch and have had more frequent sessions.

The context required for the performing of analytic work depends upon the following:

1. Motivation

2. A capacity for a reasonably trusting attachment to the analyst

3. Capacities for introspection and for distinguishing internal from external reality

4. The ability to accept the major burden of the therapeutic work

5. Relative abstinence on the part of the analyst, which I define as the discipline necessary to permit the patient to struggle with neurotically (irrationally) determined depression and anxiety without offering palliative comfort (The abstinence is relative because the analyst's friendliness, optimism, and encouragement that the tasks of treatment are attainable are necessary and known to the patient. The concept of total abstinence is a myth; efforts to attain total abstinence may well have iatrogenic consequences.)

6. The consistent interpretation of resistance, both tactical and strategic (Silverberg 1955), wherever it appears

7. Consistent interpretation of the transferential distortions and monitoring of the real component of the therapeutic (analytic) dyad in order that the therapeutic alliance be maintained

CONCLUSION

The empirical experience derived from the treatment of borderline patients underscores the crucial role of damage in the sphere of object relations sustained within the earliest years of development. Evaluation of the processes that lead to successful therapeutic results highlights the importance of the functions of attachment, trust, incorporation, object constancy, individuation, and relative autonomy. Progression through the developmental stages is observed in the form of a complex drama, which takes place upon the stage provided by the dyadic, analytic relationship (again, real and transferential). The more damaged patient forces the analyst to react to and to be aware of developmental fixations within the sector of object relations, for he or she requires concrete proof of the analyst's reliability, active involvement, concern, and effectiveness. The neurotic patient who has achieved a reasonable level of object constancy may not require such explicit validation of that which is to him or to her implicit or assumed.

Given the experience with the borderline patient, it would appear to be true that where a positive therapeutic outcome does result from the induction and working through of the regressive transference neurosis, it is not the consequence of interpretation alone. Rather, it is the result of interpretation within the context of that crucial object relationship evolved by patient and analyst. The interpretation of transference phenomena as they are encountered during the analysis and during termination is central, but it is effective only within the interplay between the real relationship and those transferential phenomena. The mythology that may inhibit the young therapist and the more tradition-bound analyst concerns the functions of the real relationship. If the analyst is so fearful of the real dangers of irrevocably damaging the analytic relationship by hostile and/or seductive behavior, his or her basic humanity may be compromised. Austerity, neutrality in the face of damaging life events, or the successful mastery of previously impossible psychological tasks are correctly perceived as hostile by the patient. Fundamental human behavior by the analyst will never damage or "contaminate" a transference. Quite to the contrary, the real relationship ultimately constitutes the reservoir of forces that enables the patient to sustain, understand, and eventually overcome the fear that accompanies and determines the irrational components of the transference.

If it is understood that the deepest roots of illness reside in the internalization of pathologic object relations in the earliest years of life and that psychoanalytic therapy is effective only when the pathologic internalizations of the past are worked through in an analytic relationship in which the analyst is a real and reliable object, can we avoid the clinical reality that treatment always be modified or adapted to the requirements of the patient's pathology? The more profound the illness, the greater will be the importance of the metaphorical parenting of the real relationship, which serves as a counterforce to the consequences of deficient or hostile parenting.

We have arrived at a time in psychoanalytic history that calls for a redefinition of therapeutic terminology. Leo Stone's contribution, *The Widening Scope of Psychoanalysis* (1954), confirmed that confronted with changing patterns of pathology, "like Freud himself, analysts were capable of flexible adjustments to changing circumstances" (Anthony 1977). In reality, these flexible adjustments constitute the modifications of technique called for by the nature of the patient's psychopathology. It is suggested that, in the service of clarity, Stone's concept be reversed in order to carefully delineate the very *narrow* therapeutic scope of *standard psychoanalysis*, as opposed to its scope as an investigatory procedure. As Knight (1954) pointed out, "as a method of therapy, it has limited application in the vast field of human psychological distress." To quote Glover again:

> ... the transference neurosis may not develop in the psychotic, psychotic character, borderline as well as the character disorders, perversions, certain psychosomatic disturbances, psychopathies, cases of marital difficulties, and the "almost normal character."

It is further suggested that the method of treatment that has been defined as psychoanalytic psychotherapy with its "parameters" and modifications represents that which is therapeutic in contrast to that which is process. Empirical experience informs us that it is the duration of treatment rather than daily sessions that is related to successful therapeutic result, that it is the disciplined and human participation of the analyst that is crucial to therapeutic process, that abstinence and neutrality need only be relative and partial, and that a "full-fledged, regressive transference neurosis" is not required for durable change.

Psychoanalytic treatment, based upon the factors of unconscious mental functioning and analysis of resistance, transference phenomena, and dreams within a controlled setting that permits a reliving and reexamination of the injurious experience of the past, engenders unique therapeutic outcome. Reliable change, which ultimately depends upon the modification of distorted, pathogenic, and pathologic internalized representations of the self and object world, can be achieved on a treatment schedule of two to three sessions per week and, at times, in the face-to-face setting. As in Robert Knight's view:

> In the last analysis, there is only one psychotherapy ... with many techniques ... resting upon a basic science of dynamic psychology ... and those techniques should be used which are clinically indicated for each individual patient (p. 64).

REFERENCES

Anthony, E.J. (1977) The Boring Patient. *Psychiatric News.* September 15, 1977.

Balint, M. (1950) Symposia on the Termination of Psychoanalytical Treatment and on the Criteria for the Termination of an Analysis. *Int. J. Psychoanal.* 31:78–80.

Dince, P.R. (1977) Partial Dissociation as Encountered in the Borderline Patient. *J. Amer. Acad. Psychoanal.* 5(3):327–345.

Dince, P.R. (1978) Factors Inherent to the Treatment of Borderline Patients. In press.

Gill, M. (1954) Psychoanalysis and Exploratory Psychotherapy. *J. Amer. Psychoanal. Assn.* 2:771–797.

Glover, E. (1955) *Technique of Psychoanalysis.* International Universities Press, New York, pp. 374–386.

Kernberg, O. (1967) Borderline Personality Organization. *J. Amer. Psychoanal. Assn.* 15:641–685.

Knight, R. (1954) *Psychoanalytic Psychiatry and Psychology.* International Universities Press, New York, pp. 97–109.

Mahler, M. (1975) *The Psychological Birth of the Human Infant.* Basic Books, New York, pp. 76–108.

Pfeffer, A.Z. (1961) Follow-up Study of a Satisfactory Analysis. *J. Amer. Psychoanal. Assn.* 9:698–718.

Silverberg, W.V. (1955) Lectures in Psychoanalytic Technique. Comprehensive Course in Psychoanalysis.

Stern, M. (1968) Fear of Death and Neurosis. *J. Amer. Psychoanal. Assn.* 16:3–31.

Stone, L. (1954) The Widening Scope of Indications for Psychoanalysis. *J. Amer. Psychoanal. Assn.* 2:567–594.

Wallerstein, R. (1965) The Goals of Psychoanalysis. *J. Amer. Psychoanal. Assn.* 13:748–770.

Weil, A. (1953) Certain Severe Disturbances in Ego Development in Childhood. *Psychoanal. Study of Child* 8:271–287.

5

CHARACTER, COGNITION, AND THERAPEUTIC PROCESS

JOSEPH BARNETT, M.D.
New York Medical College,
William Alanson White Institute, New York, and
New York University

The concept of character has always been undervalued by theorists. Commonly defined as the aggregate of traits that distinguish a person, character has been seen as superficial and peripheral to the main concerns of psychoanalysis. The early instinct-versus-defense model of psychoanalysis defined character as expressions of or defenses against instinctual pressures. As a result, character has usually been assigned an epiphenomenal role—at most, it has been considered a derivative of the functions of the ego and superego. It has remained an ambiguous, poorly defined notion, peripheral to our theories of mind and of therapy.

The recent growing concern of psychoanalysts with epistemic and cognitive issues, however, is beginning to effect a change in the orientation toward the concept of character. This concern promises significant reevaluations of the concept and of its importance to psychoanalytic theory and practice.

This chapter will examine the nature and function of character as a structural phenomenon related to the architectonics of knowing. It will extend observations that have been made regarding the central significance of cognition to the understanding of the functioning of the mind and the relationship of the concept of character to issues of cognition. It will also examine the implications of these views for issues of psychodynamics and the therapeutic process.

Psychoanalysis is the study of what, how, and why the individual knows and does not know. Its theoretical premises include both the fact that early experience affects knowing and meaning and that subsequent behavior and mental functioning reflect these earlier patterns of meaning. In essence, psychoanalytic therapy may be considered an exercise in personal epistemology, in which the patient's ways of knowing and systems of meaning are explored and understood in order to correct dysfunctional mental processes and behaviors.

Because its roots lie in clinical observation, psychoanalysis, more than the academic psychologies, has recognized the importance of sensate experience on the organization of meaning in a person's life. Yet, like the academic psychologies, psychoanalytic theory too narrowly defines cognition as being related simply to processes of thinking. Affect, or feeling, has been considered an opposing phenomenon to thought, which has led, unfortunately and arbitrarily, to the creation and institutionalizing of the dualism of thought and feeling.

This dualism and its attendant dialectics have assumed unwarranted prominence in psychoanalytic theory and practice. In our conceptualizations of personality, cognition is equated with thought and is then contrasted with affect as an exclusive process. Rapaport (1951), for example, considers thought and affect as alternate results of delay in the gratification of drive tension. The implications of "either—or" in the production of thought or affect pattern many of our clinical and therapeutic concerns. Clinically, although it is often contrary to observable clinical data, the implied dialectics of this approach to thought and affect dominates our attitudes toward the problem of character. The oversimplification of this approach leads to theoretical and clinical impasses.

It has been suggested, therefore, that use of the term *cognition* be expanded to incude all those processes involved in experiential knowing (Barnett 1968). Cognition, so considered, would include a range of knowing from the more direct, sensory, and immediate awareness of experience to the more linguistically structured and syntactically organized awareness. Knowing might then be said to occur on a continuum, the points of which differ primarily in their degree of sensate or syntactic structure. The more syntactically structured an experience, the more we might be said to comprehend it. Sensate experience would be knowing on a level of apprehension rather than comprehension. By custom, the more immediately apprehended aspects of experience are referred to as *feeling* and the more linguistically structured, as *thought*. Thought and affect are not opposing, mutually exclusive, aspects of mental life but rather are formal and structural reflections of a continuum of knowing, existing in intimate interchange and reaction to each other and to the actional system.

CHARACTER AS A CENTRAL STRUCTURAL CONCEPT

To be truly dynamically significant and not just a nosological afterthought, character must be distinguished from presenting style (Shapiro

1965)—it must be freed from its definition as merely an aggregate of superficial traits. Character is an underlying structural phenomenon whose design and formal attributes determine much of an individual's mental life. From a structural perspective, character may be viewed as a behavioral and cognitive reflection of the organization of experience in a person's life. Character is a template, formed by the impact of historical experience. It functions to determine the individual's perception, interpretation, and organization of ongoing experience, as well as designs of expectation and anticipation, behavioral tendencies, and interpersonal operations.

In its cognitive aspects, character represents relatively durable patterns of relationships between sensate and syntactic experience and the organization of these patterns into systems of apprehension and comprehension. It reflects the individual's ways of knowing and systems of meaning. Ideally, the state of cognition in character organization would be an expanding interchange between levels representing both sensate and syntactic structure, with each level enriching and renewing the other, and each dependent on the other for optimal functioning. This ideal model would be an open-ended system in homeostasis with the environment, restricted only by the inherent limitations of the human organism.

From a practical viewpoint, however, the study of character is more often the study of the limitations and distortions imposed by various sources on these systems during their development. The delineation of a character type implies the existence of a skew in the organization of experience, a dysfunctional relationship between sensate and syntactic experience that leads to closure rather than to open-ended homeostasis. To distinguish, therefore, between hysterical characters and hysterical neuroses—or between obsessional characters and obsessional neuroses—would be arbitrary and would ignore the fact that both are structural deformations differing only in extent or in the cultural or personal bias of the observer.

DYSFUNCTIONAL CHARACTER FORMATIONS

Dysfunctional character organizations have consistent areas of "not knowing," or innocence, which function as predictable systems. These systems of innocence imply historically and dynamically created areas of difficulty in cognitive organization. The effect of these systems is to block the interchange between apprehension and comprehension, to create closure of cognition, and to restrict opportunities for growth. Knowing is interfered with at various specific levels of cognition, and the creative interplay between apprehension and comprehension is limited by the confines of a rigid template.

In normal living, affective experience is of both external and internal importance to the personality. Affect is used expressively for reaction and communication and intrapsychically as data for thought and syntactic organization of experience; that is, affect normally gives rise to *expression* and *impression.* Expression involves the direct, presyntactic communication of affects, such as in gesture, posture, facial expression, crying, and laughing. Impression refers to the perception and storage of the sensate data of experience, which become important sources of experience for syntactic organization and comprehension.

In dysfunctional character formations, however, affective experience is used either explosively or implosively. *Explosion of affect* is a cognitive dynamism in which a forceful ejection or voiding of apprehended experience takes place before adequate structuring or thoughtful integration of experience can occur. *Implosion of affect* is a cognitive dynamism in which affect is forced inward on the cognitive processes, disorganizing them. Both explosion and implosion interfere with the normal cognitive ordering of experience, but they do so differently. In affective explosion, the apprehended data of experience are discarded before adequate syntactic structuring and comprehension can take place. In implosion of affect, on the other hand, the very processes necessary for adequate organization are disorganized, with the result that apprehended data are contained but left simply as raw data. These dynamisms are reflected in characteristic ways in dysfunctional characters.

Two basic types of dysfunctional character formations can be defined structurally—the explosive disorders and the implosive disorders. Explosion of affect is the dominant cognitive dynamism in the hysterical disorders, the acting-out personalities, and the impulse disorders. Affective implosion characterizes the obsessional disorders, the paranoid character disorders, and the depressive personalities.

Explosive and Implosive Disorders

Explosion of affect finds its most direct expression in the hysterical character neuroses (Barnett 1968 and 1971). The hysterical character typically expels affective experience before adequately structuring it syntactically. A historical fear of affect and associated feelings of helplessness lead the patient to void large areas of apprehended experience prematurely and often in substitutive forms. This expelled, undigested affective experience, whether it be good or bad, is then used to shape the sweeping generalizations and crude formulations that characterize the hysteric's transitory comprehension of experience, which is unrefined by the effect of impression. The lack of organization and the premature voiding do not allow for the differentiation and ordering of the meaning of experience. As a result, the hysteric's comprehension of experience is simple and imprecise. Furthermore, the rapid riddance of emotional reaction deprives the hysterical person of essential material for use in integrating experience with signficant others into stable realizations of their identities. The hysteric's images of others can shift abruptly from adoring idealization to hateful contempt and cynicism. Communication then, is, related more to sensate experience than to syntactic experience and consequently is often exaggerated and highly colored emotionally.

The hysteric's assets also can be linked to the use of apprehended experience. The development of this aspect of cognition leads to an empathic sense of interpersonal events and transactions, an expressive ability to convey affective experience to others, and an ability to chance action and commitment—all of which are typical of the hysteric.

The obsessional personality is the most characteristic example of the phenomenon of implosion of affects (Barnett 1966a). Raised in a climate of ambiguity, where explicit avowals of love and concern covered implicit rejection or hostility, the obsessional person has learned to fear the implicit in interpersonal situations. By imploding the affective experience of these interactions, the individual who uses obsessional operations disintegrates cognitive organization and the meaning of events. Fearing specific cognitive configurations that are implicit in interpersonal situations and that might challenge existing self-concepts, the obsessional person avoids making anxiety-provoking interpersonal inferences. He or she maintains disruption of these inferences by imploding preexpressive affects into the inferential processes that organize the implications of ongoing experience. The individual becomes syntax bound, excessively literal, and legalistic because of the disturbances in the processes of thought. Adept in the recitation of a stereotypic, ideologic dogma regarding the conduct of human relations, and often even correct in proforma behavior, the obsessional person can be party to emotionally intensive positive or negative interpersonal interchanges without even vaguely grasping their meaning. Ambiguous referential systems based on the individual's past experience persist and lead to the indecisiveness, ambivalence, and lack of commitment characteristic of the syndrome. Because of the implosive use of preexpressive affects and their disorganizing effects, the obsessional person may feel like a chaotic and turbulent caldron of affectivity, which nonetheless serves poorly as data of experience.

The impulse disorders and the acting-out personalities are related cognitively to the hysterical disorders in their utilization of explosion of affect. Like the hysteric, the impulse neurotic voids apprehended experience, but this is done largely through action rather than feelings. Comprehension of experience again is imprecise, but there is an added dimension to the maintenance of innocence by the impulse neurotic, namely, the input of information about the significance of the impulsive actions. The acting-out person, disclaiming intention of the effect—on others or on himself or herself—of unfortunate behavioral and actional operations, can repeatedly violate the simplest canons of socially acceptable interpersonal relations without the slightest appreciation of the meaning or impact of the violations. The basic organization of the two character types around affective explosion accounts for the frequent blending of hysterical and impulse disorder phenomena in clinical cases.

The paranoid character disorders are closely related to the obsessional disorders in that they both utilize implosion of affects to disorganize ongoing inference-making in interpersonal situations. Both try to avoid knowing, because of central damage to their sense of self and their very precarious self-esteem. Whereas the obsessional person substitutes static, clichéd and stereotyped judgments for ongoing inferences, however, the paranoid person substitutes arbitrary inferences that are based on the person's existing assumptions of a threatening and hostile interpersonal environment. It was recently suggested that the roots of such isolating cognitive assumptions lie in specific types of family ideologies or belief systems (Barnett 1978a). The similarities in obsessional and paranoid cognition account for the tendency of these two types to overlap clinically. Paranoid phenomena frequently appear in obsessional patients, and most paranoid characters utilize obsessional mechanisms.

The depressive personality represents another variety of implosive character. Unlike the obsessional and paranoid characters, the depressive person is openly identified with his or her low self-esteem. The depressive person uses this damaged sense of self openly in interpersonal operations that are designed to claim attention and sympathy from others, to exploit them in covert power operations and dependent demands for care, and to punish them for real or imagined hurts. Like the obsessional and paranoid characters, depressive persons obscure and deny the meaning of their behavior, in that they deny the use to which they put their damaged self-images. Data that might furnish them with understanding are promptly employed in a mea culpa operation that compounds the malfunctioning cognitive system.

Depression may also be used as a symptom by any dysfunctional character type. Symptomatic depression should be distinguished from the depressive character itself. In the obsessional, for example, a low-grade depression is almost constant. Overt or covert depression accompanies implosion of affects and is most severe in interpersonal situations that provoke the most implosion—that is, where there is the greatest need for maintaining innocence. In the paranoid character, as in the obsessional, depression is frequent and is related to implosion, but it seems to be relieved somewhat by the arbitrary inferences that are expressed in response to threatening situations.

In the explosive disorders, where affective explosion prevents adequate comprehension of experience, depression accompanies the blocking of explosive phenomena, that is, with the occurrence of relative implosion. In the hysteric disorders, this occurs when explosion of affect is blocked, whereas in the impulse disorders and the acting-out personalities, depression accompanies the blocking of exploded action.

Character, then, is a superordinate rather than a subordinate system. It is a structural or formal concept that reflects the pattern of relationships between sensate and syntactic experience and the corollaries of meaning of such experience as well as the patterns of action designed by these systems.

Patterns of cognition have more extensive effects on intentionality and motivation than is envisioned by those who adopt the epiphenomenal view of cognition, or by those who limit their conceptions of motivation to instinctual-drive forces alone. Intentionality and motivation stem from meaning rather than from drives. For the very reason that character designs knowing and meaning in the individual, it also designs intentionality and motivation. Klein (1967) has shown that a train of thought especially when it is repressed, may have the the quality of peremptoriness necessary to create motivational power. This separation of the notion of motivation from a necessary relationship to instinct and energy is an important theoretical step. Implicit patterns of thought or affect and the meaning that they convey to the person are the ultimate sources of motivation.

THE SELF AS A COGNITIVE CONCEPT

The concept bridging the designs of knowing and meaning on the one hand and the designs of action and behavior on the other is the self. Already a central conceptual tool in post-Freudian theory and practice, self is of growing importance to almost all theoretical persuasions in the field of psychoanalysis. Most theoreticians either explicitly or implicitly view the self as a cognitive concept. The term also has been defined as the recognition, both felt and thought, of one's meaning to the interpersonal environment, to one's inner and outer world, especially in terms of one's roles and functions (Barnett 1978a). Self is not just another structure of the mind, to be compared or equated with ego, as it often is. Self is a cognitive experience. Self, as experienced by the person, has its sensate (felt or sensed) aspects as well as its syntactic (comprehended) components. Which aspects of the self are apprehended, which are comprehended, and which fall within the individual's systems of innocence are determined by the design of the person's cognition. Both the structure and the limits of the experience of self are patterned by the formal aspects of character structure. Significant modification or growth in the experience of self must be prefaced by changes in cognition and character.

The function of self as a bridge between the designs of cognition and the designs of action is related to the fact that self is perceived in terms of roles and functions in the environment. Roles and functions imply actional relationships with the environment, and the self therefore mediates the personal meanings that are the necessary and the sufficient cause for both intention and motivation. Cognizing self, according to this view, provides the person with the basic template for action vis-á-vis the environment and its inner representations. Sullivan (1953) recognized this structured aspect of the actional system in personality and its relationship to self in his construct of the *self-system*, which he defined as the organization of operations designed by the individual in his or her attempt to avoid anxiety in interpersonal relations. Although anxiety is an important determinant of meaning in experience, the phenomenon like the instincts, is too limited to account for all motivation.

IMPACT ON THERAPEUTIC PROCESS

Such a broadened view of the significance of character to mental functioning should, of course, have considerable impact on the approach to the therapeutic process. It is certainly inadequate to consider character analysis as merely a prelude to the task of analyzing the Oedipal conflict, the transference neuroses, or even the self-esteem. Nor should changes in character be considered merely by-products, occuring incidentally to progress in the analysis by whatever measures current theortical orientations offer. A theory of therapy where character finds its niche only in the analysis of resistances or of the defenses also is inadequate. The task of analysis *is* the task of character analysis—it is impossible to conceive of truly successful analytic work that does not entail significant change in the person's character structure.

With regard to resistances, it is difficult to see them as being specific to the analytic situation, as is usually claimed. Differentiation should no longer be made between character resistances and other types of resistances, because all are characterological, both in origin and intent. The patient's resistances follow the skewing of mental functioning and behavior that is meant to maintain systems of innocence. Resistances involve interpersonal operations intended to subvert collaboration and to avoid exposure of the self to the self and to others. They are not specific to the analytic situation in that they are a class or category of interpersonal operations also seen with regularity in the patient's interactions with other people in which interpersonal collaboration or intimacy is required. Internalized resistances to one's own mental processes also follow this rule and are constructed in accordance with the conditions of relatedness to internalized and personified others. One may be resistant to performing certain tasks even when alone, when the task implies collaboration or exposure to an internalized figure like a parent or an idealized aspect of self. In practice, the analysis of resistances marks the beginning of the analysis of character and the earliest view of the core of the patient's neurotic problems.

Transference, too, seems to indicate characterological problems and is not specific to the therapeutic situation. The process- and cognition-oriented concept of parataxic distortion (Sullivan 1953) that is used in interpersonal theory is preferable to the more static, content-oriented concept of transference used by the more classical theories, because it better describes the effect of dysfunctional knowing systems on the perception and interpretation of the patient–analyst dyad. Additionally, it is easier to utilize the concept of parataxic distortion in interpersonal situations other than the analytic encounter, where I feel transference phenomena occur constantly.

COGNITIVE REPAIR

Because analysis is always character analysis, and because the nature and function of character are so involved with issues of knowing and meaning, it becomes necessary to address more directly in our theories of therapy the issue of cognition. Accordingly, the central task of psychoanalytic therapy can be defined as *cognitive repair* (Barnett 1966b and 1972).

Cognitive repair implies the correction of the distortions and imbalances in the person's systems of knowing and meaning and the repair of those dysfunctional or nonfunctioning mental processes and operations that maintain systems of innocence and prevent integration of meaning with experience and action. Without such a concept as an integral part of our theories of therapy, there is too much danger that new experience cannot occur, that insight cannot be integrated into experience, that the patient will continue the dysfunctional patterns of the past, and that analysis will become futile and interminable (Barnett 1978b).

Cognitive repair is a process involved with cognition but oriented by character. The dominant trends in the patient's character indicate the dysfunctional patterns of cognition and their integration into experience and action. These dysfunctional patterns, outlined previously, provide us with a guide for the necessary operations of a psychoanalytic therapy that is oriented toward cognitive repair.

In the explosive disorders—the hysterics, the impulse neurotics, and the acting-out personalities—cognitive repair is directed toward the systems of innocence created by the patient's failure to adequately structure experience syntactically. The analyst's stance must be to foster what Forest (1977) calls containment of the patient's affectivity, which is utilized to empty the self of the apprehended data of experience before adequate syntactic organization and comprehension can occur. Actually, the methods of analytic therapy aid us in this endeavor, particularly when they stress the need to attend to detail and channel associations to meaningful conclusions. Guiding the patient to dwell on and analyze emotional experience and to relate present experience to that of the past aids containment and impression of affect. In effect, psychoanalysts are geared to the task of increasing syntactic organization at least implicitly. It is probably because of this emphasis in the structure of analytic therapy that patients with explosive character disorders, such as the hysterics, fare so well in treatment.

More explicit and extensive concern with cognitive repair would improve results and expedite significant change in explosive characters. These patients tend to overvalue their affectivity and apprehension of experience. They believe that what they feel must be right. Unfortunately, without syntactic refinement they often miss the mark of their perceptions. Emphasis on conceptual examination and analysis of their perceptions of self and others aids in the process of refinement of experience. It is also useful in introducing them to more syntactic modes of comprehension, which can permit increased validation of experience with others and therefore decreased isolation.

Explosive characters frequently use sweeping generalizations in their reactions to interpersonal situations toward the same end of avoiding comprehension and maintaining innocence. The hyberbolic nature of these responses, larger than life as they are, must be related to their need to maintain innocence and to minimize the reality of events, thus avoiding the true impact of experience on them. Characterologically, a major purpose of these excessive responses is to discard the initial perception entirely because of the magnitude of the overreaction. The analyst's task is to aid such patients in their understanding of these processes, while at the same time preserving the valid core of their responses.

The profoundly dependent needs that are so central to the origin of explosive characters are often conventionalized and rationalized as needs for intimacy. The symbiotic concept of self of these patients and their excessive need for interpersonal contact to deny their real problems with intimacy need to be explored in therapy.

The implosive characters—the obsessionals, the paranoids, and the depressive personalities—are those patients who are least likely to emerge from psychoanalytic therapy with effective insight and change in character. These are the patients who swell the ranks of our therapeutic failures or who most often come for reanalysis. Our neglect of the cognitive disorders of these patients and our failure to deal with the characterological templates of meaning and the dysfunctional thought processes that maintain them are largely responsible for our frustrated therapeutic efforts. The primary theoretical focus on fear of feelings and the methodology that focuses on haphazard detail and on unlimited free association miss the point of the cognitive difficulties of these patients. The very design of our treatment and its concerns often reinforce, or even create, the dead, sterile intellectualizations that caricature real insight as well as the obscurantism that is at the heart of the neurotic's characterological problems.

Repair of the cognitive faults of implosive characters requires that analysts address the need of these characters to maintain innocence, to avoid knowing and comprehending experience. Their dynamics involve a need to obscure and hide through deviousness, inhibition, and denial. Such dynamics must be demonstrated to the patient, along with the specific operations that make them possible.

From the onset, therapy with implosive characters should be a search for clarity. These patients desperately do not want to know. Their innocence is organized around their self-contempt and fear of knowing their interpersonal significance and is maintained by defects in interpersonal inference-making, which might organize their awareness. Careful definition of the defects in inference-making is necessary in the early phases of therapy. Mapping of the areas in which these processes are disturbed gives clues as to the historical and developmental origins of the systems of innocence. These clues can be pursued with attentive questions, to elicit specific information from which viable inferences may be drawn. The stereotypic labeling that the patient uses in place of these inferences must be recognized as such and related to the context of the patient's life experiences.

Ambivalence, doubt, and indecision are cognitive symptoms of considerable importance to the attempt to resolve the dysfunctional thought processes of these patients. These symptoms are related to the presence of ambiguous referential systems. These dual lexicons—public and private definitions of the meanings of interpersonal events and concepts, often directly contradicting each other—must be conceptualized, clarified, and traced to the early history in the family and the events that helped to create the more private and dissociated referential processes.

Furthermore, these patients need help in defining the family ideologies that molded their beliefs, dogmas, values, and myths, as well as their cognitive operations that prescribe and proscribe what they may know and what they must not know.

This outline of concerns regarding cognitive repair is meant to indicate a direction for explicitly dealing with the cognitive disorders, which are the core issue of neurotic living. Character is a central structural concept that can aid psychoanalysts in understanding the epistemic issues at the heart of neurosis and their relationship to actional systems. The concepts of character and cognition presented can be integrated into psychoanalytic theories and into our designs of therapy with considerable advantage. With these concepts we can help our patients to make fuller use of their capacity for coordinated sensate and syntactic knowledge. Our patients' utilization of their experiences is the key to their gaining meaning and significance in their lives.

REFERENCES

Barnett, J. (1966a): On cognitive disorders in the obsessional. *Contemp. Psychoanalysis*, 2:2, 122–134.

Barnett, J. (1966b): Cognitive repair in the treatment of the obsessional neuroses. In *Proceedings of the Fourth World Congress of Psychiatry, 1966*, Excerpta Medica Foundation, Netherlands, 752–757.

Barnett, J. (1968): Cognition, thought, and affect in the organization of experience. In *Science and Psychoanalysis*, Vol. 12, ed. J. Masserman, Grune & Stratton, Inc., N.Y., 237–247.

Barnett, J. (1971): Narcissism and dependency in the obsessional-hysteric marriage. *Family Process*, 10:1, 75–83.

Barnett, J. (1972): Therapeutic intervention in the dysfunctional thought processes of the obesssional. *Amer. J. of Psychotherapy*, XXVI, No. 3, pp. 338–351.

Barnett, J. (1978a): The dynamics of interpersonal isolation. *J. Amer. Acad. Psychoanalysis* 6:1, pp. 59–70.

Barnett, J. (1978b): Insight and therapeutic change. *Contemp. Psychoanalysis*, 14:4, 534–544.

Forrest, T. (1977): Personal communication.

Kelin, G. S. (1967): Peremptory ideation: Structure and force in motivated ideas. In *Motives and Thought*, Psychological Issue Vol. 5, No. 2-3, ed. R. R. Holt, International University Press, Inc. N.Y., 80–130.

Rapaport, D. (1951): Toward a thoery of thinking. In *Organization and Pathology of Thought*, ed. D. Rapaport, Columbia University Press, N.Y., 689–730.

Shapiro, D. (1965): *Neurotic Styles*, Basic Books, Inc., N.Y.

Sullivan, H. S. (1953): *The Interpersonal Theory of Psychiatry*, W. W. Norton & Co., N.Y.

Part Three

PSYCHOANALYSIS OF THE BORDERLINE PATIENT

6

VULNERABILITY TO SCHIZOPHRENIC AND AFFECTIVE DISORDERS: IMPLICATIONS FOR PSYCHOANALYTIC THERAPY IN BORDERLINE PATIENTS

Michael H. Stone, M.D.
Medical College, White Plains, New York

Not long after the analytic pioneers began applying the Freudian method to neurotic patients, interest developed in possible applications within the realm of the psychoses. Maeder (1910) and Bjerre (1912) were among the first to write of their experiences in using psychoanalysis with paranoid schizophrenics. The presence of psychosis—that is, of a serious defect in the capacity to test reality—was unmistakable in their cases; hence there were no moments of uncomfortable surprise, midway in the therapy, when signs of a deeper disturbance suddenly became apparent to the analyst.

DEVELOPMENT OF THE CONCEPT OF BORDERLINE

A number of other analytic writers, however, having begun work with what they supposed to be classically analyzable cases, did note, in a few of their patients, manifestations of a psychotic condition that contraindicated further pursuit of conventional psychoanalysis. Still other analysts began to describe patients with whom classical analysis failed, or got bogged down, even in the absence of florid psychotic signs. It was out of the experience with this latter group of patients that the concept of a borderline case began to take shape. From the vantage point of the analyst, the term *borderline* designated specifically a region between neurosis and psychosis, as these terms were then understood. At other times, borderline was used to differentiate patients with clear-cut schizophrenia from less severely ill patients in whom stigmata of schizophrenia were discernible but not of an intensity that would satisfy whatever criteria were in current use for the unequivocal diagnosis of schizophrenia.

Clark (1919) and Moore (1921) used borderline in both senses: too ill for classical analysis and close approximation to either a schizophrenic or a manic-depressive psychosis. Moore, in particular, was impressed by the frequency of severe affective illness in the families of depressive border-lines or of schizophrenia in those borderline patients whose clinical picture was reminiscent of schizophrenia. He felt that both the borderline and the full-blown variants deserved classification under the same heading, since the thread of hereditary predisposition seemed to run through both the mild and the severe forms. In the absence of convincing statistical data, Moore had only his clinical impressions to rely on. It should be recalled, however, that the notion of hereditary predisposition in the more serious types of functional mental illness was an article of faith in 19th-century European psychiatry.

A second generation of psychoanalysts, already much more exclusively psychological and much less biological in orientation than their predecessors, found it threatening to acknowledge the possibility of a hereditary factor in psychotic, let alone, borderline conditions, because of the aura of hopelessness then attached to the idea of genetic underpinning. Thus Glover (1932), noting the analogy between dreams and psychosis, spoke of how "all of us are larval psychotics, and have been so since age two" (p. 841). In the 1938 paper of Stern, which led to the popularization of the term borderline within the analytic community, mention is made of depressive attributes in some cases and of paranoid and other schizophrenic attributes in others, but only a passing reference is made to the operation of a constitutional factor.

Deutsch (1942) considered the "as-if" personality for the most part a "preschizophrenic" condition, implying that such patients might eventually succumb to clearly recognizable schizophrenia. Knight (1953) was also at pains to differentiate borderline states from schizophrenia, the supposed parent condition to which many of the borderline causes belonged. Other writers were impressed by the stability of the borderline condition over time (Schmideberg 1947; Frosch 1964): many borderline patients remained free, even after years of follow-up, of the grosser signs of psychosis. If a break with reality occurred, it was ordinarily very brief—perhaps only a few days—in duration. Since borderline conditions were not often transitional phases on the way to or from symptomatic psychosis, they deserved to be viewed, in Frosch's opinion, as separate entities. Regarding their heterogeneity, he had this to say (Frosch 1964, p. 82):

When we use the term borderline, we are obviously referring to conditions which are borderline to psychosis. . . . If they do decompensate . . . they may reveal a recognizable clinical syndrome such as schizophrenia. On the other hand, the psychotic picture . . . may run the gamut of all known psychoses, paranoid, manic-depressive, and the rest.

Frosch suggested that many of the in-between conditions then described under a bewildering array of headings—Zilboorg's *ambulatory schizophrenia* (1957), Bychowski's *latent psychosis* (1953), Beck's *schizophrenia without psychosis* (1959), and so forth—could be meaningfully subsumed under the label he proposed: *psychotic character.* Frosch outlined the characteristics of the psychotic character using ego-psychological and object-relational frames of reference. One noted, for example, a relative preservation of the capacity to test reality, a higher level of object-relations than that found among symptomatically psychotic persons, and a resiliency such that any psychotic symptom-production tended to be transitory.

CRITERIA FOR DEFINING BORDERLINE CASES

In the 1960s the borderline conditions were teased apart still further from the classical psychoses of which the earlier generation of analysts had assumed they were the dilute versions. Grinker, Werble, and Drye (1968) speak of the borderline conditions as distinct from schizophrenia, a position also taken by Kernberg (1967). The borderline state is described by Grinker and his collaborators largely in phenomenological terms—that is, readily observable abnormalities in behavior, work capacity, and relationships—and by Kernberg, in psychostructural terms. The latter represents the continuation of a trend in psychoanalytic nosology emphasizing internalized object-relations, a trend noticeable already in the Deutsch article mentioned previously.

Kernberg's criterion-set delineates, in essence, a level of adaptation, namely, an intermediate level between neurotic and psychotic, where the following characteristics are identifiable:

- Good reality testing in the presence of poor ego-integration

- High vulnerability to frustration ("low anxiety tolerance")

- Impulsivity and poor scholastic or occupational performance ("impaired capacity for sublimatory channeling")

- Primitive defenses (splitting, projective identification, and denial)

- Either unstable or superficial object-relations

Kernberg's definition does tend to rule out chronic schizophrenia (where reality testing is chronically poor) but does not exclude the milder expressions of the schizophrenic genotype, such as described, under the heading "borderline schizophrenia," by the psychogeneticist Kety (1968). Numerically, however, if the typical Kernberg borderline patient has affiliations to any classical psychosis, they are to the affective disorders (Stone 1977). The same is probably true for the borderline cases defined according to the criteria of Grinker (one of whose four subtypes is even called *anaclitic depression*) or, more recently, of Gunderson (1975). The borderline personality disorder of Gunderson emphasizes manipulative suicide threats and a good social facade (thus demarcating the syndrome from chronic schizophrenia) but a poor work capacity (thus distinguishing the syndrome from the classical psychoneuroses).

Besides the phenomenological, psychostructural, and psychogenetic usages alluded to above, the term borderline is also used within another frame of reference: the psychopharmacologic. Klein (1969) has defined a number of syndromes within the borderline range of severity, predominantly of affective coloration. Recently, more precise definitions of these syndromes, namely, that of hysteroid dysphoria, are being elaborated by Klein, in conjunction with Spitzer and his co-workers (1978). Spitzer, in turn, has begun to refine a checklist of signs and symptoms occurring with particular frequency in conditions to which the psychoanalytic and psychiatric communities have been applying the borderline label (1978). The Spitzer checklist, of particular utility as a first step in objectifying the clinical impression of a borderline state, is geared toward the discrimination of a largely schizotypal versus a largely affective subtype and thus is wedded to the notion of a spectrum within both the schizophrenic and manic-depressive realms.

This notion is carried a step further in other work (Stone 1977, 1978, 1978a): as a result of seeing a number of pedigrees of schizoaffective patients in which schizophrenia was noted in one parental line and manic-depression in the other, the existence of a phenotypic (and possibly even of a genotypic) continuum of "psychoses" has been suggested, ranging from unequivocal schizophrenia to what might be called predominantly schizophrenic schizoaffective illness, on to an evenly balanced type, and then to predominantly affective schizoaffective illness, and finally to the "pure" unipolar and bipolar affective disorders. This notion finds support in the impressions of the psychogeneticist Stabenau (1977).

It is possible to find individual patients not only in every compartment of such a continuum but also at either the psychotic or the borderline level. In an effort to measure more accurately the balance between schizophrenic and affective features in any given case, a weighted rating scale was devised by Cohen and his co-workers (1972) in connection with their study of monozygotic twins, at least one of whom had a psychotic disorder. At the New York Hospital–Westchester Division, the reliability of a modified version of the Cohen scale is currently being appraised. The working hypothesis is that for otherwise similar patients at the psychotic or borderline level, the more nearly the symptom picture inclines toward the affective pole, the better the prognosis; the more it inclines toward "pure" schizophrenia, the worse the prognosis, at least with respect to the likelihood of any benefit from intensive psychotherapy. Accurate measure of symptom balance is an important component in the evaluation of this hypothesis.

The literature already contains a number of reports bearing on this issue; the results are conflicting. To some extent this lack of agreement may be a reflection of variation in patient samples. Welner et al. (1977), for example, marshalled evidence to the effect that schizoaffective psychosis had an outcome, using work and personal relations as indexes, no better than ordinary schizophrenia, suggesting that the presence of an affective component did not predict superior outcome. It would appear, however, that the patients in Welner's sample were nearer to chronic schizophrenia phenomenologically than were the more "affective" schizoaffectives of Clayton (1968) and of Sovner and McHugh (1976) or even the original schizoaffectives as first described by Kasanin (1933), the majority of whose patients had some degree of perplexity in the acute state and went on to make rather good recoveries.

The criteria embodied in the diagnosis of a borderline condition according to the most popular current usages are outlined in Tables 1 through 4. From inspection of these tables, the relative specificity of the

Table 1
Kernberg's Borderline Personality Organization

A. Essential characteristics
  1. Seriously impaired ego-integration, with presence of sharply contradictory attitudes about important aspects of self and others (Erickson's syndrome of "ego diffusion").
  2. The capacity to test reality is well preserved.
B. Nonspecific signs
  1. Heightened vulnerability to frustration (lowered anxiety tolerance).
  2. Poor control of impulses.
  3. Poor sublimatory capacity (manifested as poor occupational, scholastic, or avocational function).
C. Primitive defensive operations
  (Defensive pattern predominated by lower-level defenses such as splitting, denial, projective identification, etc., rather than higher-level defenses such as rationalization, reaction formation, etc.)
D. Significant impairment in object-relations (with superficiality, exploitativeness, turbulence)
E. Poor integration of values and ideals (poor superego integration)

Table 2
Gunderson's Borderline Personality Disorder

A. Essential characteristics
   1. Lowered achievement
   2. Impulsivity, including the propensity to alcohol or drug abuse or to sexual promiscuity or deviation
   3. Manipulative suicide threats (viz., wrist-cutting intended primarily to wrest attention from others)
   4. Mild psychotic episodes (sometimes precipitated by intensive psychotherapy; more apt in any case to be expressed as severe derealization/depersonalization than as widespread delusions)
   5. A high degree of socialization
   6. Disturbances in close relationships (with a tendency to be depressive in the presence of the important other and to become panicky, enraged, or suicidal should the latter threaten to leave)
B. Psychological tests tend to show:
   1. Intactness on the structured portions
   2. Primitivity of responses on the unstructured portions

Table 3
Diagnostic Criteria for Hysteroid Dysphoria
(developed by D. F. Klein, M.D., 1978)

A. Essential characteristics
   1. Intolerance of personal rejection, with particularly severe vulnerability to loss of romantic attachment.
   2. A depressive, painful, crashlike reaction to interpersonal rejection, associated with either a, b, or c.
      a. Overeating of sweets.
      b. Retreat to bed with naps.
      c. A sense of leaden paralysis and inertia.
   3. The depression is nonautonomous and anaclitic. Patients can usually be brought out of it by well-meaning attention, but will occasionally be rejecting of help.
   4. Depressive reactions are usually short-lived (one to two weeks), but very frequent and repetitious, leading to severe life disruptions. There are very occasional prolonged depressions, and only the very occasional depression appears endogenous.
B. Associated factors (need three)
   1. In normal state, is any of the following: histrionic, flamboyant, intrusive, seductive, narcissistic, demanding.
   2. Abuses alcohol episodically when depressed.
   3. Abuses stimulants when depressed; may become habituated to stimulants.
   4. Negative reaction to phenothiazines.
   5. Normal mood is expansive and active.
   6. Overidealization of love objects, with poor social judgments.
   7. Applause is highly stimulating.
   8. Makes suicidal gestures and threats.

Table 4
Spitzer Borderline Checklist

A. Identity disturbance
  1. Schizotypal items
    a. Odd communication
    b. Ideas of reference
    c. Suspiciousness or paranoid ideation
    d. Recurrent illusions; sensing the presence of a force or person not actually present
    e. Magical thinking (viz., superstitiousness, clairvoyance)
    f. Inadequate rapport (aloof, superficial, etc.)
    g. Undue social anxiety or hypersensitivity to real or imagined criticism
    h. Social isolation
  2. "Unstable" items
    a. Unstable and intense interpersonal relationships
    b. Impulsivity in two or more areas (spending, sex, alcohol, gambling, etc.)
    c. Inappropriate intense anger or lack of control of anger
    d. Physically self-damaging acts
    e. Affective instability
    f. Chronic feelings of emptiness or boredom
    g. Severe problems tolerating being alone

Gunderson and Klein syndromes will be seen more clearly. Both are largely contained within the realm of borderline *structure* as defined by Kernberg. Besides the item "identity disturbance," a patient, to qualify as borderline according to the checklist of Spitzer et al., should have at least five additional items. These need not be from the same subsection (schizotypal or unstable), although if almost all the applicable items were from one subsection, this would heighten the likelihood that the patient was within one or the other major spectrum.

The Characterologic Dimension of Diagnosis

Thus far we have concentrated on two main dimensions of diagnosis: one relating to *constitutional* (especially, hereditary) factors and the other, to overall *level of function* (neurotic/borderline/psychotic). Full discussion of psychoanalytic intervention and of prognosis in the borderline realm requires attention to a third diagnostic dimension, namely, the *characterologic*. This dimension may be understood as being composed of two categories: *character* per se—one's habitual facade and reaction-style in relation to others—and *temperament*—one's inborn predisposition to react in a particular manner to external and internal stimuli, which may be noticeable even in the absence of others.

Temperament has particular relevance to borderline conditions, because many of the nonpsychotic relatives of clear-cut manic-depressives or schizophrenics exhibit one or another abnormality of temperament. A significant percentage of these relatives function at the borderline level (as defined by Kernberg). Similarly, the psychotic patients themselves often show various abnormalities of temperament during the premorbid and interpsychotic phases of their life-course. Kraepelin (1921) outlined four such temperaments noted amongst manic-depressives and their relatives: the depressive, the manic, the irritable, and the (rarer) cyclothymic. Kraepelin estimated the frequency of these temperaments as about 40 percent in manic-depressive patients. In an analogous fashion, other temperamental abnormalities—especially the paranoid and the schizoid—are to be found in a large proportion of schizophrenics and their relatives. There is less specificity to the temperamental type than to the major disorder: Bellack (1976) has cautioned that only a little more than a fourth of schizophrenics show "schizoidia;" Abrams et al (1974) have drawn attention to the paranoid subgroup of manic-depressives, who are sometimes confused with schizophrenics.

The presence of manic temperament or of cyclothymia has been felt by many to militate against the use of analytically oriented psychotherapy (cf. Kernberg 1975). Jacobson (1953, p. 50), taking Nunberg to task for his pessimism, felt, however, that patients may be amenable to a psychoanalytic approach " ... even when in a depressed or hypomanic state, provided ... that we know we are dealing with a basically psychotic case and do not neglect differential diagnostic considerations." This objection aside, the majority of analysts find hypomanic and cyclothymic patients—because of the denial of illness and the characterological rigidity so common in these groups—as generally poor candidates for analytic psychotherapy. Occasionally a borderline and even a neurotic patient with one of these temperaments gets referred for analysis but goes on to develop full-blown bipolar illness. In still other cases, a patient with a rigid obsessional character structure—but who shows only faint signs of one of the Kraepelinian temperaments—may catch the analyst unawares and succumb to a manic psychosis (Stone 1978b).

With respect to character typology, Kernberg (1975) has made the point that certain characterological dispositions augur well among borderline patients for analytic ("expressive") psychotherapy. These include the depressive/masochistic, the infantile, the hysteric, and the obsessive. Others—the hypomanic and the antisocial—have much more ominous prognostic overtones. In an intermediate category are to be found the paranoid, the schizoid, and the narcissistic. (How much some of these personality types are to be considered manifestations of temperament rather than of character is not always easy to distinguish; they may also be affected by sociocultural factors.) Although it is not possible to well-order the many personality types in common parlance according to their responsiveness to expressive therapy, a rough approximation has been presented in diagrammatic form (Stone 1978a).

In contemplating intensive psychotherapy for a patient in the low-to-intermediate range of function, the tridimensional approach sketched previously would suggest that the most favorable responses would be obtained in patients who are (1) predominantly depressive rather than manic or schizophrenic, (2) borderline in psychostructural level rather than psychotic, and (3) temperamentally, depressive rather than cyclothymic, schizoid, and so forth and, characterologically, obsessive, hysteric, infantile, and so forth, rather than antisocial or severely narcissistic. ("Depressive," incidentally, is used, to add to our confusion, as a constitutional label, a temperamental subtype, and a character type.)

It is important to recall that in almost all series, borderline patients will be female twice as often as male (cf. Spitzer et al. 1978), a ratio also noted among unipolar depressives (many of whom show borderline structure). Female borderline patients often suffer severe premenstrual tension and in some instances are even prone to psychotic episodes during this phase of the cycle. The premenstrual tension may be accompanied by one or more of the following: rage outbursts, self-destructive acts, suicidal ruminations, histrionic behavior, and chaotic sexual activity. The biologic component may be of primary etiological significance with respect to this impulsivity. The psychological concomitants (namely, minor rejections in everyday life or in the transference situation), although possibly significant as triggers, should not be regarded as sufficient, in and of themselves, to precipitate these attacks. These "minipsychotic" episodes in premenstrual borderline women often do not yield to psychological interpretations no matter how deftly and firmly made; a combined approach, including appropriate medications, is usually required.

CLINICAL CASES

In order to illustrate the diagnostic and prognostic points in the preceding section, some vignettes from a series of borderline patients will be offered, arranged in continuum fashion from those nearest the polar concept of schizophrenia to those whose conditions most closely approximate the pure affective disorders. This is not to imply that borderline conditions may all be placed somewhere within a universe of schizophrenic and manic-depressive spectra. Many patients exhibiting borderline psychic structure, for example, have neither the clinical stigmata nor any close relatives with either type of psychosis. Some come from backgrounds of severe emotional deprivation or physical abuse (cf. Searles 1969).

The proportion of cases related to the classical psychoses will vary from series to series. Among the hospitalized borderline patients at the New York State Psychiatric Institute, more than half had one or more close relatives with such disorders, usually affective in nature (Stone 1977). One young woman, diagnosed originally as borderline, suffered her first manic episode (in what then became recongizable as bipolar illness) four months after her admission. Some of the patients fulfilled the criteria for unipolar depression; others had four or more positive items from the "unstable" category of the Spitzer checklist and a smaller number were "schizotypal." The term borderline tends, in any case, to be applied to younger patients who have scarcely entered the ages of risk for either schizophrenia (15–45 years) or manic-depression (20–60 years). Abuse of marijuana and other psychoactive drugs may also contribute to the development of borderline-type psychopathology in certain adolescents, including those with perinatal "minimal brain damage" (Stone 1973).

It should also be borne in mind that a schizotypal borderline patient or even a classically schizophrenic patient with excellent vocational skills, high motivation, and favorable characterological features will tend to do better (both in expressive therapy and in everyday life) than will a "less disturbed" borderline patient who is free of schizophrenic signs but who shows poor psychological-mindedness and motivation or unfavorable characterological features.

Pertinent demographic and diagnostic data on 10 borderline patients are presented in Table 5. Two patients were chosen from each of five arbitrarily defined regions within the phenotypic continuum between the "pure" schizotypical, with *no* affective features (Region 1), to the pure affective types, with no typically schizophrenic features (Region 5). Region 3, for example, would include schizoaffective patients in whom the balance between the two types of symptoms seems about equal.

Table 6 summarizes the history of emotional illness in the families. Information was more complete for the first-degree relatives (here, parents and siblings only; none of the patients had a child past age ten) than for second-degree relatives (grandparents, aunts, uncles, nieces, and nephews). Although these patients were not part of a controlled study, it is of interest that the affected relatives of those nearer the schizophrenic end of the spectrum were themselves mostly schizotypal; relatives of the patients in Regions 4 and 5 had mostly affective disorders. This tendency of these conditions to "breed true," though with some overlap of diagnostic categories, has been noted by many investigators (cf. Odegaard 1963 and Gershon et al. 1976).

Additonal data regarding treatment and outcome are provided in Table 7. Although all had begun as office patients, three had been hospi-

Table 5
Diagnostic Data on 10 Borderline Patients

	Patient									
	1 (21,M)[a]	2 (25,M)	3 (26,F)	4 (24,F)	5 (36,F)	6 (29,F)	7 (19,M)	8 (24,F)	9 (34,F)	10 (28,F)
Diagnostic Data										
Satisfies criteria for borderline as developed by:										
Kernberg	+	+	+	+	+	+	+	+	+	+
Gunderson	–	–	–	–	–	+[b]	–	+	+[b]	+
Klein (hysteriod dysphoria)	–	–	–	–	–	+	–	+	+	+
Kety/Spitzer	+	+	+	+	+	+	+	+	+	+
Schizotypal items[c]	b,c,f,g,h	c,f,g,h	a,b,c,f,g,h	a,c,e,g,h	c,e,g,h	c,f,g,h	c,f,g,h	b,c,f,g,	b,c,f,g	g
Unstable items[c]	c		b,f,g	c	e,f	a–g	c,f	a,b,c,e,f,g	b,c,e,g	c,e,g
Temperament[d]	S/P	S	S/P	S	D	D	S	mainly D	I	D
Region in Sz-MDP Continuum	1	1	2	2	3	3	4	4	5	5

[a]Age when first seen and sex are in parentheses.

[b]Includes the attribute of showing a normal pattern on the WAIS in the face of poor performance on unstructured portions of a psychological test battery.

[c]See Table 7-4.

[d]Key: C = cyclothymic, D = depressive, I = irritable, P = paranoid, and S = schizoid.

Table 6
History of Emotional Illness in the 10 Patients' Families

Patient	Affected First-Degree Relatives	Affected Second-Degree Relatives
1	1 out of 3 (chronic paranoid schizophrenic)	Unknown
2	1 out of 4 (schizotypal borderline)	Unknown
3	2 out of 4 (both alcoholic; one also schizotypal borderline)	Unknown
4	2 out of 4 (both chronic undifferentiated schizophrenic	3 out of 8 (1 paranoid schizophrenic; 2 alcholic)
5	2 out of 5 (1 paranoid schizophrenic; 1 schizoaffective	1 out of 13 (schizotypal borderline)
6	1 out of 2 (schizoaffective)	2 out of 7 (1 schizoaffective, manic type; 1 schizotypal borderline)
7	1 out of 5 (unipolar depression)	
8	4 out of 4 (2 schizoaffective; 1 paranoid-schizophrenic; 1 unipolar depressive)	2 out of 6 (1 unipolar depressive; 1 paranoid schizophrenic)
9	3 out of 5 (all alcoholic; 2 with depressive episodes)	Unknown
10	2 out of 4 (both with unipolar depressive disorder)	Unknown

talized briefly (maximum, four weeks) early in the course of treatment. These three patients also exhibited the hysteroid dysphoria syndrome. Each patient was rated when first seen according to the 100-point, anchored scale, the Global Assessment Scale (Endicott et al. 1976), which is a modification of the Menninger Health-Sickness Rating Scale (Luborsky 1962). Another rating was made after two years, the minimum length of psychotherapy in this group. Some patients (numbers 3, 5, and 12) have been followed more than 10 years. Although increments of less than 10 points ordinarily imply a lack of significant improvement, even greater increments would be needed to substantiate improvement in patients evaluated initially when *acutely* ill. Since the scale is designed to reflect behavior and symptoms only during the week before the rating is made, a transient psychotic episode at the beginning of treatment will give an artificially low estimate of general premorbid function. With this in mind, it will be noted that in half the patients there was no significant improvement (patients 1, 2, 3, 5, and 7 showed increments of 5 points or less); the other half showed significant and in some instances dramatic improvement (increments ranged from 14 to 35 points). There was a trend in this group of borderline patients for those at or near the schizophrenic pole to show little or no improvement and for those near the affective pole, to show substantial improvement.

The trend noted in Table 7-7 reflects my impression that expressive psychotherapy in borderline patients who show vulnerability to one or to a mixture of the classical psychoses will prove most beneficial where affective (rather than schizophrenic) symptoms predominate. Optimally, the affective symptoms should be mostly depressive. If manic symptoms or traits of the "manic" temperament overshadow the depressive components, it seems unlikely that analytically oriented therapy will contribute much to whatever improvement supportive therapy (and, where indicated, the appropriate medications) may effect.

Final answers about the efficacy of intensive psychotherapy in borderline patients with vulnerability of this sort will emerge only from carefully controlled, randomized studies. One such is currently in progress in two cooperating centers (the McLean Hospital and Boston State Hospital) in the Boston area, under the direction of Alfred Stanton.

In the material that follows, five of the ten borderline patients are described in greater detail. One patient has been selected from each of the five regions into which the phenotypic continuum between schizophrenia and manic-depression has been arbitrarily divided. All the patients had

Table 7
Treatment and Outcome of the 10 Borderline Patients

Treatment and Outcome	Patient									
	1	2	3	4	5	6	7	8	9	10
Ever hospitalized	−	−	−	−	−	+	−	+	+	−
Mode of psychotherapy[a]	E	E	M	E	E→S	M	E	M	S→E	E
Medications used										
Antidepressant	−	−	−	−	+	+	−	+	−	−
Phenothiazine	−	−	−	−	+	±[b]	−	±[b]	±[b,c]	−
Global Assessment Scale										
Initial score	46	53	48	40	51	20	44	38	29	47
Score at two years	51	53	50	62	56	47	47	69	64	61

[a]E = predominantly expressive psychotherapy; M = mixture of expressive and supportaive; S = mainly supportive
[b]± = only occasionally
[c]Only during hospitalization

completed high-school; all but two, both of whom were wives of professional men, had completed college. (Patient 7 received his degree during the course of therapy.) Frequency of sessions varied between two and three per week.

Patient 2: A Schizotypal Borderline Patient

A 25-year-old unmarried man sought psychiatric help because of vague complaints about "not having found himself" and "not living up to his potential." He was one of two children born to a couple widely apart in age and from different religious and cultural backgrounds. The father, an elderly professor, had ceded most of the child-rearing functions to the mother, who was a tempestuous and irascible woman given to episodic rage attacks. During some of these outbursts she would be verbally abusive and physically cruel to the children; her usual punishment, even for minor offenses, would consist of locking the patient in a closet for many hours at a time. The mother was treated for a schizoaffective disorder when the patient was 15 years old; five years later she left the father and subsequently divorced.

The patient had always been shy and seclusive, had almost no friends, and had never competed in the usual school athletic contests. There had been no physical relations with either sex. He completed college but had no enthusiasm about pursuing graduate studies, although for years he had been urged, especially by his father, to get his doctorate and enter academic life.

Although in moderate distress over his lack of success in the social and vocational realms, he showed little motivation for psychotherapy. He recognized the nature of his problems but assumed from beginning to end that nothing could be done about them. To this air of defeatism was added a subtle mockery of psychotherapy: he in effect dared me to budge him from the immovable conviction of his own untreatability. Of his rich inner life he conveyed only the barest outlines, and at that I had to rely on his dreams; of spontaneous speech there was almost none. I always had to interrupt the silence after about three or four minutes, or else he would surely have allowed the whole session to pass by without a word being spoken.

As always happens with the largely silent patient, the therapist's own thoughts go off in a thousand directions. The silent session is a breeding ground for fantasy. One begins to feel, based on subtle cues from the patient's facial expression and bodily gestures, that one "knows" what is going on in him inwardly. One uses one's own reactions—of boredom, exasperation, despair, impotence—as indexes of what the patient is experiencing but is unable or unwilling to relate. Occasionally I would make an interpretive remark, in hopes of making him aware of his "projective identifications" where I was concerned, namely, his seeing me as "defeated," "contemptuous," and so forth. At other times I would suggest to him, "You must fear change more than you fear the status quo—could that be why you act in such a way as to ensure that nothing happens in your sessions?" Or, if there were a dream about exposure and entrapment, I would say, "I think your silence may reflect the intense shame you seem to feel about some of your experiences, urges, and so forth, as though to share them were to confirm the worst. My guess is that you would discover how your mental life is much nearer the ordinary than the unique." Or, "Are you telling me, through all this silence, you're so convinced you can't be helped, that you've decided to pick up a few scraps of satisfaction in demonstrating how I, too, am ineffectual and hopeless?" (This picture, by the way, conformed to his image of his father.)

There was always a remarkable discrepancy between the vividness of his dreams—filled as they always were with scenes of terror and escape, humiliation at the hands of ferocious women, homosexual assault, and alienation from others—and his unbreachable taciturnity. One such dream, related in the 15th month of treatment, portrayed him as buried alive in some foreign outpost. This was followed with the revelation of his having been punished as a child by being locked in a closet. I welcomed this revelation as a sign of trustfulness and of cooperativeness on his part, such as might betoken the formation of a genuine therapeutic alliance. Not so. My sympathetic remarks to the effect that he still must be reeling from the impact of those terrifying hours of dark confinement met with his customary bland denial, "Oh no. That was a long time ago. That has nothing to do with my life as it is. It was scary at the time, but I don't think it bothers me now."

After two years the patient broke off treatment, having concluded, unfortunately quite correctly, that it was not getting anywhere. At no time had he manifested any "target symptoms" of the sort considered amenable to psychoactive drugs; accordingly none were prescribed. Instead one saw only the unchanging, and apparently unchangeable, schizoid temperament—suspiciousness, apathy, and the curious mixture of rich and violent inner life with feelings of emptiness and boredom. He remains a social isolate, employed, well below his intellectual capacities, at a secure but uninteresting job. Treatment had little influence on the sharp contradictions in his perceptions of himself, although his impressions of others grew more realistic.

Patient 4: A Schizotypal Borderline Patient with Affective Features

A twenty-four-year-old single woman sought help because of recurring episodes of depression, accompanied by general feelings of self-doubt and indecisiveness regarding life goals. She was employed as an instructor in English in a junior college, having completed her master's degree and about half the requirements for her doctorate. It had become difficult for her to keep up with her assignments; she was conflicted about a love relationship, which, after four years, had become stagnant. Her fiance kept postponing decisions about marriage; she was no longer sure she wanted him but could not bring herself to separate from him either.

She came from a well-to-do, but bleak and at times chaotic, family. Her mother had a postpartum schizophrenic breakdown and had never been fully functional since; she was largely unavailable to the patient throughout her childhood. The father was successful in business, but at home he was stern, authoritarian, and uncommunicative.

In the early phase of therapy the patient gave frequent expression to feelings of alienation from those around her; at times this approached the level of derealization, as though the rest of the world and the people in it were strange, indecipherable, and, often, threatening. She became tearful during many of the sessions, contemplating what seemed to her to be the insuperable task of overcoming her wariness of others and her tendency to search for meanings within meanings, which rendered relationships even of the most superficial kind intolerably complex and burdensome.

On several occasions she experienced momentary psychotic episodes in the sessions, of a distinctly paranoid flavor. She would feel "imprisoned" in the office or would see me as a "violent" person intent upon hurting her physically. A few such episodes were characterized by extreme confusion about identity, even as to gender.

This patient was exquisitely alive to nuances of emotion and was highly motivated for therapy, seeking not only relief from her distressing symptoms but also a chance to achieve what Levenson (1978, p.30) has called the true goal of psychotherapy: "greater comprehension" of her life and "engagement with the real world and growth."

It had always been difficult to understand her, because of the diffuse, rambling nature of her speech. Sometimes, in an effort to educate me about the peculiarities of her inner life, she would give old words a new twist or tack on improper endings, as when she would refer to the "anxietyness" of certain social gatherings (that is, their tendency to make her feel anxious).

Interpretive work occupied only a portion of the sessions, especially in the beginning, since it was so often necessary to ask for clarifications and simplified versions of what she was trying to get across. She utilized her dreams well, however, and was able to work consistently on transference themes. Even during the long phase in which she concentrated upon feelings—of abandonment and deprivation—concerning her mother (or myself-as-depriving-mother), she never passed beyond tearfulness and grief into despair or suicidal ruminations. In part, this may have been a reflection of her temperament, which was predominantly schizoid and was depressive only to a mild degree. In part, this was a testimonial to the many strengths in her personality, which included, besides a keen intelligence, considerable perseverance and candor.

After two years of psychotherpy, much of the contradictoriness in her feelings had been resolved and the minipsychotic episodes had ceased. She no longer functioned, psychostructurally, at the borderline level. Yet there were still the eccentricities of speech, intense shyness, and heightened anxiety in social situations that had contributed to the original impression of "borderline schizophrenia." In place of solid diagnostic signs, what was discernible now was merely a vulnerability to this type of illness.

Patient 6: A Schizoaffective Borderline Patient

This patient was married to a lawyer and had two children. She had been referred because of a strong preoccupation with suicide that had emerged in the context of a deteriorating marital situation. The marriage had been built largely on a foundation of physical attraction, combined with a desire—in each partner—to escape an intolerable family. There were few shared interests and little communication beyond superficialities. This not-always-amicable truce had become strained by a mounting conviction in the patient, despite the absence of any compelling evidence to this effect, that her husband was unfaithful.

Her behavior became increasingly erratic and irritable; her mood alternated between rage and despondency. The first few sessions were characterized by puzzling silences and a peculiar combination of openness on some subjects with secretiveness on others. Not long afterwards she made a suicide gesture, consisting of scratching one wrist with a knife. She was then hospitalized, but, because she threatened to "save up her pills," no medications were at first prescribed.

Within the safe environment of the hospital, she was able to reveal the nature of her anxieties and something of their causes. It developed, for example that her parents had divorced after as many years of marriage as she and her husband had now accumulated. She had reason to suspect that her father had carried on a number of extramarital relationships and had assumed that in her own marriage the same set of circumstances would be reduplicated—and on the same timetable. Of the latter she had no conscious awareness; interpretation of this curious "anniversary reaction" did, however, strike her as valid. Her suspiciousness diminished considerably after the connection was made.

A complicating factor in our work lay in our sharply divergent values concerning self-revelation. For me, candor was an essential ingredient in the movement toward integration on a higher plane. For her, because of several shattering experiences of betrayal years before, candor could be seen as leading only to humiliation and exploitation by others. The gentlest of transference interpretations had precipitated, during the early phase of therapy, brief panic attacks and threats of interrupting treatment. I learned to develop respect for the need to go at her pace, not mine. A special language evolved between us to deal with this withholding. She would indicate to me in roundabout ways that she was growing troubled by things (presumably feelings about me) that she was not ready to share with me. I would caution her not to feel pressured in this regard, advising her to concentrate instead upon whatever factors seemed to be operating and that interfered with her becoming more open. I would reassure her, citing the example of the tortoise and the hare, that since the "speedy" revelation of her secrets was utterly intolerable to her, to proceed slowly was surely the fastest road to recovery.

Eventually a rhythmic pattern became discernible in the sessions. The beginning of the cycle would be devoted to the exploration of a particular conflict (centered around a parent or her husband). A series of dreams would be reported, discussion of which led to the precise clarification of the conflict. The riddle solved, the cooperative spirit of the preceding sessions would give way to indifference, although her mood would brighten to near-euphoric levels.

After a few weeks of such comfort, all her external relationships grew more tranquil, life went smoothly, and there was, or so she insisted, "nothing to talk about." Now the dreams pointed clearly to transference themes—with a commingling usually of loneliness and lustful feelings—about which she could say very little. Anxiety reappeared and intensified. To admit being pent up with feelings of so "personal" a nature, however, would already constitute too dangerous a revelation. Instead, the feelings would not be so much "acted out" (cf. Frosch 1977) as transformed into hostility and displaced onto various members of the family. Suddenly her life would be turbulent all over again: there would appear to be "real" problems *elsewhere* than in our relationship. Narcissistic aspects of her personality came to the foreground; her otherwise considerable capacity to care about others would go temporarily into eclipse. She would again threaten to break off treatment. Exhortation by her family and confronting interpretations by me would save the day, as she reluctantly agreed to resume the work.

The cycle now complete, a new area of conflict would emerge, on a level one notch higher than the preceding. Cooperative effort would resume, only to be interrupted by another spell of dangerous comfort, when there was "nothing left" to reveal, except feelings connected with the transference. By the time five or six such cycles had passed, the strength of her suicidal impulses had waned significantly. She made sufficient gains in overall function so that attention to transference matters was no longer threatening.

The first occasion of this sort became a turning point in the course of therapy. The subject concerned her forlornness before a vacation, any reaction to which had been vigorously denied during similar separations in the past. To the earlier separations she had reacted with denial and giddiness, reminiscent of the bipolar-II manic patient (cf. Dunner et al. 1976). It is of interest that she had one first-degree relative with a shizoaffective disorder and a second-degree relative with Lithium-sensitive bipolar illness. Although initially, schizophrenic and affective signs seemed present in about equal mix, the affective began to predominate. This patient also presented the picture of "hysteroid dysphoria" (see Table 7-5). Tricyclic antidepressants were added to her regimen; episodically, small doses of a phenothiazine were also given, for acute anxiety. The course of her life was much less stormy after these medications were prescribed. If she stopped taking them, as she would sometimes do when she began to feel well again, depressive symptoms would reappear within a week. Typical of borderline patients, with affective symptoms, she had a tendency, under stress, to abuse alcohol (cf. Rado 1933 on "pharmacothymia" in impulsive patients). Here, the tendency was mild, not requiring special technique of treatment.

After two years the patient had made significant gains in autonomy and self-discipline; the episodes of anxiety, rage outbursts, and erratic behavior were spaced more widely apart and were muted in their amplitude. There is still fluctuation of mood and function, corresponding to a fluctuation in the Global Assessment Score from the mid-40s to the high 50s. This patient represents one of the most challenging types of clinical situations still amenable to expressive psychotherapy. As she improved, she shifted diagnostically, partly because of "occasion variance" (presenting a truly different picture at different times) and partly because therapy affected certain groups of symptoms more than others. Initially an evenly mixed schizoaffective disorder, her condition at times exhibited some of the features of "hysterical psychosis" (Hollander and Hirsch 1964) and then leveled out as an affective condition with depressive features.

Patient 8: A Predominantly Affective Borderline Patient with Some Schizotypal Features

A 24-year-old woman was referred for psychotherapy for depression over a broken engagement. Her symptoms, which included brief panic-episodes and intolerance of being alone, in addition to crying spells and despondency, interfered with her studies at a university, where she was working toward a doctorate in art history. Shortly before her fiancé left her, she also began to feel that certain acquaintances on campus were snickering behind her back about her loss and poking fun at her because of her fundamentalist upbringing. A mild tendency to magical thinking—out of keeping with her educational level—was also noted.

Many members of her immediate family had severe emotional disorders themselves. Several members of the maternal line had been hospitalized for affective illnesses (bipolar in one instance, unipolar in two others) and the father, although successful in business, had suffered a paranoid schizophrenic break some years before and had died when she was 16. A brother and a paternal uncle had had "schizoaffective" episodes.

A few weeks after she began treatment she suddenly became rageful, suspicious, and negativistic. She developed persecutory delusions concerning the Mafia and the FBI. Hospitalization was necessary, but, once admitted, she soon acknowledged having taken large quantities of Tuinal.® Discontinuance was accompanied by the rapid clearing of the psychotic symptoms. Unwilling to remain in the hospital beyond a week, she resumed therapy, which was at first stormy and unproductive because of her continued suspiciousness and rage outbursts. Elavil® (150–250 mg/day) led to a gradual calming and lessening of her panic attacks.

Themes dealt with in her twice-weekly sessions unfolded in the following sequence: (1) the death of her father and their ambivalent relationship; (2) attachment to a lover who resembled the father, as a substitute for the mourning process; (3) her initial dread and subsequent idealization of me; and (4) fear of dependency. The latter topic made itself manifest through a series of anxiety-provoking dreams in which she saw herself as "seduced" by a "beautiful, middle-aged lesbian," subsequently identified as her lonely and depressed mother. Much time was also devoted in her sessions to fostering better techniques for coping with loneliness and for withstanding the pressure to date inappropriate men, as an antidote to the loneliness.

This patient had a marked tendency to become irritable and panicky before her menses. She gained five to seven pounds the week before her period began. These symptoms were alleviated by diuretics given premenstrually and by temporarily augmenting her Elavil® dosage.

Two years after the commencement of therapy, sufficient integration had occurred in object-relations and in her self-image so that she advanced, psychostructurally, from the borderline to the neurotic level. She completed her thesis and was engaged to a man more suitable than her first fiancé. Despite these gains (and the 30-point rise in her Global Assessment Score), certain signs of vulnerability remained: there were times when being alone still led to suicidal ruminations and panicky feelings (the temptation to abuse barbiturates reasserted itself at such moments); she still occasionally had nightmares in which she pictured herself as dismembered or dead. Although Flemenbaum (1976) has cautioned that frightening dreams occur particularly often after large single doses of tricyclics given at bedtime, these dreams would recur episodically in this patient even after she was off all medication.

Considering the multiplicity of first- and second-degree relatives with schizophrenia or affective illnesses, it may be legitimate to attribute her vulnerability to heightened risk for *both* forms of functional psychosis.

Patient 10: A Borderline Patient with Features of Affective Illness

A 28-year-old married woman was referred for analytically oriented psychotherapy because of increasing irritability in connection with her five-year-old son. Although unable to admit it, in the beginning, her most serious problem was with her husband, hostility to whom had been for some time displaced onto the boy.

Raised by a fanatically devout and sexually inhibited mother, the patient had developed serious inhibitions of her own. Shortly after she entered therapy, for example, she noted a small pimple on her son's penis. Though quite worried about it, she could not bring herself to mention the word *penis* when phoning the family physician and therefore did nothing about the lesion. Though at first tearful, panicky, and preoccupied with ruminations about suicide, she agreed to continue in treatment only on the condition that we never discuss sex. To circumvent a power struggle with the patient, who was in such urgent need of help, I accepted her proviso but on the following terms: I told her that I would not bring up the subject nor force her to discuss sexual themes in any way, *but* that if at some point in the future—and we could not predict how she would feel toward it months hence—she found herself wishing to make me aware of some problem in the area of sex, out of respect for the shift in her attitude, I would listen to what she had to say and would deal with it as tactfully as I knew how.

Two sessions later she began to pour out volumes of long-pent-up material about guilt over premarital sex, unresponsiveness during intercourse, and her fears that giving birth somehow damaged her internal organs.

At almost every session the patient reported dreams, the content of which was often violent and harrowing. Especially in the dreams immediately preceding her menses, she would see herself as mutilated, often as the result of an attack by a crocodile or a tiger. Initially, she could not be budged from the position that her sexual inhibitions were not really a "problem," because the Church, according to her, was opposed to pleasureful sexuality anyway. There seemed to be no way around this resistance, until she reported a dream, following sex with her husband, in which she was in "Hell," being tortured by her mother, who was whipping her on the back with an elongated rosary. This gave me the opportunity to interpret to her that the Catholic Church, with its 983 million adherents, was, despite its monolithic reputation, too large an organization to hold such a solitary and rigid view about sex and that—as was clear from her dream—it was not the Church she saw as punishing her but her mother. In this fashion she gradually became able to confront the true source of her sexual guilt and no longer invoked religious beliefs as a defense against the recognition of her own sexual impulses.

The chief characterological features in this borderline patient were the depressive-masochistic and the infantile. Depressive features, besides the tearfulness, panic episodes, suicidal ruminations, and dysphoria already alluded to, included, in the first weeks of treatment, weight loss of 10 pounds and anorexia. Her anxiety became particularly intense when alone or alone with her child, whom she feared she would injure in an unguarded moment. Many attributes of the "depressive temperament" were also noted, as well as several of the traits mentioned by Wittenborn and Maurer (1977) as persisting—beyond acute episodes—in depressed women. Included among these were excessive worrying and overconscientiousness.

This patient had been the brightest and the most popular of four sisters. The mother and the patient's eldest sister had both received courses of electroshock therapy for major depressive disorders. The patient's panic-attacks were limited to the first few months of treatment and could usually be terminated after a brief conversation with me on the phone. Occasionally, small amounts of Mellaril® or Elavil® were also required, but not on a consistent basis. By the end of the first year of treatment, the prevailing mode in the sessions had shifted from supportive/expressive to purely expressive. A highly motivated and psychologically minded patient, she made rapid strides, exploring, in turn, fear of her rather seductive father, sexual feelings toward him, guilt toward her mother for harboring such feelings, hatred toward her mother for going on long vacations with the father during her infancy, and last, her strong yearning for closeness with the mother. The homosexual overtones of this last and most primitive layer of feeling were particularly uncomfortable for her to explore and resolve. When this task was finally accomplished, she became, ironically, more eager for sex and her husband, toward whom she was now as irritable for his "indifference" as she had once been on account of his "demandingness." Now functioning at the neurotic rather than the borderline level, her interest in the outside world expanded considerably; she made steps to further her education in preparation for a career. Whereas she identified at first only with her mother's professed value-system (which relegated women to a life of "Kinder, Kirche, Küche"), an advanced degree and work were no longer incompatible with her image as a woman.

It is of interest that, despite satisfying the criteria for the "hysteroid dysphoria" syndrome, her personality assets and her amenability to intensive psychotherapy were both so great as to render antidepressant medication less necessary than is ordinarily the case with this syndrome.

SUMMARY AND CONCLUSION

In psychoanalytic parlance, the term *borderline* has been used to describe a group of conditions intermediate in severity and heterogeneous in etiology. Initially, the boundaries between the borderline realm and its two neighbors on either side, *neurotic* and *psychotic*, were imprecise. Eventually this imprecision detracted from the value of the borderline label. Faced with the need to improve precision, one inevitably confronts the paradox that specificity can be bolstered only at the expense of coverage, and coverage enhanced only at the sacrifice of specificity.

This problem has been outlined in some detail by Blashfield (1973). Kernberg, for example, has redefined the term so as to capture most intermediate-range conditions within more precise boundaries, yet in a manner tha continues to gather in etiologically diverse entities. Klein's hysteroid dysphoria is a fairly specific syndrome, even with respect to distal etiology, but covers only a fraction of the borderline realm as defined structurally by Kernberg. Gunderson's "borderline personality disorder" answers more closely than the other usages to the particular set of patients (especialy, hospitalized patients) who inspire the most optimism with regard to intensive, analytically oriented psychotherapy. The Gunderson usage provides greater coverage than Klein's term, but is largely included within the Kernberg definition, since the latter contains all cases that are amenable to "expressive" therapy and many—for example, severe alcoholics, sociopaths, rigid paranoid disorders, or hypomanic character disorders—that are not.

The relationships of these different terms may be illustrated, for purposes of clarity, by means of a modified Venn diagram, as shown in Figure 1. Note that the broadest definition of borderline is that represented by Spitzer's borderline checklist. This region is even larger than Kernberg's borderline personality organization because a fair number of "schizotypal borderlines," in the geneticist's sense (cf. Kety et al. 1968), demonstrate psychotic *structure*, within Kernberg's psychostructural framework. That is to say, certain schizotypal borderline patients, however free they may be of grossly delusory ideation or hallucinations, nevertheless exhibit rigidly held and demonstrably unrealistic views of themselves and other people, thus qualifying in structural (though not in phenomenological) terms as psychotic. The more specific syndromes of Gunderson and Klein are situated within the borderline domain, partly within the affective region and to a lesser extent within the region where no affiliation to the classical psychoses is discernible. Some Gunderson-positive cases are also schizotypal with psychotic structure (by Kernberg's definition); for this reason the Gunderson region extends further into the schizotypal area than does the Kernberg region.

Confronted with a patient in the intermediate realm of psychopathology, the clinician cannot afford to choose among the various competing systems now wearing the flag of *borderline*. The analyst should, instead,

FIGURE 1.

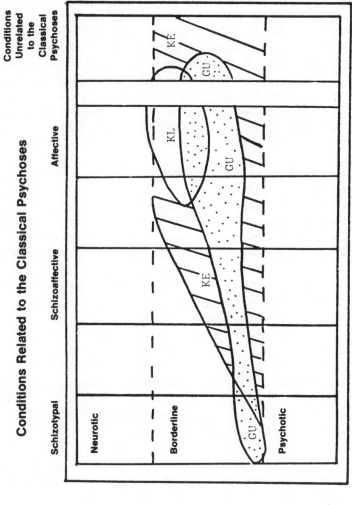

The universe of all psychiatric patients is here divided phenom-enologically—that is, according to signs and symptoms. The *Bor-derline* realm contains all those considered borderline according to the Spitzer checklist. Within this realm are the regions of Kernberg (KE), Klein (KL), and Gunderson (GU).

be aware of all the usages, in order that partisanship to one does not blind him to the advantages of another. The situation here is analogous to what we see within the realm of schizophrenia, where, as Strauss (1973, 1977) has recently pointed out neither a purely typological nor a purely dimensional model is altogether sufficient. The nuances of our patient's clinical picture—especially in the case of the borderline patient—will be best appreciated by the diagnostician who employs a categorical/typological and a dimensional approach simultaneously.

Similarly, one should be able to compare the patient's condition against a number of diagnostic yardsticks, not just one. It will be important to know whether the patient meets the stricter, or the more specific, criteria or merely the looser and less specific criteria. The less any given case satisfies the strict criteria, the more one must employ dimensional measures. This is a complex task, as Strauss (1973, p. 448) also cautions, but one that seems unavoidable in the borderline realm, where, by definition, the criteria for the most well-defined nosologic entities cannot be met.

As each prospective borderline patient is evaluated, there will be one description among the more precise usages currently in vogue, that most closely approximates the patient's condition. Selection of optimal treatment methods will depend to a great extent upon the establishment of this "best diagnostic fit." The more closely a case resembles Klein's description of hysteroid dysphoria, for example, the more likely it is that psychoactive medications will contribute significantly to recovery. In fact, to withhold medication from certain borderline patients of the dysphoric type, on the grounds that such intervention may intrude upon the "purity" of an otherwise expressive approach, may be quite hazardous.

The functional psychoses are being seen more and more as manifestational diseases for which combined genetic and nonspecific constitutional factors are necessary, though not sufficient, preconditions (Zubin and Spring 1977); that is, they are the expressions of increased *vulnerability*. Borderline patients, however defined, often present either clinical signs or family histories suggestive of heightened vulnerability to one—or to both—of the classic functional psychoses. The size and nature of this proportion will, as mentioned earlier, vary from one patient sample to another, though among borderline patients considered good candidates for analytic psychotherapy, as many as two out of three may exhibit this vulnerability.

There are many schizotypal borderline patients, for instance, that one encounters in office practice who (1) never require hospitalization, (2) have a number of similar and more obviously schizophrenic relatives, and (3) even manage to satisfy the psychostructural criteria for borderline. Their adjustment is marginal—especially with regard to intimate relationships—but stable. The more affectively ill borderline patients are also seen in office practice; in hospital practices they appear to outnumber the schizotypal borderlines, perhaps because the suicidal tendencies of some of the affective patients make hospitalization mandatory.

Many impulsive patients, including those who abuse alcohol or the illicit psychoactive drugs, have a close kinship, symptomatologically or genetically, to manic-depression. Borderline patients of this type will often "act out" in the transference situation, but the biologic component of their acting out may be so strong, that interpretation alone cannot reverse the pattern. Medication is essential in these cases. Whether tricyclic antidepressants, phenothiazines, or Lithium® should be used will depend on the degree of proximity to the "classic" psychosis for which each drug is traditionally prescribed. In certain schizoaffective cases, a combination of drugs may, at least temporarily, be indicated; here it becomes important to assess dimensionally whether the symptom picture is predominantly affective or schizophrenic or whether it is evenly divided.

In the psychiatric literature, sufficient attention has not thus far been paid to the frequent overlap of acting-out and vulnerability to affective illness. The presence of certain syndromes, especially those that interfere seriously with everyday life, should also alert the clinician to the likelihood of both borderline structure and heightened vulnerability. Examples of these are agoraphobia and anorexia nervosa. Association between anorexia nervosa and primary affective disorder has been suggested in some recent articles by Barcai (1977), Berg et al. (1974), and Cantwell et al. (1977). In some borderline patients who appear neurotic when first seen, the presence of a more serious disorder is presaged by frightening dreams, in which the dreamer pictures himself as either having died or having been mutilated (Stone 1979).

Though vulnerability implies genetic predisposition, it does not imply hopelessness or lack of responsiveness to intensive psychotherapy. The pessimism of the previous generation of analysts was predicated on misconceptions about the genetics of mental illness, insufficient development of confrontational techniques for dealing with denial, projective identification and other primitive defenses, and unavailability of effective psychopharmacologic agents. Recent advances in psychogenetics, psychotherapeutic technique, and psychopharmacology have made possible bold and felxible techniques, in which knowledge from all these disciplines is integrated for the effective treatment of many borderline patients.

An appreciation of the dimensional as well as the categorical approaches to diangosis is also important in the evaluation of borderline patients. The fully developed affective psychoses, for example, are characterized by good remissions (the *restitutio ad integrum* of Kraepelin) in contrast to the schizophrenias, where chronicity is the rule. It would appear that among the borderline variants of these conditions, amenability to intensive psychotherapy and overall prognosis are better the more the intrinsic symptomatology inclines toward the affective. This impression constitutes a hypothesis that must now be tested by careful studies including randomized studies at clinical centers that afford access to the many varieties of borderline patients depicted in the literature.

REFERENCES

Abrams, R., Taylor, M. A. and Gaztanaga, P. (1974) Manic-depressive illness and paranoid schizophrenia. *Arch. Gen. Psychiat.* 31:640–642.

Barcai, A. (1977) Lithium in adult anorexia nervosa. *Acta. Psychiat. Scand.*, 55:97–101.

Beck, S. G. (1959) Schizophrenia without psychosis. *Arch. Neurol. & Psychiat.*, 31:85.

Bellak, L. (1976) A possible subgroup of the schizophrenic syndrome and implications for treatment. *Amer. J. Psychother.*, 30:195–205.

Berg, I., Hullin, R., Allsopp, M., O'Brien, P. and MacDonald, R. (1974) Bipolar manic-depressive psychosis in early adolescence. A case report. *Brit. J. Psychiat.*, 125:416–417.

Bjerre, P. (1912) Zur Radikalbehandlung der chronischen Paranoia. Jahrb. für psychoanal. u. psychopathology. Forschungen, 3:759–847.

Blashfield, R. (1973) An evaluation of the DSM-II Classification of schizophrenia as a nomenclature. *J. Abnl. Psychol.*, 82:382–389.

Bychowski, G. (1953) The problem of latent psychosis. *J. Amer. Psychoan. Assoc.*, 1:484–503.

Cantwell, D. P., Sturzenberger, S., Burroughs, J., Salkin, B. and Green, J. K. (1977) Anorexia nervosa: An affective disorder? *Arch. Gen. Psychiat.*, 34:1087–1093.

Clark, L. P. (1919) Some practical remarks upon the use of modified psychoanalysis in the treatment of borderland neuroses and psychoses. *Psychoan. Rev.*, 6:306–308.

Clayton, P., Rodin, L. and Winokur, G. (1968) Family history studies III. Schizoaffective disorder, clinical and genetic factors, including a one to two year follow-up. *Comp. Psychiat.*, 9:31–49.

Cohen, S. M., Allen, M. G., Pollin, W. and Hrubec, Z. (1972) Relationship of schizoaffective psychosis to manic-depressive psychosis and schizophrenia. *Arch. Gen. Psychiat.*, 26:539–545.

Deutsch, H. (1942) Some forms of emotional disturbance and their relationships to schizophrenia. *Psychoan. Q.*, 11:301–321.

Dunner, D. L., Fleiss, J. L. and Fieve, R. R. (1976) The course of development of mania in patients with recurrent depression. *Amer. J. Psychiat.*, 133:905–908.

Endicott, J., Spitzer, R. L., Fleiss, J. L. and Cohen, J. (1976) The Global Assessment Scale. *Arch. Gen. Psychiat.*, 33:766–771.

Flemenbaum, A. (1976) Pavor nocturnus: A complication of single daily tricyclic or neuroleptic dosage. *Amer. J. Psychiat.*, 133:570–572.

Frosch, J. (1964) The psychotic character. *Psychiat. Q.*, 38:81–96.

Frosch, J. (1977) The relation between acting out and disorders of impulse control. *Psychiatry.*, 40:295–314.

Gershon, E. S., Bunney, W. E., Jr., Leckman, J. F., Van Eerdewegh, M. and De Bauche, B. A. (1976) The inheritance of affective disorders: A review of data and of hypotheses. *Behav. Genet.*, 6:227–261.

Glover, E. (1932) Psychoanalytic approach to the classification of mental disorders. *J. Mental Sci.*, 78:819–842.

Grinker, R. R. Sr., Werble, B. and Drye, R. C. (1968) *The Borderline Syndrome.* New York: Basic Books.

Gunderson, J. G. and Singer, M. T. (1975) Defining borderline patients: An overview. *Amer. J Psychiat.*, 132:1–10.

Hollander, M. H. and Hirsch, S. J. (1964) Hysterical psychosis. *Amer. J. Psychiat.*, 120:1066–1073.

Jacobson, E. (1953) Contribution to the metapsychology of cyclothymic depression. In Greenacre, P. R. (ed.): *Affective Disorders.* New York: International Universities Press, pp. 49–83.

Kasanin, J. (1933) Acute schizoaffective psychoses. *Amer. J. Psychiat.*, 97:97–120.

Kernberg, O. F. (1967) Borderline personality organization. *J. Amer. Psychoan. Assoc.*, 15:641–685.

Kernberg, O. F. (1975) *Borderline Conditions and Pathological Narcissism.* New York: J. Aronson.

Kety, S. S., Rosenthal, D., Wender, P. H. and Schulsinger, F. (1968) Mental illness in the biological and adoptive families of adopted schizophrenics. In Rosenthal, D. and Kety, S. S. (eds.): *Transmission of Schizophrenia.* Oxford: Pergamon Press, pp. 345–362.

Klein, D. (1978) Personal communication.

Klein, D. and Davis, J. (1969) *Drug Treatment and Psychodiagnosis.* Baltimore: William and Wilkins.

Knight, R. (1953) Borderline states. *Bull. Menn. Clin.*, 17:1–12.

Kraepelin, E. (1921) *Manic-depressive Insanity and Paranoia.* Edinburgh: Livingstone.

Levenson, E. A. (1978) Two essays in psychoanalytical psychology. *Contemp. Psychoanal.*, 14:1–30.

Luborsky, L. (1962) Clinician's judgments of mental health. *Arch. Gen. Psychiat.* 7:407–417.

Maeder, A. (1910) Psychologische Untersuchungen an Dementia Praecox-kranken. Jahrb. für Psychoanalyse, 2:234–245.

Moore, T. V. (1921) The parataxes: A study and analysis of certain borderline mental states. *Psychoan. Rev.*, 8:252–283.

Odegaard, Q. (1963) The psychiatric disease entities in the light of genetic investigation. *Act. Psychiat. Scand.*, Suppl. 169:94–104.

Rado, S. (1933) The psychoanalysis of pharmacothymia. *Psychoan. Q.*, 2:1–23.

Schmideberg, M. (1947) The treatment of psychopaths and borderline patients. *Amer. J. Psychother.*, 1:45–55.

Searles, H. F. (1969) A case of borderline thought disorder. *Internat. J. Psychoanal.*, 50:655–664.

Sovner, R. D. and Mc Hugh, P. R. (1976) Bipolar course in schizoaffective illness. *Biol. Psychiat.*, 11:195–204.

Spitzer, R. L., Endicott, J. and Gibbon, M. (1978) Crossing the border into borderline personality and borderline schizophrenia: The development of criteria. *Arch. Gen. Psychiat.* (In press).

Stabenau, J. R. (1977) Genetic and other factors in schizophrenic, manic-depressive and schizoaffective psychoses. *J. Nerv. & Ment. Dis.*, 164:149–167.

Stern, A. (1938) Psychoanalytic investigation and therapy in the borderline group of neuroses. *Psychoan. Q.*, 7:467–489.

Stone, M. H. (1973) Drug-related schizophrenic reactions. *Internat. J. Psychiat.*, 11:391–441.

Stone, M. H. (1977) The borderline syndrome: Evolution of the term, genetic aspects and prognosis. *Amer. J. Psychother.*, 31:345–365.

Stone, M. H. (1978) *The Borderline Syndromes: Constitution, Coping and Character.* New York: McGraw-Hill. (In press).

Stone, M. H. (1978a) Psychodiagnosis and psychoanalytic psychotherapy. *J. Amer. Acad. Psychoanal.,* 7:79–100.

Stone, M. H. (1978b) Toward early detection of manic-depressive illness in psychoanalytic patients. *Amer. J. Psychother.,* Vol. 32:427–439.

Stone, M. H. (1979) Dreams of fragmentation: A manifestation of vulnerability to psychosis. *Psychoparmacol. Bull.* 15:12–14.

Strauss, J. (1973) Diagnostic models and the nature of psychiatric disorder. *Arch. Gen. Psychiat.,* 29:445–449.

Strauss, J. S. and Gift, T. E. (1977) Choosing an approach for diagnosing schizophrenia. *Arch. Gen. Psychiat.,* 34:1248–1253.

Welner, A., Croughan, F., Fishman, R. and Robins, E. (1977) The group of schizoaffective and related psychoses: A follow-up study. *Comp. Psychiat.,* 18:413–422.

Wittenborn, J. R. and Maurer, H. S. (1977) Persisting personalities among depressed women. *Arch. Gen. Psychiat.,* 34:968–971.

Zilboorg, G. (1957) Further observations on ambulatory schizophrenia. *Amer. J. Orthopsychiat.,* 27:677–682.

Zubin, J. and Spring, B. (1977) Vulnerability: A new view of schizophrenia. *J. Abnl. Psychol.,* 86:103–126.

7

ADOLESCENCE, ADOLESCENT PROCESS, AND BORDERLINE STATES

Sherman C. Feinstein, M.D.
Michael Reese Hospital and Medical Center, Chicago, and Pritzker School of Medicine, University of Chicago

Changing concepts, even in psychoanalytic metapsychology, pose a fundamental difficulty. Change, which involves the acquisition of new knowledge, demands the loss of old concepts. Since dealing with loss is a dilemma of the human condition, abandoning a worthless concept might be delayed, sometimes indefinitely, because of great ambivalence around mourning the loss of a comfortable conceptualization.

Conceptual areas that have experienced delayed growth and development because of ambivalence around change are adolescence and adolescent process and borderline states. It is particularly interesting to see what has happened to a conceptualization that was of great interest to those psychoanalysts who participated in the Grinker studies at Michael Reese Hospital's Psychosomatic and Psychiatric Institute a decade ago (Grinker, Werble, and Drye 1968).

Grinker has great disdain for impreciseness and fuzzy thinking and believes that psychoanalytic metapsychology is unscientific and counterproductive. He teased out by careful observation a group of patients who presented a broad spectrum of behaviors that he considered to be borderline—something between the neurotic constellation and schizophrenia that is capable of mimicking both of these states on good days or bad but is, in fact, neither of these diagnostic states in pure culture.

Kernberg (1978), who has described Grinker's studies as phenomenological rather than dynamic, has elucidated the borderline personality to a high state of organization so that it emerges as a discrete diagnostic entity that can be differentiated from normal, neurotic, and schizophrenic adjustments. Other authors use the borderline concept in even more creative fashion. Appearing in recent readings have been such variations as borderline quality, borderline patient, borderline adjustment, borderline reaction, typically borderline, and the penultimate—that one of the effects of working with borderline patients is to be made to feel like a borderline analyst.

In keeping with the theme of changing concepts in psychoanalysis, this chapter will attempt to illustrate how current structural concepts of ego psychology and borderline states were delayed from being understood earlier because of essential myths and distortions about adolescence and, in particular, about adolescent process and the borderline state.

THE HISTORICAL DEVELOPMENT OF ADOLESCENCE

The failure to recognize adolescence as a separate stage of development did not occur by accident but has a long history related to marked discomfort about adolescent process and the emergence of sexual and aggressive impulses. What is a natural change of status from dependency to semidependency to final independence and what depends upon a change in roles in the family must now be evaluated from an appraisal of the dynamic state of an adolescent's stage of separation-individuation. The imposition of societal demands on a psychic system not yet ready to master the changes demanded of it can result in conflict owing to the regressive aspects of change at the service of ego mastery. Artificial demands for independence imposed on an immature psychic system lead to fixation, inhibition of growth, and conflictual crises. These result from failure to resolve the final developmental tasks that are normally engaged in providing structuralization of the ego and character formation.

Adolescence has long been viewed as a problematic period of life. Kett (1977), in his study of the history of adolescence, points out that in its premodern form adolescence was associated with behaviors manifested by the aristocracy, knighthood, and numerical classifications of the ages of man. He notes that Rousseau was one of the first authors to postulate changes at puberty, which were described as a "twice over birth." This concept was to play an important role later in influencing psychoanalytic metapsychology and, inadvertently, to inhibit conceptualization of adolescence as a separate development phase. Sexual maturation was seen as overburdening the system, with masturbation as the main cause of depletion of energy.

Rousseau (1712–1778) had profound influence on European thought. In his novel *Emile* (1762), a treatise on education, he described the ambivalence of adolescence by suggesting that fluctuating moods were the result of antagonism between the "social affections" released by puberty and a residue of "self-love" from childhood. Any frustration of basic wishes was seen as an attack on the self. He advised that "sexual curiosity" and "secular knowledge" not be stimulated in order to guarantee a noiseless transition from childhood to youth—a prolongation of innocence was considered the final solution. These ideas had long-term effects on adolescent theory and, in addition, affected attitudes toward women even more than men. For example, school demands, which were seen to produce bad effects, were seen as dangerous to females who dominated secondary education since males left school to go to work. Menstruation demanded prolonged periods of rest, which interfered with educational process as a means of avoiding the development of hysteria. Therefore, early concepts of adolescence were intertwined with a romantic view of childhood and fears of overpressure and overstimulation. Medical authors warned about the dangers of too vigorous socialization, widespread absorption in trivial interests, dietary indiscretions, and parental indulgences.

Of great importance historically was the work of Hall (1904), who saw adolescence as a struggle between biological maturation and social imperatives resulting in powerful expressions—such as religious conversions, common epiphenomena in the early 1900s—which served as a preparation for maturity. The rise of sexual potency with pubescence convulsed the child and created what was then considered adolescent storm and stress.

It was at this time that the era of the adolescent dawned in Europe and America. Demographic and economic factors resulted in the concepts and institutions that dominated work with adolescents long after the theories that led to their development were disproved. Echoing Rousseau, Hall viewed the adolescent as a new slate, torn by dualisms that disrupted the harmony of childhood, which were manifested by hyperactivity and inertia, social sensibility and self-absorption, and lofty intuitions and childish folly. Misbehavior and eccentricities should be viewed as normal outrowths of biological maturation. Recommended attitudes were toward a prolongation of adolescence to maximize growth and minimize precocious sexual development. The free play of idealism, altruism, moodiness, religious enthusiasm, inertia, and even serious acting out (delinquency and running away) were to be considered expressions of instinctual demands and should not be repressed. Adolescence was a recapitulation not of childhood but of neoatavistic acquisitions of the race viewed from a Darwinian perspective.

In the 19th century, puberty had been seen as a period when children acquired more energy and, therefore, greater capacity for good or evil. Adolescence, then, was associated with psychological turbulence and moral incapacity. By the 20th century, adolescence was seen as something spontaneous, dangerous, and to be avoided if possible by emphasizing passivity, regulating sparetime pursuits, and prolonging education.

These historical reflections are sharply in contradistinction with current attitudes, which stress the continuity of development from childhood to adolescence and the importance of considering adolescence a separate stage of life with the considerable task of character formation as its final accomplishment.

PSYCHOANALYTIC AND PSYCHOTHERAPEUTIC ASPECTS OF ADOLESCENT PROCESS

Adolescence represents an important period in the growth and development of the individual. The longitudinal, observational approach has confirmed the etiological importance of infancy in normal emotional development. The Oedipal period, during which the identificatory processes receive their greatest stimulation, continues to affect developmental growth. However, adolescence as a developmental stage may achieve the same degree of significance as an etiological precursor of later development as has been assigned to the infantile period (Feinstein, Giovacchini, and Miller 1971). This importance becomes manifested by the actions that result from the unique disruptive aspects recognized as the tumultuous and impulsive reactions of every normal adolescence, where symptoms are usually individual, mild, and episodic and become more significant when early developmental defects lead to psychopathological solutions with their multiple, severe, chronic symptomatology.

Although adolescence may be currently thought of as a continuation of structural development of the ego leading to the completion of development tasks resulting in the synthesis of character, which provides a cohesive unity of the personality, from a historical point of view adolescence has suffered from the same misconceptions metapsychologically as it did in previous centuries, when it was considered nothing more than a phase of childhood that was better repressed, denied, or neutralized by prolongation and minimization.

Freud (1900, 1915, 1923) was primarily concerned with the vicissitudes of instincts, which was consistent with his id-psychological frame of reference. He saw adolescence as obscure and described earlier instinctual patterns as becoming subordinated under genital dominance (Giovacchini 1978). Jones (1930) may have contributed most to the delay in psychoanalytic understanding of adolescent process by dismissing it simply as a recapitulation of childhood and a disagreeable excursion by the ego on its way to maturation.

Gitelson (1948), in a discussion of the essentials of therapy in adolescents, provides a useful review of historical development at that time. He noted a general tendency to shy away from direct psychotherapy of adolescents and instead to provide supportive and group help. While not questioning the possible theoretical and practical value of these efforts, he raised the possibility that this tendency might represent a defensive maneuver on the part of preserving the therapist's psychic integrity from the onslaught of the adolescent's resurgent primitive anxiety or the fear of recognition of satisfaction from the adolescent patient's relationship with his therapist. He believed that a "particular kind of empathic capacity" was required to deal therapeutically with adolescents and that it took "particular and different kinds of adults" to treat various types of adolescents and their problems.

Gitelson compared the treatment of narcissistic and borderline disorders in adults to the treatment of adolescents and noted that some analysts were beginning to find it possible "to close the emotional gap resulting from the limited transference capacity" and to deal with "real" and "here and now" attitudes of these patients rather than repetitions of the past. He saw the goal of therapy with adolescents as facilitating character synthesis rather than psychic analysis and defined the special therapeutic skills required as an ability to tolerate mistrust, the capacity to develop empathy, and the tolerance and ability to make narcissistic contact, especially in crisis situations.

A growing recognition of adolescence as a phase of development increases the focus on the further development of the self and on object-relations structures of the ego and the adolescent tasks to be accomplished. During adolescence, aggressive and libidinal motivations must be dealt with. This includes the modification of unconscious concepts of parents, the assumption of a value system, clarification of gender identification, and the selection of an educational or career role (Gardiner 1959).

With the demand for the continued remodeling of ego structures pressing from both emotional and physiological sources, some attention must be directed to the manner in which these adolescent tasks are accomplished (Feinstein and Ardon 1973). Eissler (1958) wrote that the ego, during adolescence, has a "second chance" to review and revise previous solutions to the oedipal conflict selected during latency development. This is carried out by "liquefaction" of some ego structures, during which regressive features are certain to appear. Anna Freud (1958) described a defensive regression to the ego state of "primary identification," a response to intolerable anxiety produced by potentially close and threatening object relations. Geleerd (1961) viewed the adolescent as dealing with both the intense demands of object relationships and the heightened physiological processes resulting in continuous states of alertness and vigilance and an increased sensitivity to stimuli. The adolescent uses the mechanism of partial regression to the undifferentiated phase of object relationships as an essential step in furthering ego development.

Geleerd regarded this partial ego regression as a normal phenomenon and explained that the ego needs to withdraw various object cathexes in order to prepare itself for adult object relationships. It is during this process that the ego may show a spurt in development, accompanied by increased growth and mastery of intellectual pursuits, as well as a general widening of interest in human endeavors. However, during these developmental maneuvers, the adolescent may be described as "altruistic and egocentric, devoted and unfaithful, gregarious and solitary, blandly submissive to a leader and defiant of authority, idealistic and cynical, sensitive and callous, ascetic and libertive, optimistic and pessimistic, enthusiastic and indifferent" (Gitelson 1948). These wide-ranging affective responses may be understood as equivalent depressive reactions to the loss of previous ego states. As Mahler (1972) writes, "inherent in every step of independent functioning is a minimal threat of object loss," a state that encourages, at times, the use of desperate defensive operations to avoid even the possibility of any perception of separateness or loss. It is these experimental defensive operations that make adults uncomfortable as both aggressive and sexual impulses in the adolescent become apparent.

Erikson (1956) used the term "ego identity" to denote the results of certain gains achieved by the end of adolescence. These derivatives of preadult experiences, accomplished in order to become ready for the tasks of adulthood, connote eventually a persistent sameness within oneself (self-sameness) and a persistent sharing of some kind of essential character with others. Erikson described the psychosocial schedule of ego growth as including the following: (1) mechanisms of introjection and projection, which depend on a satisfactory mutuality between mother and child; (2) childhood idenitifactions, which depend on satisfactory and trustworthy family experiences; and (3) identity formation, which arises from the repudiation of childhood identifications and the assumption of new configurations with both internal and societal recognitions.

The clinical picture of identity diffusion is recognized in young people who are unable to utilize the social or intrapsychic moratoria provided. A composite description illustrates the "phase specific" aspects of Erikson's approach, which emphasizes the life task shared by this group of patients. The time of breakdown is related to adolescent demands for simultaneous commitment to physical intimacy, competition, and psychosocial definition. The resulting regression is manifested by an inability to make decisions, a sense of isolation and inner emptiness, an inability to achieve relationships and sexual intimacy, a distorted time perspective resulting in a sense of great urgency as well as a loss of consideration for time as a dimension of living, an acute inability to work, and, at times, the choosing of a negative identity, a hostile parody of the usual roles in one's family or community.

Anna Freud (1958), describing adolescence as "a neglected period, a stepchild," referred to the difficulty of drawing the line between normality and pathology. She views adolescence as an interruption of peaceful growth that resembles a variety of emotional upsets. Adolescent reactions approximate symptom formation and merge, almost imperceptibly, into borderline states of almost all mental illnesses. While in earlier writings adolescent disturbances were described in terms of their similarity to adult neurotic and psychotic syndromes, Freud (1946) revised her concepts, describing psychopathology not only in terms of id impulses and fantasies but also on the basis of the adolescent's struggle with parental images, which were previously repressed but not stimulated by the adolescent process of attempting to further break the ties that impede efforts toward further growth and development.

The more recent literature on adolescence includes research efforts to correlate demographic and intrapsychic understanding through the use of psychoanalytically oriented interview techniques and alliances developed by the investigator and subjects over a long period of time. It was from such investigations that Offer (1969) concluded that turmoil was not an inevitable normal pathway for adolescents but was only one route for passing through adolescence. A cluster of middle-class adolescents was isolated, whose development was continuous and undisturbed; the antecedent of this group's nonturmoil path is believed to have been nonstressful childhood with maximal developmental opportunities. Offer's work is of great importance in establishing the concept of normalcy in adolescence and thereby helping to delineate the parameters of behavior related to early experiences of reliability and trust as well as the family system's capacity to help the young child to deal with loss or separation experiences in a creative, ego-building fashion. It is those examples of continued acceptance of conscious parental values that help to clarify the vicissitudes of adolescents whose early developmental experiences were only partially successful and only partially completed. In those cases in which adolescence represents a significant disruption of the psychic equilbrium, the incomplete development led to massive breakdown of synthetic efforts, with resulting pathology.

ADOLESCENCE AND THE BORDERLINE STATE

Efforts at clarifying diagnostic considerations in adolescence are most difficult because of the rapid developmental, psychosomatic, and psychosocial changes that characterize this period of life. In addition, adolescents present clinicians with a challenge, because current troubled behaviors indicate some change in capacity to cope with stress and because previous stable efforts to resolve reality demands are no longer functional. Aggression, which once was comfortably handled, is now expressed more intensively toward family members, school and community authorities, and friends. On the other hand, the teenager may become passive and withdrawn, gradually eliminating many well-established activities.

These are early indicators of the increasing use of regression as a device to deal with internal and external stresses on the already burdened ego structure. If the aggressive reaction can be considered under the general rubric of "adjustment reaction," and if recognition of stress and therapeutic efforts to respond to the plea for help are properly instituted, there is usually a rapid resolution of the stress reaction, and one can be reassured that the adolescent is passing through an identity crisis or phase. If regressive behavior persists, a more serious mental process must be considered, and the adjustment response is now to be perceived as an "alarm signal" indicating deeper conflict and the need to further explore diagnostic aspects of the personality structure (Kernberg 1978).

The current interest in the clarification of structural criteria in borderline states is of particular importance in the consideration of and the therapeutic efforts for disturbed adolescents. From an historical view, it clarifies the importance of considering the developmental point of view along with longitudinal, observational studies and reduces the use of empathy as a research tool to a proper focus on issues of transference and countertransference. From a diagnostic point of view, there is a developing general agreement that the borderline syndrome is a personality organization characterized by deficient self and object constancy derived from a developmental defect in ego functions, which usually is precipitated in early childhood but which can occur in later life. The descriptive and diagnostic characteristics of this form of severe character pathology include the following: the presence of identity diffusion expressed as a lack of integration of self and object representations; continued use of primitive defenses, particularly splitting (a defect in object relations where internalized representations and reality are not fused but continue to split into the good and the bad); and the maintenance of reality testing, even after a transient psychotic episode is experienced (Kernberg 1978; Grinker 1975, 1978). In defining the overall characteristics of the borderline syndrome, Grinker et al. (1968) found anger as the main affect, along with defect in affectionate relationships, absence of indications of self identity, and the presence of depressive loneliness.

CONCLUSIONS

These formulations, both descriptive and dynamic, pose a serious problem for the clinician attempting to quantify the adolescent patient. As Giovacchini (1978) points out, the adolescent has had only a short time to adjust to his or her new pubertal ambience, is faced with intense feelings he or she has to learn to control and integrate, suffers from insufficient transformations of an identity sense, and hovers on the edge of psychotic thinking, from the danger of identity diffusion. The lack of integration from these transitional phenomena makes the adolescent in regressive crisis from internal and external stresses look and act very "borderline."

Careful use of development and structural concepts, however, can eventually clarify whether the adolescent is pursuing (1) a normal pathway through adolescence, which may be tumultuous or impulsive but is characterized by maintenance of self and object relationships; (2) a neurotic pathway, with internalized intrapsychic conflicts resulting in symptom formation; (3) a schizophrenic pathway, in which careful, long-term contact will eventually reveal a disorder of thinking; or (4) the borderline syndrome, in which defective personality organization is present with a considerable degree of internal consistency and stability and is not a regression as a response to internal or external conditions of stress.

REFERENCES

Erikson, E. H. 1956. The problem of ego identity. *Journal American Psychoanalytic Association.* 4(1):56–121.

Eissler, K. 1958. Notes on problems of technique in the psychoanalytic treatment of adolescents. *Psychoanalytic Study of the Child.* 13:223–254.

Feinstein, S. C., Giovacchini, P. L., and Miller, A. 1971. Introduction. *Adolescent Psychiatry.* 1:13–15. New York: Basic Books.

Feinstein, S. C., and Ardon, M. 1973. Trends in dating patterns and adolescent development. *Journal of Youth and Adolescence.* 2(2):157–166.

Freud, A. 1946. *The Ego and the Mehcanisms of Defense.* New York: International Universities Press.

Freud, A. 1958. Adolescence. *Psychoanalytic Study of the Child.* 3:255–278.

Freud, S. 1900. The interpretation of dreams. *Standard Edition.* Volumes 4 and 5. London: Hogarth Press, 1955.

Freud, S. 1915. Instincts and their vicissitudes. *Standard Edition.* 14:117–140. London: Hogarth Press, 1957.

Freud, S. 1923. The ego and the id. *Standard Edition.* 19:12–66. London: Hogarth Press, 1962.

Gardiner, G. E. 1959. Psychiatric problems of adolescence. In S. Arieti, ed. *American Handbook of Psychiatry.* New York: Basic Books.

Geleerd, E. 1961. Some aspects of ego vicissitudes in adolescence. *Journal American Psychoanalytic Association.* 9:394–405.

Giovacchini, P. L. 1978. The borderline aspects of adolescence and the borderline state. In S. C. Feinstein and P. L. Giovacchini, eds. *Adolescent Psychiatry.* Chicago; University of Chicago Press.

Gitelson, M. 1948. Character synthesis: Psychotherapeutic problems of adolescence. *Journal American Orthopsychiatric Association.* 14:422–431.

Grinker, R. R. Sr., Werble, B., and Drye, R. C. 1968. *The Borderline Syndrome.* New York: Basic Books.

Grinker, R. R. Sr. 1975. *Psychiatry in Broad Perspective.* New York: Behavioral Publications.

Grinker, R. R. Sr. 1978. The borderline syndrome. In S. C. Feinstein and P. L. Giovacchini, eds. *Adolescent Psychiatry.* Chicago: University of Chicago Press.

Hall, G. S. 1904. *Adolescence.* New York: Appleton.

Jones, E. 1930. Psychoanalysis and biology. In *Essays in Applied Psycho-Analysis.* London: Hogarth, 1951.

Kernberg, O. 1978. The diagnosis of borderline conditions in adolescence. In S. C. Feinstein and P. L. Giovacchini, eds. *Adolescent Psychiatry* Chicago: University of Chicago Press.

Kett, J. F. 1977. *Rites of Passage.* New York: Basic Books.

Mahler, M. 1972. On the first three subphases of the separation-individuation process. *International Journal of Psychoanalysis.* 53:333–338.

Offer, D. 1969. *The Psychological World of the Teenager.* New York: Basic Books.

Rousseau, J. P. 1933. *Emile.* New York: Dutton.

8

TRANSFORMATION OF INTERNAL OBJECT FANTASIES DURING THE PSYCHOANALYSIS OF A BORDERLINE PATIENT

Frank Crewdson, M.D.
New York Medical College

The purpose of this chapter is to demonstrate changes in internal object relations in a borderline patient during a five-year psychoanalysis. Selection of the case material is chronological and is limited mostly to a description of the appearance and transformation of the several key self and object paradigms that emerged. Kernberg, in a recent article, on intrapsychic change in the psychotherapy of the borderline, wrote that "a borderline patient in intensive psychoanalytic psychotherapy expresses his psychopathology with a limited repertoire of predominant primitive internalized object relations." (1) He also stresses that transformation of these primitive object relations is possible primarily through the medium of the transference.

Benny, as he will be called, had failed by age 22 to develop sufficiently as a separate individual to function more than marginally in the community. He was from a close-knit, extended Italian family. His mother was a dependent personality, as was her brother. They both relied heavily on an older sister who lived next door. There is no history of schizophrenia in the family.

There is a history of controlling and infantilizing behavior toward Benny and his two younger brothers, with encouragement to remain at home and no encouragement for outside activities. His father is successful in his families' business but was remote from his sons; he, however, actively encouraged the therapy.

Benny finished high school with a low average but has proved to be intelligent in his analysis. His lack of educational and vocational success and his negative self-image had resulted in a depression for which he sought therapy.

As a patient, he was well suited to a study of internal object relations because of readily available fantasy material. Though his reality testing was impaired during periods of object loss, he was able to form a good therapeutic alliance and to identify with the analyst and the analytic work; for instance, he early on kept a diary in his struggle to understand the "changes" that he was going through.

His motivation for analysis was high, because of the subjective pain of his defective self-image and the ease with which he could be triggered into frightening loss of identity states. He was seen face-to-face twice a week for five years. Early in the analysis, he formed a close relationship with Rose, whom he later married.

PART 1—THE DANCER

Benny, at age 24 and in the second year of his analysis, clearly revealed fantasies of intense yearnings for reunion with the symbiotic mother, the mother before separation.[2] These fusion fantasies were provoked by a brief separation from Rose, the real object to whom he had remained attached after leaving his mother's house the year before.

Speaking of the fusion fantasies, he began by saying that a weird thing was going on:

> I am losing myself in fantasies of this dancer, just as though she were available to me. I picture being inside of her. I imagine that it's safer inside and I feel so lonely and deprived because I realize I can't have that.

This wish for merger was triggered when a dancer seductively enveloped Benny with her long hair. He then described, while fantasizing, a confusion of the identity of the dancer with his mother:

> Without these women, I am nothing. Mother, don't deprive me. It's too lonely out here. I would love to be the dancer's son, to be inside her. My mother was bad to bring me into the cruel world.

Casting the dancer in the role of the symbiotic mother he yearned for and also having images of the bad mother who turned him out into the cruel world, he experienced chaotically two sets of self and object images.

In one, he imagined himself as safe and protected, engulfed by an ideal mother; in the other, he felt separated, deprived, abandoned, and hurt, rejected by the bad mother.

Though reality testing was impaired during this period of fantasizing and of projecting his inner self and object images onto the external person of the dancer, he managed to face the "harsh reality" of not getting her. He said, "She is not available for the laying on of my primal wishes," and "I'm the guy who didn't get what he wanted but who gained strength."

A separation from Rose had provoked an abandonment depression with underlying fears of death. As a maneuver to avoid the unacceptable idea of object loss, he turned to defensive fantasies of merger with the mother, which included being a baby yet to be born. He also expressed angry feelings against his cruel mother who had pushed him into the outside world.

PART 2—THE CORE PATHOLOGY

The focus now will be sharply on a key episode that occurred two years later in the early sessions of the fall of the fourth year of Benny's analysis. Since the dancer episode, he had married Rose and was firmly in a dependent attachment to her. In the fall, she began to complain about his analysis resuming. She focused all of her dissatisfactions on his having to be in analysis, which she saw as a disabling dependency. He was caught between what he interpreted as threats of absolute rejection and his ever-growing involvement in analysis.

In describing the key session here, in which there was identity fragmentation and the emergence of a very distinct mother-son internalized object relation that had previously been out of awareness, it is important to realize when assessing his ego function that Benny was working within the therapeutic relationship and was remembering, reporting, and observing and thus not functioning at a psychotic level. The significance of the session in following his object relations is that prior to this he had largely managed to maintain an illusion of oneness in his attachment to Rose, not perceiving her as a separate individual. Now, the valued relationship to the analyst was a threat to that unity.

Some of the material emerged as a retelling of fantasies of being in an analytic session, as though the emergence of such frightening fantasies required the reassuring presence of the analyst. Benny said:

> In the fantasy yesterday, I was telling you about losing Rose. I wanted to whine out. You were encouraging me to bring it out. I was standing,

trying to be brave, but I sank to the floor, slowly succumbing to isolation. Going through those feelings of losing Rose, I felt doomed. Wow, this has been with me so long, always away from my mother.

The next fantasy reported occurred while he was sitting in the waiting room, and he again imagined a session. The fantasy had the character of a dissociated state:

> I was with you, you were telling me to bring it out. There was a "me" crying like a baby. The room shook. The vicious voice of my mother came out of me: "Shut up, you little bitch bastard!" There were two parts to me: the mother cursing and screaming; me, the baby, crying. You were shocked and scared. Then, in order to get what I wanted from you, I had to take it from you; I had to kill you.

Still in fantasy, through projective identification, he had momentarily seen me as the ungiving mother and was expressing both his rage at her refusal to give and the ruthless quality of his demand, so voracious that he would kill to be fulfilled.

Later, at home with Rose, realizing that he was using Rose to represent the mother in his fantasy, he nevertheless felt angry and rejected when she watched television instead of letting him enjoy closeness to her. He had a fantasy then, in which he killed her, saying: "I was so angry at her leaving me. I imagined killing her, getting the most out of her, consuming her." With the threat of abandonment by Rose, the previously dissociated and impacted self and object relationship became conscious. Clearly, he experienced Rose's rejection as an abandonment and actually felt doomed to nonexistence.

The constellation of identifications that emerged from the dissociated state included that of a deprived, hurt, crying baby, who was enraged at the rejecting mother. Also, aggressive impulses emerged to kill the frustrating mother to get love from her, to consume her. The vicious mother image contained some qualities of controlling behavior and anger actually present in his mother, but the degree of anger was a projection of his own murderous rage. The primal fantasy of the deprived, enraged baby murderously attacking and consuming the rejecting mother with consequent loss of the mother seems to be the core psychopathology previously dissociated. The merger reunion fantasy with the symbiotic mother now appeared to be a defensive fantasy.

A year later, in the fall of the fifth year of analysis, again with threats of abandonment by Rose, another fantasy of maintaining a bond with the maternal object appeared, this time without the ego disorganization seen before. The fantasy:

I searched for a beautiful woman, told her that I would be in total submission to her, would be her slave. I would be nobody and I would
sleep handcuffed on the floor in the basement. She could come whenever she wanted. She would give me food only if I gave her good sex.
There was security in it.

This theme of totally giving over the self, hands tied, to a dominating,
exploitative mother figure in exchange for the security of being bound to
her was the predominant theme in the transference.

In order to better follow the upcoming activation in the transference
of the three internalized self and object relations that have so far
emerged and that were activated in the transference, their appearance
and significance will be reviewed. Each self and object unit was triggered
by a separation threat to the dependent attachment to Rose. In Part 1,
Rose separated, an abandonment depression ensued, and fantasies of a
merger with an ideal mother figure followed. Also, Benny saw himself as
deprived and thrust into the world by a cruel mother.

In Part 2, again provoked by a separation threat from Rose, a deeper
abandonment depression ensued, with thoughts of death and, by this
time, feelings of security with the analyst. The deprived-child-pushed-
into-the-world-by-a-cruel-mother fantasy from Part 1 greatly intensified,
and a dissociated image of a vivid quality erupted into consciousness: the
crying baby cursed at by the screaming mother. A further terrifying element merged—that the frustrated and enraged infant wished to kill and
consume the mother figure.

A short time later, again provoked by a separation threat from Rose,
a minor abandonment state ensued but was coped with by the defensive
fantasy of the slave handcuffed and at the disposal of the dominating
woman. This clever fantasy opened the way to the possibility of change
within the transference, wherein the submissive self-image of the slave
began by degrees to oppose and rebel against the image of the dominating master, a role now perceived to be played by the analyst.

The original merger fantasy, acted out with Rose, provided a defense
against both the abandonment depression and the cruel mother-deprived
child scenario. The unmitigated and dissociated killer baby—screaming
mother dyad could not be lived with. The slave fantasy—as well as containing the satisfactions of food and sex—created the necessary components for the beginning of an active separation from the mother figure,
and the components appeared immediately in the transference.

PART 3—TRANSFERENCE: PROTEST

In contrast to the prior relationship with the analyst, in which the transference was of a transitional object type as described by Modell[3] a well-

defined transference began in the fifth year, with the patient attributing new characteristics to the relationship; for instance, that he wanted me to direct him or felt that I was intolerant of his self-expression. He perceived me as begging to give him my valuable information, that is, to feed him. Not tolerating positive statements from me, he said, "When you give me credit, I realized I was being hard on myself, as though my mother was talking in an angry voice and cursing at this little boy."

Thus connected directly to the cursing mother image and the dominating mother image, Benny was animating old scenes of helplessness, of being fed and of being the slave in a relationship with the angry and controlling mother. Other material confirmed the idea that he experienced a threat of abandonment should he be assertive. He asked, "Are you sure I'm not too strong?"

One can see the dramatic directness with which this belief in a controlling mother is reenacted in the transference. The created illusion that the analyst is the dominating mother is a temporary denial of the real identity of the analyst and provides an arena for change within the relationship. In this context, Benny began suddenly to protest the imagined control exercised by the analyst.

He said, quite unexpectedly,

> When you talk, I lose my identity. I put out my ideas and I feel robbed. Let me talk! I come here and feel like an accomplished person; I say my things and wind up feeling empty. I want to do things my way and not have to come here and hear your glorious words and keep alive your life system.

He then had a fantasy of the analyst begging Benny to be allowed to give him his valuable information in order to maintain his own (the analyst's) life systems.

Then, demonstrating the movement that can occur in the transference relationship, he said, "I really *changed* that session around. I felt before that I wasn't coming out with my ideas, but I let out my protest and it was OK with you. You grinned and were pleased that I was asserting myself." Such a sequence—protest, expectation of disapproval, and reality testing—repeated many times, undermined and modified the extreme images of the power of the object and the helplessness of the self in the original fantasy. He explained that he had felt that, for selfish reasons the analyst *needed* Benny to feed information to and that when he spoke, Benny felt taken over. This derived, in part, from the real personality of the mother, whose main purpose in life was to feed her family.

I made a correct interpretation that he was protesting and not listening in order to avoid being taken over or engulfed, fearing loss of his identity. Then, *only* because I had spoken, he shifted to a transference perception of me, listening in stony-faced silence with no hint of expression as to whether my words registered. He then abruptly began on an unrelated topic. He explained later what had happened: "You changed everything by talking. I didn't listen." He felt that my spoken words were an overwhelming threat to his sense of self, and we determined that this pattern of not listening, not responding, and changing the subject was a means of fortifying himself against this dreaded emptiness.

Then, Benny began to identify with the overpowering mother image. He said, "I am afraid I am too threatening to you; I am getting stronger. Maybe I will step on people." He then reported a masturbation fantasy in which he had forced himself on Mary, a friend, and made her see things his way. He said, "It was exciting: I took away her identity, and she had to be whatever I wanted her to be."

In the midst of this shift and reversal of identification, an event only observable in the analytic process occurred. He started the session by saying how effective he had been during the day in his work role. He did look stronger. I remained silent. He said, "I feel nervous suddenly, unsure. I looked at you and I felt empty, an immediate put-down. Suddenly, nothing I did today was important."

Addressing him as my analytic collaborator, I asked, "How does that work?"

"The way I was seeing Mary—manipulating and exploiting her, robbing her of her identity—I could project that onto you. You could control me—I would lose the identity that I built up today."

There is a coherent progression in this sequence that demonstrates how the self-object unit, once activated in the creative illusion of the transference, can be transformed as the patient measures his distorted perception of the analyst against glimpses of the real identity of the analyst; this, repeated many times, provides awareness of the tendency to project inner states onto external objects.

In time sequence, the structure of this section can be outlined as follows:

1. The analyst speaks; Benny loses identity. The difficulty in maintaining the self in the presence of the object is in focus, a problem in self and object differentiation, complementary to the dominant object, helpless self dyad.

2. Benny realizes that it is OK to speak. Glimpse of analyst's real identity.

3. Analyst speaks a self and object differentiation interpretation.

4. The defense of not listening and changing the subject is discovered. Seeing this trait will alter the rest of the analysis.

5. Benny identifies, in reversal of self and object roles, with the dominating object, who has the power to engulf Mary (in his fantasy).

6. Benny becomes aware of the power of the dominating object to engulf the self (through the fantasy in step 5) and realizes that he can and does project that image onto the analyst.

The observer self, within the medium of the transference, becomes aware of the distorted perception of the analyst and the self and of how inner images color outer or external real objects. The transformation takes place over time and is accumulative.

PART 4—TRANSFERENCE: DEFIANCE

The just-described transference work occurred at the beginning of the fifth year; the resolution of this transference paradigm began about six months later and was ushered in by increasingly defiant sessions in which Benny talked powerfully of confronting me and stopping the analysis. At one point he said, "I came here looking for something to fight about, to tell you off, to quit, to humiliate you, to dominate you. My power has taken effect on Rose, too; she is too weak for me." He further said, "I have to be defiant and nonresponsive—that is the way I say 'this is me.'" He gained power by identifying with the dominant side of the dyad.

Then, he softened his attitude to me and said, "I was so negative to you, and you were coming out with some good stuff—I even thought it was worth the fee today."

It became clear that he had been striving to maintain the upper hand in the relationship, to avoid being dominated and engulfed again by the analyst. His softened attitude immediately resulted in a reversal from the omnipotent self to the helpless self. That night he dreamed that a doctor had tried to give him a pill. If he had taken it, the doctor could do whatever he wanted to with him—have sex with him, manhandle him. He said, "The next day, I was weak, an asshole; I submitted to your golden treatment, I was wiped out. I didn't dominate; I wanted to give up everything." At this point, only these two modes of functioning seemed possible—strength through domination or submission leading to weakness. The defective self-image, which was painful to face after the period of omnipotence and strength, elicited a memory of being hurt and bleeding as a child.

The insight provided by the sequence of powerful negativity (identifying with the original maternal object) and of the sudden reversal of roles as he identified with the weak self-image—a sequence that had been seen repeatedly since the transference began—again produced change. The appearance of the truly painful defective self-image especially motivated change. He said, "I am beginning to question much more what I am succumbing to and what it makes me."

A feeling of importance, of equality, and, again, of being able "to do his own thing" without being submissive followed. Shorter sequences within single sessions occurred, in which Benny began by being defiant *or* by feeling weak—the two alternatives—but ended with a positive identification derived from doing the analytic work, which gave him awareness that a third alternative was possible: coexistence. "I feel good about you and I appreciate being able to analyze those things," he said, again showing the growing importance of positive feelings to the real analyst.

His growing identification with the analyst and the pain of the defective self-image combined to allow functioning at a new level, as he called it. He said,

> I am doing very well. I did analytic work of my own. We have done good work together, and I used it as a technique to maintain my identity when Rose began to criticize me. I have always felt unworthy; I have accepted her version of me. I have to look at reality. It's not all me. She has her problems too.

PART 5—WHY CAN'T I BREAK AWAY?

"Since I have seen you last, I've maintained my strength. Two weeks ago I rose to a different level. I felt more responsible and important. The feeling stayed."

This is the theme of Benny's new identity, and with this firmer sense of self, he is able to perceive others more clearly—an example of improved self and object differentiation. He described Rose, for instance, in a fuller and more realistic way.

I made a short statement about the maintenance of his identity, which had the effect of pulling him back into the regressive transference. He said, "I'm trying hard to stand firm and not be wiped out by you. I felt OK when I wasn't seeing you, but all of a sudden, I feel weakened."

In the next session he said,

> I don't like the role I play. When I came into that session I was reduced to a helpless patient. I hated you. I acted out that role and felt belittled.

I have struggled, though, and haven't lost myself. I want to break away so badly. I feel like I am sacrificing and missing out on things. Why can't I break away? What role am I going to play? Helpless? And let you feed me information or stand up for myself? I don't need you. I am functioning independently. I have maintained my identity completely.

The free play between a new sense of identity and questioning the regressive transference roles is evident. Can he function independently? Why does he play a helpless role when he comes into my presence? Why can't he break away? These are all very creative questions, which he is intensely involved with.

The time had arrived and Benny was ready to express and work with the irrational beliefs and associated emotions in the transference. As he did this, he shifted back and forth in an intricate and fluid way between perceiving himself and the analyst with good reality testing in their real identities and regressively perceiving himself and the analyst in terms of the long-activated submissive self and dominant object roles. In order to change, he had to express the blocked-off feelings of anger toward being forced to submit, in order to maintain the bond to the dominating object.

The intricate changes as they occurred in this session will be played through, with parenthetical comments that will be a guide to understanding them.

I wanted to break away from you and stop therapy, but I came back. (He wanted to free himself from the illusory domination of the controlling analyst, but he still needed him.)

But you wanted to pry some more. You need me more than ever. I hate this whole scene. (This is projection of his own need onto the analyst.)

I am stronger than ever. I have an inner strength. It's only me doing things. (That is true; but he still has the illusion that he needs the object to function.)

I left here last time and decided I had to help myself, but you would put that down. (This is the illusion that the object rejects his independent strivings.)

I just imagined you saying to me that *I* needed *you* and I said "the hell I do, I don't need you! I can be independent!" Then, I fell to the floor showing my helplessness. I could walk out, damn it, but I would fall to pieces a block away. (He moved here toward acknowledging that it is Benny who needs the analyst—not the projected version heard earlier. He further reveals clearly for himself that in spite of his actual firmer identity, he still fears disintegration should he separate from the object.)

If I break away, I will lose what I have built up with you. He cries. (He does not fully know yet that what he has internalized through identification with the analyst will stay with him when he terminates.)

I want to leave so bad. I could do it on my own. I feel like I have to express all these feelings. (The observing self is aware of the reality situation of being in a session working out a problem. Having expressed anger and having acknowledged his irrational beliefs, he now shifts completely out of the transference.)

I don't feel overwhelmed now. I could like myself now. When I come here, I am reduced to a helpless patient.

I then spoke for the first time in this session: "In fantasy you feel like a helpless patient, but in reality you have functioned very effectively in this session."

He said, "I feel good now. I didn't feel a loss of myself. I am OK. All I want is to be accepted and to be able to express my identity in my own way."

As it turned out, with all the prior transference work behind him, this session was the turning point. A firm sense of self, with improved object differentiation, flowed from the correction of the basic irrational idea that he needed the object to function. He achieved a separate status as an individual.

Many observable changes quickly emerged and have persisted. Benny achieved an insight into his previous mode of relating and his vulnerability to submission. He continued this process by comparing his firmer independent state with the past tendency to weaken and collapse when confronted by a strong individual.

His sense of identity included an entirely new image of himself. In describing why he thought another person would like him, he said, "He would appreciate my maturity, my being able to understand him. He would like that I am solid and together." I said, "Do you see yourself that way?" He answered, "Yes—also funny, deep, and complicated." Identification with the analyst and the analytic work was evident in this and other material.

Resolution of the transference brought improved self and object differentiation, which was most evident in the new perception that he had of our relationship:

> I definitely have found myself. I won't go back to being wiped out by anyone. I wanted to come here. I thought, "Frank could add to my good feelings (instead of feeling robbed). He will be right there. I can come feeling good and he won't take it away." I see you sharply in focus—right there.

Along with the improved reality testing and self and object differentiation, which depend on a firm sense of identity, he also revealed a genuine capacity to love: "I feel really good about you. I know I have taken part of you with me."

DISCUSSION

This chapter is designed to give an understanding of how a young male patient with a severe degree of borderline psychopathology, living in a state of dependent attachment first to his mother then to his wife, participated in the psychoanalytic process and achieved separate functioning and an improved sense of identity.

Presented in longitudinal perspective, with the case material stemming from the patient, the natural unfolding process of psychoanalysis is apparent. From the perspective of time, the first four years involved maintaining attachment to external maternal objects on whom inner object images were projected. Also involved was the growing therapeutic relationship to the analyst, whose "holding" and "mothering" functions[4,5] provided a secure base from which to build sufficient ego strength (primarily reality testing) to undergo structural change. The fifth year brought activation in the transference of the previously seen fantasized object relations and a relatively rapid resolution of them.

The novel point of view of the chapter is the focus on fantasized object relations and their transformation as well as their activation in the transference. Grotstein states:

> The meticulous detailing and classification of internal object fantasies . . . constitute one of the truly important, pressing needs in clinical research so that a technology of fantasies and objects can keep pace with the gains of ego psychology, . . . telling the biographical narrative of object relationships[6] · · ·

Though the unfolding of the fantasized object relations is detailed in the chapter, it will be summarized here. The long-term fantasy of reunion with the object, as was seen dramatically with its projection onto the dancer, and other merger fantasy material not included are understood as a wish to deny the separateness of the object[4,6], a defense against separation anxiety.[2] Also, Benny's living out the fantasy of merger and remaining attached to his mother was not adaptive for normal living and led to his seeking therapy.

Separation anxiety and abandonment depression were seen at the same time as the dancer fantasy but not with the full intensity with which they erupted from the dissociated state in the fourth year with the coming into awareness of the cursing mother and crying baby images. The enraged baby wishing to kill the mother figure in order to consume her and merge with her is a more primitive and frightening version of the fantasy of reunion originally seen.

This was called the core of the patient's psychopathology because of its devastating nature and because the self and object relation depicted was primitive and had been long dissociated, only to emerge when sufficient ego strength and trust in the analyst had dekeloped; furthermore, clinically, it was the major turning point in the analysis, becuase from then on, the transference quickly developed and was worked through.

The fantasy of the slave helplessly bound to the object is representative of an internal change in object relationships. In this fantasy the omnipotent maternal figure needs *him* for the maintenance of her "life system"—a projective identification—and keeps him available to satisfy her needs. It thus provides a bond (updated reunion fantasy), but also a position from which he can rebel.

It is contended that the eventual activation and working through of the transference in the fifth year depended on the prior appearance and partial transformation of the fantasied internal self- and object-images: first, the fantasied reunion with the object to deny separation; second, the core separation fantasy, with rage and consuming the objective to maintain merger; and third, the slave fantasy, which was much less primitive and open to change (through rebellion) toward separation-individuation.[2]

This chapter is an attempt to give substantive and clinical expression to frequently incomprehensible concepts of internalized object relations. It also demonstrates the structural changes possible within the analytic process—in this case, those stemming from the transformation of fantasied object relations as they were first expressed in the patient's actual relationships to outside figures and then as they were expressed in the transferential relationship to the analyst.

REFERENCES

1. Kernberg, O. F.: Structural Change and Its Impediments. In *Borderline Personality Disorders*. New York: International Universities Press, Inc., pp. 275–306, 1977.

2. Mahler, S.: *The Psychological Birth of the Human Infant*. New York: Basic Books, Inc., 1975.

3. Modell, A. H.: *Object Love and Reality*. New York: International Universities Press, Inc., 1968.

4. Winnicott, D. W.: *Collected Papers*. New York: Basic Books, 1958.

5. Modell, A. H.: The Holding Environment and the Therapeutic Action of Psychoanalysis. *J. Amer. Psychoanal. Assn.*, 24:285–307, 1976.

6. Grotstein, J. S.: The Psychoanalytic Concept of Schizophrenia: I. The Dilemma. *Int. Jour. of Psycho-Anal.*, 58:403–425, 1977.

Part Four

CHILDHOOD

9

ATTACHMENT, DETACHMENT, AND PSYCHOANALYTIC THERAPY
The Impact of Early Development on the Psychoanalytic Treatment of Adults

DAVID E. SCHECTER, M.D.
William Alanson White Institute, New York, and
Einstein College of Medicine, Bronx, New York

This chapter is from a series of papers on the emergence of human relatedness and the nature of human attachment.[1] All of the papers were based on the premise that observations of normal ethologic and psychic developments can contribute to the deepening of psychoanalytic theory and therapy (Schecter 1968a, 1968b, 1971, 1973, 1974, 1975a, 1975b). The time is now ripe for the integration of several fields of study: ethology, ego development, interpersonal relations, object relations, and psychoanalysis. The attachment of the human infant to its mother—and the reverse (Klaus and Kennel 1976)—can be observed from these five points of view.

Detachment—the turning away from human relationship—can also be so described. This chapter will briefly summarize the process of attachment in humans and will delineate the defense system of character detachment and its relevance to psychoanalytic theory and practice. *Character detachment* is seen as a network of defenses and coping mechanisms that become relatively stable and structuralized, that is, chronic in the personality. The structural network of detachment functions protects the organism and the psyche against those painful affects that are associated with human attachment. In this sense, character detachment can be seen as a primary and rather awesome defense against the very process of human relatedness itself.

Detachment is not simply "good," or "bad": it can be relatively adaptive or maladaptive in relation to the individual's total psychosocial situation. Significant aspects of character detachment can be found in persons bearing every psychiatric diagnosis. Character detachment can be subjectively experienced as "never again," as far as close human relationships are concerned. The defenses are related to persistent and usually unconscious anticipation or fear of the various forms of psychic pain. The detachment defense attempts, for example, to convert the fear of being abandoned (ego-passive fear) to an active movement away from relationship. The greater the depth of detachment, the greater will be the sense of futility, that is, no hope for a "good relationship." Also, the earlier in development detachment occurs, the greater will be the potential pathologic consequences. Detachment—as used in this paper—can be observed in *any* stage of development. This is in contrast to the narrower concept of "schizoid detachment," which connotes a severe and lasting detachment process between mother and child beginning in the stage of infancy. Detachment is observed in varying degrees when a child, adolescent, or adult suffers the loss of a beloved person. To some degree the process of mourning uses aspects of detachment as part of its repertoire. Diagnostically, it is therefore crucial to observe whether the detachment is of early origin and is deep and almost total (schizoid), or whether it is occurring in selective areas in a character disorder or neurotic personality. The prognosis and therapy are obviously quite different, depending on the preceding diagnostic criteria.

Detachment as described here can, at certain times, be part of a healthy coping with a difficult situation or a certain stage of development. For example, puberty-age children almost classically go "underground" and in varying degrees cut off their affective relationship to their parents, while they might intensify their bonds to their chums. Also, the midlife parents, whose children are on their way out into the nonfamily world, will affectively detach themselves from certain kinds of closeness to their sons and daughters. Older-age detachment may be quite adaptive, for example, in the sense of the Oriental form of detachment from an anxious "overattachment" to life itself.

The last section of this chapter will examine the psychoanalytic situation and technique that are appropriate for working on the areas of character detachment. The therepeutic goal, briefly stated, is to reestablish human attachment in those areas where relatedness has been "frozen" or cut off. With "re-relatedness" in these areas, dissociated aspects of the personality—including its strengths and talents—can be reintegrated, giving rise to a situation where "activity affects" can emerge (Schachtel 1959).

However, analysts must be alert to periodic and perhaps necessary regression to intrapsychic fusion or symbiotic fantasies with internal objects to fill the extreme isolation of the very detached person. They must also learn to distinguish the ensuing "pseudoindependence" and the "arrogant self-sufficiency" from healthy progression toward authentic autonomy and interdependency. The final therapeutic goal is to bring back from dissociation the fractured parts of the self which can be restructured and integrated under "one roof," that is, under the roof of the total self and under control of the ego.

Object relations theory has helped to make respectable the empathic "real" relatedness of analyst to analysand (Bromberg 1976). The model of analyst as "interpretive mirror" is being replaced by the model of participant-observation (Sullivan 1953). Moreover, with the observation and studies of early infant-parent relationships, the analyst's empathic capacity is broadened and deepened to include preverbal and nonverbal feeling states.

ATTACHMENT AND THE CONSTANCY OF RELATIONSHIP

On the ethologic level of observation, *attachment* can be defined as a unique relationship between two people that is specific and enduring through time (Klaus and Kennel 1976), though not necessarily at the level of mental representation. Attachment behaviors include fondling, kissing, cuddling, and prolonged gazing—behaviors that serve both to maintain contact with and to express affection toward a specific individual. Close attachment can persist during long separations of time and distance, even though at times there may be no visible sign of its existence, indicating the infant's "memory bank" for good attachments.

The particular stages of formation of the first human bond to the level of object constancy have been described in detail elsewhere (Schecter 1973, 1974). Suffice it to repeat here that the process is not based primarily on reduction of need tension. Rather, there is an evolution of two-person interactions where tension rises and falls in rhythmic fashion. This is true for mutual smiling, for eye-to-eye "choreography" (D. Stern 1971), and for playful interaction, including peek-a-boo (Schecter 1973). These processes require an interpersonal model that is quite different from, for example, the reduction of oral-drive tension.

In earlier papers, several hypotheses were put forth concerning human development that were based on direct observations in natural family settings. Summarized briefly, these hypotheses are as follows:

1. Social stimulation and reciprocal interaction, often playful and not necessarily drive-connected or tension-reducing, constitute a basis for the development of specific social attachments and relationships between infant and others.

2. Early reciprocal stimulation and response can be seen as the precursors to *all* human communication.

3. The early ego functions and structures constitute the building blocks of human development and are necessary precursors to moral development and social collaboration, which, in turn, constitute the fabric of our society. It is safe to predict that until society and its responsible institutions take care of the needs of its infants, children, and adults, we will suffer ongoing generational family and social disorganization.[2]

In the later stages of constancy development, the child not only can discriminate and selectively value his mother but also has begun to represent her mentally with qualities of increasing permanence and objectivity. The mother continues to be preferred and central to the child's life, even in the face of cruelty and frustration or during a limited absence. This centrality of mother constitutes the achievement of constancy of relationship, which also implies object-person constancy as well as a growing sense of continuity and sameness in the self (self-constancy).

The relationship is now represented mentally (intrapsychically) and is invested with intense affect; it develops growing stability over the years. Analysts tend to think that there is a critical—or at least optimal—period for such constancy of relationship to be defined and maintained, with growing stability and an increasing number of persons (during the second and third years and onward). Mental health is predicated on these developments, and they pertain to the parent as well as the child. The warps and deficits in ego and interpersonal development derive in large part from a failure to achieve a level of constancy of relationship with one or more persons early in life.

The work of individual development and of therapy consists of integrating the polar splits of good mother and bad mother into the felt concept "my mother." As Sullivan (1953) suggests, the learning of language and its word symbol "mother" facilitates, and in part coerces, the integration of the good and bad polarities of experience. The further task of both development and therapy is to be able to endure and maintain the constancy (continuity and sameness) of the relationship, of the self (self-identity), and of the object (object constancy) despite the prevalence of ambivalent affects toward mother. Constancy of relatedness[3] can be defined in part as the capacity to maintain the integrated relationship (internal) to the mother in the face of the conflicting affects such as love and hate. The love object will not be exchanged and is not interchangeable even under conditions of cruelty.

The development of constancy of relationship is only begun in infancy. It is still highly unstable in early childhood.[4] It is really a lifelong developmental task to retain and modify the previously described constancy under the vicissitudes of separation-individuation and of ambivalent feelings. A fresh or sharp loss or disappointment threatens to test the stability of constancy, and, clinically, there is a splitting of parent or spouse and/or self into "all good" and "all bad."[5] Eventually, in analytic therapy of deeply detached persons, there develops a spontaneous desire of wanting the various compartments of the self to be under "one roof," whose subjective expression includes "my self" or "all me."

The clinical relevance of the concept of constancy of relationship is enormous. To the extent that this capacity has been developed in a stable way, there will be less tendency to splitting of the object—person or of the self into all good or all bad—tendencies that are seen in the borderline character and in paranoid and shizophrenic persons. Moreover, such constancy anchors and centers the self during its process of separation-individuation, thereby leading to increased ego autonomy and to less tendency to regresssion to fusion states when under stress. Also, constancy of relation protects against a sense of total loss or abandonment (for example, when this occurs in reality with the external object), since the internal constant relationship, if strong enough, will help to mourn the loss of the external object-person.

DETACHMENT

Now that the process of human attachment has been described in a condensed way, the process of detachment will be examined.[6] Detachment is an attempt to anesthetize psychic pain. Detachment implies a "never again" or an "I don't care" affect as far as one's relation to specifically loved persons.[7] It attempts to neutralize the anxieties that accompany relationships—the anxiety of separation, of loss of love, or of yearning but without hope, for example.

Detachment in its broadest sense has a biological base in development. Sullivan (1953) describes the phenomenon of "somnolent detachment" in the infant, which occurs when he or she is overly anxious or over stimulated, as in pain. The infant's biologic defenses include both falling asleep and visual aversion, literally a turning away from a source of anxiety such as the angry mother. These biologic mechanisms are seen here as the anlagen to the psychic defense of detachment.

Interest in defensive detachment has derived from Bowlby's (1973) description of the young child's reactions to separation. Bowlby used the term *detachment* to describe the third stage of a two-year-old's reaction upon physical separation from mother due to the child's hospitalization. After the initial stages of stormy, angry protests followed by despair (sadness, regression, and loss of interest in the environment), a third stage—detachment—was characterized by "improved spirit," with an active avoidance of mother, or by a distinct "cooling" of the strong specific attachment behavior usually shown at this age toward mother.[8]

The detached child was described as committing himself or herself less and less to succeeding figures and becoming more self-centered and more preoccupied with need satisfaction such as desiring sweets and material things. The parallel—phenomenologically and etiologically—between (1) the direct observation (by camera) of Bowlby's detachment phase following actual separation and (2) characterologic detachment in adults is quite striking.[9] It seemed that Bowlby's description of the detachment phase needed to be understood as a process that could be conceptualized on two levels: (1) the behavioral ethologic level (pre- and post-representational) and (2) as intrapsychic defense.[10]

The latter intrapsychic detachment defense can be seen as becoming available to the child not only after real physical separations but, on another level, after the realization of a greater sense of psychic separatedness during the separation-individuation processes in childhood[11] and in later stages of development.

It is in the processes of detachment and normal separation-individuation that the internal capacity for constancy of relationship becomes most critical. The more stable the constancy and the deeper the structure of the loving superego, the less traumatic will be the separation anxiety and the ensuing detachment defense.[12] In a sense, it can be said that a firm, healthy constancy of relationship in some degree immunizes child and adult reactions to the effects of loss, separation, and abandonment. If a good relationship is internalized in one's self, he or she will be able to endure separation and loss without the need for extreme detachment. That person will also be helped to mourn aspects of the primary relationship that are being lost, including omnipotence and symbiosis.

Detachment may be observed on a number of levels, and varying combinations of classic defense mechanisms may be used, such as the following:

- Stoppage[13] of "affect flow" interpersonally and intrapsychically (*repression*)

- *Isolation* of affect from idea—for example, of the loved other

- *Denial* of attachment, that is, a disavowal of an attachment
- *splitting* of the internal object-person and of the self

Under certain optimal conditions, including a trusting psychoanalytic situation, persons with character detachment can develop a richness of affective responsiveness, a capacity for affective flow interpersonally and intrapersonally, and the capacity for constancy of relatedness, including self and object constancy.

Quite a large number of persons have been seen who have lost a parent in childhood or adolescence. Many of these have defended against the painful affect of personal-object loss via partial detachment that can, on the surface, mimic schizoid withdrawal.

Both in the schizoid personality and in severe character detachment there exist "broken," or split, parts of the self that remain to function on their own. With reattachment to certain affects and relationships, these parts of the self are rebuilt into a central self, which gains increasing input from the reverberating circuits that ensue in interpersonal relationships. Broken parts of the self are both the source and the result of great anxiety and are, so to speak, looking for a central self and ego with which to become one—that is, to "get it together."

PSYCHOANALYTIC THERAPY OF CHARACTER DETACHMENT

The main goal of psychoanalytic therapy is to reestablish attachment with the patient in those detached areas that had been frozen or cut off. As in all psychoanalytic therapy, analysts look to the healthy nondetached areas with which they can make a therapeutic alliance with the analysand. The alliance is largely based on (1) the hope of relieving psychic pain through the therapeutic relationship and (2) the shared capacity for both therapist and patients to look together with their observing egos at the whole person of the patient, including his or her interactions with the analyst and others. The analyst has the added work of keeping in touch with and analyzing his or her own countertransference. The latter reactions may include a sense of being drained or strained by the patient's resistance, especially in his or her areas of detachment. In brief, analysts use patients' strengths, curiosity, and pain to set up rapport and a working alliance.

The analysand needs the therapist to be emotionally available right from the beginning phase of the analysis, in which some detached persons may be experienced as arid, obsessional, and intellectualized in style. The analyst's attitude should be one of watchful waiting, with a mobility to move in and make connections for patients so that they can begin to see what they feel or might have felt if their detachment had not been so complete in a given area.

It is crucial to refrain from making comments that would predictably increase the resistance. The attitude of both analyst and analysand is one of "hovering" or "bare" attention (Nyanaponika 1973). It is noticed that the resistance centers around issues whose conscious awareness will bring pain. These issues usually have as their central affects anxiety and fear or depression but also, potentially, great shame and humiliation. Raw shame is one of the most potent dissociating forces, largely because it threatens suddenly to lower self-esteem and to annihilate the very sense of self. Hence the aphorism: "There is no problem so great as the shame of it."

The therapeutic principle of looking together and sharing experience has its roots in the mother-infant relationship from the second half of the first year onward. The paradigm consists of the infant focusing on some spectacle by gazing at or pointing to it and of mother responding in some sensitive way to the infant's communication.

In the observation of children and parents in their natural setting[14] it is most impressive to see the intensity of affect—and the amount of "free time"—that is experienced by parent and child. The affect can be described largely as joyful "activity affect" (Schachtel 1959), and it has the qualities of being peremptory and exclusively oriented to parent and child. In several families, fathers complained openly about feeling excluded from this private experience of mother and child, which has the quality of an exclusively shared private mythology. A whole body of play, fantasy, and reality become interwoven into a system fully known— usually—to one parent and child. Psychoanalytic therapy is, in part, also a shared mythology, in which the objective truth of the content is secondary to the peremptoriness of its being experienced as mutual and close to the subjective sense of truth about one's experience.[15] The melting down, through analysis, of the sense of shame and its coverups allows both analyst and analysand to look at areas that have been dissociated by detachment as these areas surface through dreams, fantasies, marginal thoughts, and nonobsessional free association. If this new body of experience is not foreclosed by premature interpretation and explanation, then "interpretive pointing" can be used to enhance the special sense of the therapeutic dyad looking together—as in snorkeling—in the same subterranean waters.

Interpretation and explanation can be used faultily to "wrap up" a dream, for example, before the dream and its associations are left in an "open state," that is, always with the possibility of coming back again and again to the dream from new perspectives and even of redreaming familiar dreams with new endings. The therapeutic attitude, then, is one of curiosity and exploration rather than explanation and interpretation. Explanation and interpretation are often used as "cerebralized" counter-resistance—a distancing by the analyst who is threatened by the necessary but finely titrated process of reattachment to a partially detached or "schizoid" person.

What has been noted here about sharing pathways to unconscious material using images and meanings in fantasy and dreams also applies to the exploration of the analysand's realities and history—indeed, because it is his story or her story, the one and only story each has, one that gives a sense of orientation, time continuity, identity, and drama to his or her own life. For some, if only to keep most hours interesting, there is a need to have some sense of drama and of history in its alive, current, and largely intrapsychic sense. The analytic expectation is to share experience in depth, and so the attitude in analytic therapy should strongly project this expectation. Otherwise, analyst and patient are doing something else with each other, and that had best be explored.

It is uncanny how, in a good analytic relationship, both analyst and analysand find the right "spot" to occupy in the dimensions of closeness versus distance and attachment versus detachment.[16] Analysts know intuitively not to move in too quickly, or too intimately, especially with a suspicious person. For patients, the anlyst can at first be felt as someone who is dangerous, as someone who may seduce or disarm a hard-won but extremely isolated fortress of pseudoautonomy. Nevertheless, patients have come to us for help, so that we have the right to inquire into their expectations, their needs, their fears, their shame, and their ideal wishes—but all with a sense of what each patient's defensive system can bear. A common question asked of a depressed or withdrawn patient is when he or she last felt good or hopeful. Not infrequently, as contact breaks through the detachment area via the transference and/or the real relationship, the patient may respond with a choked up feeling or with the shedding of some as yet undifferentiated tears.[17] If this human contact is felt as too threatening, the following analytic session is often distinctly cooler or more distanced or may even be cancelled.

Each participant in the analytic work becomes familiar with the "psychic space" around the self-boundary—the "ego-boundary" (Federn 1952)—and then with the boundary itself. The latter is more accurately experienced as a "membrane-around-the-self," a membrane that is semi-permeably selective; that is, certain affects and information can flow "in" and "out" in relation to given interpersonal situations. The concepts of self-membrane—and of membrane around compartments within the self—

are too important and complex to discuss in detail in this chapter.[18] Suffice it to say that analytic therapy works toward an optimal permeability of such membranes to facilitate the flow of information and affects.

The many therapeutic issues associated with character detachment tend to emerge naturally from an understanding of the phenomenology of attachment and detachment. For example, in the observation of infants and children, one has the experience of being responded to as the "bad stranger" whose presence can evoke near-panic in the six-month-old infant. This kind of experience, as well as that of separation terror, is not as likely to evoke a counterresistance in the analysis of adults when such attachment-separation stress behaviors are presented in the analytic situation. Similarly, the capacity for empathy with the more primitive, nonverbal affects can be more available in analysts who have had experience with infants and children. When one has seen "in the raw" the deep shame, humiliation, and rages of the preschooler, it is easier to recognize the "cover-up" of such affects in adults—a cover-up to protect the patient from a mortification of self-esteem.[19]

In working with adults, both a developmental diagnosis[20] and a "developmental therapy" can be used, with a particular interest in what ego strengths can be engaged for the patient's potential growth in therapy. An example of developmental therapy is seen in the long analysis that is required in the attempt to build a capacity for constancy in relationship. In deprivation or cumulative trauma (Khan 1974) of infancy and childhood, a capacity for constancy has failed to develop, or, if it has developed, it remains highly unstable in relation to the ordinary stresses of life. The building of a stable constancy of relatedness with the analyst may require many years, with up and down and in and out relationship (Guntrip 1968).

How one separates or detaches (these are different concepts) is *the* crucial factor to the next stage of interpersonal development. If one has left—or detached—with an inner sense of "badness," one brings this badness from one situation to another. This phenomenon is seen clearly in the transferences from early (original) family life to marital relations or in transference in the narrower, technical sense, in the analytic situation itself. One brings one's badness and tries to convert the analysis into a "bad relationship." Against this, the forces of the "good me," the "loving superego," and whatever available constancy of good relationship, all act to facilitate the ongoing analysis, in which the analyst "refuses" to treat the patient as if he or she were "really bad." In effect, the analyst does not follow the patient's attempt to "spoil" the relationship and thus challenges the patient's sense of omnipotent malevolence—a complex that may have resulted from extreme dissociation and detachment in earlier years. Almost every patient eventually describes the experience of the "fortress," "prison," or "shell" in association with a lack of connection to another person, a lonely or isolated state, or a lack of nourishment interpersonally—all with an underlying sense of deep futility.

In separations from or loss of a beloved person (or part of the self), the partially adaptive function of detachment is to maintain the homeostasis in varying degree and to protect the self from being flooded by painful affect. It is as if the psyche has the capacity to form or differentiate out a "membrane" to protect the self. In situations of impending danger or of loss (actual or sensed), the hypothetical membrane becomes almost nonpermeable, in effect like the so-called schizoid shell, thus cutting off the input or conscious registration and expression of those affects that are still preconsciously available within the membrane. In contrast to catharsis, the increased permeability of the membrane involves structural change.

In the study of character, analysts' language is replete with expressions referring to a person's being "hardened" as opposed to being "tender" in relation to certain affects—for example, "hardnosed" or "hardhearted" as against "tender" or "bleeding-heart." These expressions involve a number of functions that are related, but not identical, to each other—for example, the capacity (1) to empathize (2) to partially identify with another, or (3) to be *contaged* by the other's affect. Though each of these phenomena is significantly different, they have in common one aspect—the permeability of the membrane-around-sthe-self. Without sufficient permeability, one suffers excessive detachment—a possible advantage if this detachment is selective to negative affects such as a flooding of anxiety from another person. However, in general, all depends on the total personal situation and context and on the balance between attachment and detachment. The art of living, then, depends on a subtle set of regulatory ego functions, which feed back to the self signals of how that self is coping with what has been "taken in" and "expressed out" in the way of information, including its affective charge.

Psychoanalytic therapy aims to explore and to increase awareness of patient and therapist, especially in the area of needs and fears. The need-fear dilemma is not specific to schizophrenia: in some degree it is a universal human problem. If analysts gradually work into the depth of the patient's defensive structures, they discover that he or she is a being who *needs*, despite the awesome defensive "antineed" detachment structures that have become so synonymous with the patient's very identity. For this reason, analytical work at this level requires great patience and endurance, since the therapeutic alliance is involved in nothing less than a restructuring of the self-identity. Self-consciousness, shame, humiliation, and pride will be the analyst's guides to uncovering hidden and dangerously experienced needs and affects—often associated disparagingly with being childish or babyish. When patient and analyst realize in depth that their clinical struggle is part of the continuing human struggle between the polarities of symbiosis and individuation, a greater compassion and a melting away of the humiliation can result.

NOTES

[1]*Relatedness* refers to a relationship on the level of mental representation of self and other. *Attachment* refers to the broader ethologic term that includes pre- and post-representational stages.

[2]A number of observers, including Bowlby (1973) and Heinecke (1965), have studied the longer-term effects of separation and have shown that affects such as hopelessness and a sense of futility follow upon prolonged separation, especially with poor substitute care. Also, Bowlby quotes a number of studies in which a surprisingly high percentage of parents—from 27 percent to 50 percent—*admit* to threats of abandonment as a way of controlling or punishing a child. If to this is added more subtle abandonment or withdrawal-type parental behavior, it is likely that a majority of children in our society realistically experience the threat of abandonment.

[3]Burgner and Edgcumbe (1972) arrive at a parallel concept—the "capacity for constant relationships"—as it develops from the more primitive need-satsifying relationship.

[4]See Pine (1974) on the subject of stability and lability of object constancy.

[5]This would be considered "defensive splitting," in contrast to the normal polarization into "good" and "bad" experiences. See Freud's paper (1938) on splitting of the ego.

[6]Detachment in the ethologic sense refers to patterns of movement away from attachment. In the psychic sense, detachment connotes a defense against relationships on the level of mental representation. Detachment can be adaptive or maladaptive, depending on the total psychic situation.

[7]There is a lovely children's book (ages 5–7) by Maurice Sendak (1962) about Pierre who "didn't care" until he was swallowed by a lion, at which point he "cared."

[8]Other sequelae may appear as well—anxious clinging, for example—sometimes mixed with aggressive detachment and with serious negativism and oppositionalism, which may become dominant in the character. (Bowlby 1973, p. 225).

[9]This is to suggest, in effect, that the adult detachment is a homologue to child detachment.

[10]Bowlby (1973) observed that detachment from mother is more frequent in relation to mother as against father and that the duration of the child's detachment correlates highly with the length of the child's separation. Upon reunion, mothers complained that they were treated as strangers for the first few days. The separated children were afraid to be left alone and were far more clinging than they had been before the separation. Bowlby believes that after very long or repeated separations, detachment can persist indefinitely. It is this aspect of detachment that has been used in the concept of character detachment. It is

true both in Bowlby's children and in partially detached characters that detachment can alternate with intense symbioticlike clinging and/or intensely ambivalent attitudes, including being rejecting, hostile, or defiant toward mother. There is, of course, a lingering fear in the child—and later in the adult—that he or she will suffer new separations should any new attachments be made. Moreover, in the attempt to make new attachments, the child brings detachment defenses with him or her in a way that resists that attachment process itself.

[11]Mahler et al. (1975) describes a *change of affect* of a *depressive* tone that comes over the child (around 18 months) when he becomes more aware of the separateness of his experience from that of the mother's. This dawning realization—during the second year of life—can be seen as the developmental anlage to the later phenomenon of existential aloneness.

[12]Defenses cannot regulate the ego, but they can predominate in a way that does not allow the embattled ego to gain new input and energy from its interpersonal relations. With defenses predominating, the other ego functions are not available—for example, for object relations (internal and external).

[13]When detachment is heavily present, the affects may still be discovered as flowing between split-off dissociated parts of the self and internal object-persons—for example, internal persecution of the "bad me" by the "internal saboteur" or "condemning superego."

[14]Studies in Ego Development at Albert Einstein College of Medicine, Grant #HD 01155-01, National Institute of Child Health and Human Development.

[15]Levenson (1978) described the psychoanalytic process as one that does not rely only on the truth of the professed content. "Nor does it depend on the therapist's participation with the patient, but rather on a dialectic interaction of these elements. It is this dialectic between understanding and newness which makes for the core of therapeutic discourse. Metaphor is independent of time and space. It is always true."

[16]A little fable told by Schopenhauer will illustrate this relationship: A company of porcupines crowded themselves very close together one cold winter's day so as to profit by one another's warmth, and to save themselves from being frozen to death. But soon they felt one another's quills which induced them to separate again. And now when the need for warmth brought them nearer together, again the second evil arose once more. So that they were driven backwards and forwards from one trouble to the other until they discovered a safe distance at which they could more tolerably exist.

[17]An important task of the therapy is the learning by the analysand of a well-differentiated vocabulary for his or her often undifferentiated emotions. The therapist may sometimes have to offer the vocabulary and the metaphors, as in a "Chinese menu."

[18]See Landis (1970) and Federn (1952) for a searching view of these issues.

[19]In the process of growing up, disidentification and the mourning of diminishing identifications with parents can stimulate feelings of shame and disloyalty.

[20]See Anna Freud (1965), Nagera (1966), Kernberg (1976), and Horner (1975).

REFERENCES

Bowlby, I. (1973), *Attachment and Loss,* Vol. 2. New York: Basic Books.
Bromberg, P. (1976), Personal communication.

Burgner, M. and Edgcumbe, R. (1972), Some problems in conceptualization of early object relations. *Psychoanalytic Study of the Child,* 27:283-315.

Federn, P. (1952), *Ego Psychology and the Psychoses.* New York, Basic Books.

Freud, A. (1965), *Normality and Pathology in Children.* New York: Internat. Univ. Press.

Freud, S. (1938), Splitting of the ego in the process of defense. *Standard Edition,* 23:271-278. London: Hogarth Press, 1962.

Guntrip, H. (1968), *Schizoid Phenomena, Object Relations and the Self.* New York: Internat. Univ. Press.

Heinicke, C. and Westheimer, I. (1965), *Brief Separations.* New York: Internat. Univ. Press.

Horner, A. (1975), Stages and process in the development of object relations. New York: *Internat. Rev. of Psychoanalysis,* Vol. 2, Part 1.

Kernberg, Otto (1976), *Object Relations Theory and Clinical Psychoanalysis.* New York: Aronson.

Khan, M. (1974), *The Privacy of the Self.* New York: Internat. Univ. Press.

Klaus, K. and Kennel J. (1976), *Maternal-Infant Bonding.* St. Louis: Mosby.

Landis, B. (1970), Ego boundaries. In *Psych. Issues,* Vol. 6, No. 4, Monograph 24. New York: Internat. Univ. Press.

Levenson, E. (1978), Psychoanalysis—cure of persuasion. New York: *Contemp. Psychoanalysis,* 14:1 6.

Mahler, M., Pine, F. and Bergman, A. (1975), *The Psychologic Birth of the Infant.* New York: Basic Books.

Nagera, H. (1966), *Early Childhood Disturbances* New York: Internat. Univ. Press.

Nyanaponika, Thera (1973), *The Heart of Buddhist Meditation.* New York: Samuel Weiser.

Pine, F. (1974), Libidinal object constancy. In *Psychoanalysis and Contemp. Science.* New York: Internat. Univ. Press.

Schachtel, E. (1959), *Metamorphosis,* pp. 48–49. New York: Basic Books.

Schecter, D. (1968a), Identification and individuation. *J. Am. Psychoanal.* A., 16:48–80.

———— (1968b), The oedipus complex: considerations of ego development and parental interaction. *Contemp. Psychoanalysis,* Vol. 4, 1968.

———— and Corman, H. (1971), Some early developments in parent-child interaction. (Unpublished manuscript).

———— (1973), On the emergence of human relatedness. In Witenberg, E. (ed.), *Interpersonal Explorations in Psychoanalysis: New Directions in Theory and Practice.* New York: Basic Books.

———— (1974), Infant development. In Arieti, S. ed., *American Handbook of Psychiatry,* Vol. I. New York: Basic Books.

———— (1975a), Of human bonds and bondage. *Contemp. Psychoanalysis,* Vol. II, No. 4.

———— (1975b), Notes on some basic human developmental tasks. *J. Amer. Ac. Psychoanal., 3* 3 (3) 267–276.

Sendak, M. (1962), *Pierre: A Cautionary Tale.* New York: Harper & Row.

Stern, D. (1971), A micro-analysis of mother-infant interaction: Behavior regulating social contact between a mother and her 3½-month-old twins. *J. Am. Acad. Child Psychiat.,* 10:501–518.

Sullivan, H. (1953), *The Interpersonal Theory of Psychiatry.* New York: W. W. Norton.

10

ASPECTS OF THE THERAPEUTIC RELATIONSHIP IN CHILD ANALYSIS

CLARICE J. KESTENBAUM, M.D.
St. Luke's–Roosevelt Hospital Center, New York, and Columbia University

Two questions will be considered in this chapter. The first is directed toward those factors that produce change in the analysis of children: in other words, what contributes to symptom removal and leads to genuine structural change? The second question is more specific: What is the nature of the therapeutic relationship that fosters this change?

Implicit in the second question is the suggestion that child psychoanalysis is a valid *therapeutic* modality. Direct child observation has, of course, long been considered a valuable research tool for studying psychoanalytic theory. Exploration of the infantile neurosis in statu nascendi has, for example, provided for psychoanalysts an invaluable data bank for purposes of comparison with the material accumulated from analysis of adults, dependent as this is upon the remembrance of things past—often enough on the rather faulty remembrance of things past.

Research using direct child observation has led to major contributions to our understanding of object relations and cognitive development. Careful evaluation of young children has provided us with information about the origin and development of those defenses specific for each individual, built on a substrate of inborn tempermental characteristics, which help him cope with the basic psychobiological states of anxiety and depression. Child psychoanalysts as well as developmental psychologists have amassed a substantial body of data devoted to early-childhood research. Much of this material deals with psychoanalysis as process; less has been written about child analysis as *therapy*. Many adult psychoanalysts raise their eyebrows at the very thought of psychoanalyzing a child.

All would agree, of course, that disturbed children exist. But, they argue, shouldn't parental guidance and environmental manipulation suffice to create a more favorable environment for normal development? Must there not be, as in the case of "school phobia," a differentiation between a child who is experiencing separation anxiety and one who is fearful because he is getting beaten up every day on the way to school? Would not family counseling in the first instance, or change of school in the second, be enough to nip an incipient problem in the bud? Certainly, as for the majority of adults referred for psychiatric treatment—and for most people of any age—psychoanalysis is probably not the treatment of choice.

INDICATIONS FOR PSYCHOANALYSIS

The same painstaking assessment must be made before assigning a child for psychoanalytic treatment. The seven-year-old with perceptual problems, who does not demonstrate good verbal ability and lacks inner language and the use of symbols, is *not* a candidate for psychoanalysis; nor are children older than seven who demonstrate a failure of repression. These children are unable to defend against sexual and aggressive drives and so are constantly bombarded by stimuli either from within, as with psychotic children, or from without, as in the case of abused or culturally deprived children. Such children cannot master the necessary skills of reading and writing, nor can they engage in typical latency-age activities such as collecting rocks or stamps, learning the rules of games, or experiencing the give-and-take of peer relationships. For them, a different therapeutic approach is required: one that relies much less heavily on the verbal modes of communication such as might be used with cognitively well-developed neurotic children.

Neglected children, incidentally, are not distinguished by their membership in any particular class. Children of the rich are no less immune to the effects of maternal deprivation than poor children (Stone and Kestenbaum, 1974). Alpert (1954) has proposed that the treatment of such children requires a corrective object relationship with a real, nurturing figure (usually in the guise of the teacher-therapist), who can supply the nurturing environment absent earlier in the young child's life. The teacher-therapist, moreover, is there to help the child to acquire age-appropriate skills never before learned. By this process, a sense of competence and heightened self-esteem can develop.

In contrast, the neurotic child who comes for treatment because of phobias, compulsive rituals, school inhibition, or other symptoms presents a quite different picture—one associated primarily with *intrapsychic* conflicts. Merely changing the environment will not change the child's representational world or enable him or her to work through an unresolved trauma.

Indications for child analysis are similar to those in adult analysis. According to Settlage (1966), children must have achieved object constancy so that they can have an enduring relationship with the analyst. They must have enough ego autonomy and superego structure so that conflict is internalized. In other words, they must be able to tolerate some frustration in the analytic situation and be able to control their impulses. Action-prone or highly impulsive children who cannot translate their impulses into words or play are not suitable candidates for analytic therapy. In addition, children should be *motivated* for treatment. Unfortunately, many children in need of therapy are not and are dragged to their sessions by threatening parents or school authorities.

In the most favorable circumstances, children are aware of their own suffering—their inability to work in school, to play after school, to make friends, and so forth. In other words, they cannot move forward on the path of normal development because they are so busy struggling, albeit unsuccessfully, to master an early trauma or unresolved conflict. Children of this sort are not going to spend their free time very profitably, in any event; four hours a week at the analyst's office are not really removing them from activities that could be of much benefit in their present state.

The special child-analyst relationship that Settlage refers to is, of course, the transference relationship. For many years Anna Freud (1926) did not believe that children were capable of forming a transference neurosis. How can a child repeat, in the psychoanalytic situation with the analyst, the relationship with the oirginal objects of childhood, when the "original objects" are alive and well and ever present in the life of the child? Later she modified her view (1965). The child uses the analyst *in part* as a transference object but also as (1) a new object, (2) an object of externalization of intersystemic and intrasystemic conflicts, and (3) an auxiliary ego.

Aside from the qualitative difference in the transference relationship, there are more substantial differences in the analyses of children and adults, which stem from the fact that the child is a developing organism. As Sarnoff (1976) mentions, cognitive functions in general are mediated by a biological timetable. "Maturation is an ongoing process during latency," and therapists must be in touch with the cognitive levels of their patients and must be familiar with their cognitive styles. Sarnoff does not see latency as a period of drive diminution so much as a period of strengthening in ego organization, both in the areas of cognitive maturation and in the acquisition of new skills and defensive operations. These, in turn, serve to protect the child from the intensity of the potentially overwhelming sexual and aggressive drives. Typical defenses seen are those of repression, denial, displacement, reaction formation, projection, and, of course, identification. The more conflicted the child, it would seem, the more he or she would fight to keep the defenses intact. Therefore, the child does not relate this conflict with words; but instead plays them out.

THE USE OF PLAY IN CHILD ANALYSIS

The royal road to the unconscious in child analysis is not via dreams nor free association but, as Klein (1932) demonstrated through play. It is often difficult for adult analysts, whose stock-in-trade is verbal interpretation, to understand how children can play out fantasies or how they can work through areas of conflict without much more than a hint from the analyst. When a child unmercifully pummels a father doll or smashes a clay ball with a mallet, the result is more than merely a release of tension. Fantasies are being enacted, games are being won, and villains are being conquered, all in the safety of the familiar office, with an understanding adult nearby. Play furnishes the possibility for detailed insight into the child's problems and typical coping mechanisms. Nevertheless, Bornstein (1945) noted that it is preferable not to interpret children's symbolic play actions because interpretation is likely to upset the process before it is well established. Brody (1961) enumerated some of the qualities in the resistances of children in analysis: children withhold information; they deny conflict; and they invite the analyst to act out with them. Younger children may not wish to consider how close their play themes are to their own reality, but they might accept an intepretation.

Prepubertal children, however, because of their more mature thought processes, sense that they may expose themselves in play and are afraid to reveal their emotions; they often refuse to accept interpretations in any shape or form. Thus, child analysts must walk a fine line; on the one hand, they want to allow as much fantasy and play exploration as possible, while on the other hand they want to help the child to develop insight into his conflicts. The persistence of magical thinking about the spoken word is believed to interfere with children's ability to verbalize certain thoughts and feelings. Premature interpretation may often result in stopping analytic process altogether, particularly when the therapeutic bond is weak. Such a premature interpretation was made some years ago with the following result:

Amanda was eight years old when she appeared in my office, having been referred by her private girls' school's principal because of fighting with classmates and stealing small items from her "enemies." Amanda's mother had divorced the father several months before Amanda's birth; she was a beautiful but emotionally volatile woman who was, at the time of the first interview, separating from her third husband. She had been hospitalized twice for psychotic episodes, probably schizophrenic in nature.

The treatment mode Amanda seemed to prefer was doll play; she used mini-dolls to enact her fantasies. She repeated the same theme with variations in every session, namely, a baby's abandonment by a selfish mother: "A witch flew in the room—just like the witch in Snow White. She was beautiful but mean, and I hid under the bed until she went away."

"I think the witch is really Mother," I said, "and the play reminds you of how scared you used to be when Mother got 'mad' ".

Amanda immediately clapped her hands to her ears, shrieking, "No, you're wrong. *You* are the witch! I *hate* you," as she ran from the room. Fortunately, I was able to win her confidence again and treatment continued for another year. When I next heard from Amanda eight years later, she had just been graduated from high school and wanted to see me.

She was an "A" student, a poised and charming 17-year-old who could speak of the past with great feeling:

> "Do you remember that session when I became so angry with you I ran from the room? Well, you were right! I knew all the time the witch was mother and that the people in the stories were about mother and me, but I could never admit it. Somehow hearing you say it made it *true*, and I couldn't bear realizing mother was really like that. After all, she was the only mother I had."

The timing of an interpretation, as in adult analysis, is crucial. Otherwise, such an intervention will either fall on deaf ears or, as in Amanda's case, it will interrupt the flow of play. Attacking the defenses prematurely is obviously not an approach conducive to establishing a therapeutic alliance.

In the next section, case material from the analysis of a 10-year-old girl will be presented. In this analysis, interpretation was held to a minimum for nearly 18 months, but the therapeutic relationship is believed to have been chiefly responsible for the changes that occurred during treatment.

CASE ILLUSTRATION

Lillian was referred for psychiatric consultation by her fifth-grade teacher because of increasingly poor concentration, distractibility, and anxiety about school performance. She was demanding and infantile, according to the teacher; she had the habit of interrupting other children, waving her hands and repeatedly calling the other children, waving her hands and repeatedly calling the teacher's name, and asking the same questions again and again. She had few friends—two, to be exact, of whom she was extremely possessive. They were the only classmates who did not object to her need to control the play situation. She had had a full battery of psychological tests, which demonstrated an I.Q. in the superior range. The psychologist felt that Lillian's anxiety interfered with school performance. She was poor in mathematics, tending to work too quickly and to make careless errors. Lillian's parents, Mr. and Mrs. S., reported that during the past year Lillian had developed some compulsive behavior patterns at home. She had a number of bedtime rituals, which had to be followed to the letter: the slippers just so, the bedsheets exactly matched. Mrs. S. had to spend a half hour saying goodnight and answering questions, mostly concerning the prepraration of the following day's meals. If Lillian did not get her own way, she would have a temper tantrum—lasting 5 or 10 minutes—in which she would scream, shake her fists, and slam doors.

Lillian's parents were not strangers to psychiatry. Mr. S. was a retired art dealer who had done little actual work in 15 years. He had had two depressive episodes requiring electric convulsive therapy and had remained chronically depressed. Mrs. S., 20 years younger than her husband, was a highly competent accountant, whose capacity for work was nonetheless seriously compromised by her frequent depressive episodes. Diagnosed as having a manic-depressive disorder, she had been hospitalized twice—for the first time when Lillian was 10 months and again when she was two years old. During these weeks, Lillian was cared for by her maternal grandmother, who lived close by. Mrs. S. was an anxious woman, constantly overwrought, and, by her own admission, unable to deal with her daughter's demands. When Lillian was nine, her mother underwent a radical mastectomy for breast carcinoma, during which time Mrs. S. was preoccupied with thoughts of death and dying. She also expressed great concern about Lillian's condition, worrying lest her daughter "inherit" her illness. Lillian's 19-year-old brother had made a suicidal gesture the previous year and was currently receiving psychotherapy.

It is obvious that Lillian was a child at risk for future psychopathology. She had a strong family history of affective illness, with all its implications from a genetic viewpoint, as well as exposure to the environmental influences of depressed parents (Dince 1966). Despite separations and erratic mothering, she had proceeded along a proper developmental path without ostensible problems until age nine—a time that coincided with her mother's hospitalization and surgery for breast cancer. The clinging dependency and obsessional symptoms that developed subsequent to her mother's return appeared to prevent Lillian from entering into the normal activities of the latency-age child, that is, school achievement and peer reltionships. It was felt that the most effective mode of treatment would be psychoanalytic, and, accordingly, sessions were scheduled four times a week. Because of the complexity of the mother's problems, it was recommended that Mrs. S. see her own therapist, one with whom I had regular contact.

History of Treatment

The initial session was spent "getting acquainted." Lillian, an attractive, somewhat overweight 10-year-old, practically ran into the office and began to talk nonstop: "I like this office . . . is this where all the children come when they have problems? You have lots of toys. I like the puppets and dolls. May I do my homework here?" Throughout this pressured monologue there was no eye contact. In fact, Lillian behaved like a younger version of her mother, whom I had seen the day before.

"I guess you're wondering a lot about me and what our time together will be like," I responded.

"Well, Mother said you're a doctor for children's problems, and *my* problem is Miss Finn, my math teacher. She's a real witch. I *won't* go to school if I have her! I'll quit." She folded her arms and stared at me directly for the first time. "Will you make me go?"

"You act as if I'm a policeman," I answered. "I don't even know what troubles you yet. I want to hear all about the things you like, the things you hate, your happy and sad times, your friends, and lots more. Maybe Miss Finn should be here instead of you, but I can't ask her about *her* problems."

"Well, sometimes I worry and sometimes I have bad dreams. Once I had a dream that frightened me. A witch was inside my closet, and when I opened the door, a man's body with a knife stuck into it fell out. It was bloody all over and I was scared. And I have other worries—like my question problem. It's that I have to ask Mother the same thing over and over until I think I understand her."

"Otherwise you get nervous?" I asked.

"Yes. Then I feel terrible all over."

"And what do you do to make yourself feel better?" I asked.

"Well, that's the problem. Father is too tired to pay much attention. He just closes his door. Mother gets too nervous when I ask her." Lillian then proceeded to demonstrate the "question problem" in a variety of ways: "When do I come back here? What days exactly? How many minutes will I wait in the waiting room?"

I responded, "I think you're wondering, with all these problems, whether or not I'll be able to help you and whether I'll understand problems like the question problem. We'll talk some more tomorrow at three."

There was no more talk about problems, however. Lillian would not discuss them again for months.

The next six weeks were spent establishing rules and guidelines. Lillian selected the dollhouse and minidolls for her principal play activity, a medium that has been found to be particularly useful. She gave the dolls names—the Johnsons—and assigned specific personality attributes and roles as she remodeled the house to suit the doll family. She would sit cross-legged on the floor next to the doll house, hold a doll in each hand, and act out all the parts. The Johnson family consisted of two parents and three children, aged 12, 10, and 2. It was a typical idealized television family without any problems for the first three weeks. Then the story line changed. Twelve-year-old Robert, she declared, was a poor student and was constnatly getting into trouble. "He just doesn't listen. He always wants to be the center of attention. One day he chased his sister, Cathy, down a flight of stairs, causing her to have a head injury, which kept her home for a month."

I would question Lillian about the characters, their feelings, their motives. "Why is Robert so bad?" I asked.

"Oh, boys are like that," she answered. "They like to be bad." Little by little, enactments of everyday school situations appeared in the play. Whenever I attempted to draw parallels between the events in her make-believe world and her own life, she would counter with "I don't think I'll play anymore today" or "I don't like to talk about that."

It was evident from the beginning that Lillian was quite content during her sessions and, in fact, behaved as though the analytic hour was a special time—a magic time, where she could enter a private world. I was a benign observer while she enacted her fantasies without restraint. I was clearly a need-satisfying, non-judgmental new object, as long as she could be in control of the play situation. I did not challenge her and attempted to foster the developing positive transference. At this point her way of relating was, as Sandler et al. (1975) state, not so much a specific transference reaction as her "habitual mode of relating" to anyone.

Three months after analysis had begun, the themes of the fantasy play became decidedly more violent. "Robert" began having frequent tantrums and was constantly breaking dishes. This time he hurt "Cathy" so severely that she had to be hospitalized. "Mrs. Johnson" became so distraught during her daughter's brain surgery that she rushed into the operating room screaming "Stop, they are murdering my daughter!" Mrs. Johnson, in her panic, had been so upset by Cathy's accident that she had forgotten to feed the baby, "who died of starvation and neglect."

Lillian stopped playing at this point and told me, reassuringly, "Don't worry. Even though the baby's dead, something good will happen." And, indeed, in the next session, Mrs. Johnson became pregnant. Lillian's stories took on a new flavor—the themes dealt with concepts of pregnancy and birth. There were many scenes of children peeking through keyholes to learn the secrets of life. The youngest child believed babies came from the store; the oldest, from the liver and digestive tract, following the mother's swallowing a seed. Lillian began to interrupt her play for the first time with conversations about her own life.

"I know *everything* about pregnancy," she said sagely. "I learned it in life science and from my friends—but *never* from my mother. My parents never did "it" since I was born, I'm positive. She never told me about periods or anything. She's Irish, you know, and Irish people aren't supposed to know anything about sex." Mrs. Johnson finally went into labor and produced twins.

The subsequent play scenes became more and more violent. Mrs. Johnson, walking home one evening, was attacked by two "rapist-muggers" who "hit her in the liver," tied her up, and took her purse.

I pointed out that girls and women in her stories always seemed to get hurt, while boys never did. "It seems very scary but a little bit exciting, too," I said. The remark was enough to stop all doll play for two weeks. She asked to play checkers, draw pictures, or engage in any neutral activity where discussion was at a minimum.

When she finally returned to the doll play, the themes became even more violent. One such theme centered around three children who crept into a haunted house with a "No Trespassing" sign in front. The girl was frightened and wanted to run home. The boys laughed at her cowardice and entered the house. They opened a closet door and a man's body fell out, a bloodied knife still in place ("just like my dream," she added). The children then found another body—a woman's—"all chopped to pieces." Lillian stopped playing and turned toward me. "How is it I get scared even when it's make believe? Noises at night scare me, shadows on the wall, clothes on chairs."

I asked her what she did when she got scared.

"I call Mother. Only once she wasn't there—she was in the hospital—so I climbed in bed with Daddy; then I felt safer."

This was the first time Lillian spontaneously spoke of her father in a positive light; moreover, it was one of the few times she spoke of past events. Afterwards, she did begin recalling details of her early life: her hospitalization at age five for a tonsillectomy and her fear of the ether mask or her terror at being left at her grandmother's when she was younger, for example.

Other changes were beginning to become apparent as well, particularly in the relationship with me. One day, I had to cancel a session without notice. Lillian was sullen and withdrawn the next day but denied being angry or upset about the cancellation. She refused to talk or play, indicating that, in any case, her sessions were boring.

"I think you're angry with me for cancelling the session," I told her.

"Well, maybe just a *drop* disappointed," she replied. This led to a discussion of what people do when they are angry. "My parents don't talk to each other for days. Neither one will say he's sorry."

"No wonder you don't want me to know you're angry, if you think *I'd* get angry back. I could see how we wouldn't talk for days or weeks."

Other manifestations of our relationship revealed themselves in her play. She had seen other children entering and leaving my office. The doll figures in her stories began to exclude children from their school cliques. One member was always jealous of a new girl in class. When questioned about the doll-character's feelings, Lillian replied, "Cathy doesn't mind Linda alone, or Susan alone, but she can't stand being together at the same time, because she's the one who always gets left out. But she just pretends she dosn't care. She doesn't like anyone to know her real feelings."

"You know, Lillian," I said, "sometimes when you get disappointed or angry (like the time I canceled our session or when another child played with the dolls) you pretend you don't mind it. It's so important for you to feel 'OK' that you pretend not to notice when something bad happens."

"It's usually better to pretend," she insisted.

"I know you are very wise and see a lot of what goes on around you—how Mother gets upset sometimes or Daddy gets tired and withdraws, and I know you pretend not to notice. But what are you really feeling inside?"

"Nothing!" she answered, angrily.

Lillian had by now been in treatment for more than a year. The therapeutic relationship had undergone important changes. Whereas at the outset she used me chiefly as a need-satisfying real object, she now related to me as a transference object as well. Lillian's reaction to the canceled session and her jealousy of the other patients were both manifestations of the transference relationship; likewise, her need to reassure me, when the baby in her story "died," that "soon something good will happen."

Her mother, she recognized, was quite fragile, not only unable to care for two at a time but barely able to care for herself. Lillian had never so much as uttered a word against her mother, either in fantasy elaborations or in real-life accusations. Her use of denial and projection was still very frequent. Yet, in the daily unfolding of her stories, she presented to me a panoply of fantasies—fantasies of bodily injury (especially to women), of masochism, of pregnancy and birth, of the primal scene of separation, of abandonment, and of death (as with the mother who was so distraught that she let her baby die). I did little except explore and clarify. Only occasionally would I offer interpretations, and these usually fell on deaf ears.

At a certain point, Lillian decided to give up doll play for a time and to write a novel. The new story concerned Billy, a five-year-old boy, who was believed by his family to be retarded. He had no language and seemed to be lost in his own world. Billy had frequent temper tantrums and could only be comforted by his dog, Spot. One day Spot was killed by a car. Billy was inconsolable, rocking and staring into space for hours. Finally, his 11-year-old sister, Mary, decided to take him to a specialist. Dr. Kayo, "a nice lady who helped children with problems," told Mary, "Billy was born with a problem, but he's not retarded." She outlined a treatment plan: "Billy needs to be encouraged to play. Do not leave him alone, but give him a lot of attention." Mary spent more time with Billy. Finally one day he uttered his first word: "Spot." The family was overjoyed and presented Billy with a new puppy on his birthday. He began to speak in sentences and soon became a normal, happy boy.

It was obvious (even to Lillian) that Dr. Kayo was a representation of myself. It was through the 11-year-old Mary (following the doctor's instructions) that Billy became well. After composing this "novel," which took several weeks, Lillian brought into the sessions much more information about her life outside sessions. She related having organized a secret club with two friends at school—a writer's club. The members were all supposed to collaborate on books and stories in order one day to become famous authors. On Valentine's Day I received a poem that she had written and illustrated with a picture of a princess surrounded by flowers and birds. "To my friend Dr. Kestenbaum, with love," read the inscription.

The analysis had by now proceeded for 18 months. Lillian had changed a great deal.

Her symptoms—the compulsive questioning, the bedtime rituals, and the tantrums—had, during the first six months of treatment, completely disappeared. Her school work had improved considerably, and the teacher's reports were excellent. She still had difficulty with some classmates but had acquired several new friends. Physically there had been changes, too. She was taller and slimmer; breasts were beginning to develop. She spent her sessions drawing pictures of teenage girls and speaking freely about events in school. Her father, who was artistic, began to spend time helping her with her art work. He frequently corrected her figure drawings. One day she showed me a picture of a ballerina: "Daddy says her breasts are too big; my teacher says they're too small. What do *you* think?"

I asked her, "How is it you don't draw her the way *you* think she should look?" What do *you* think of the breasts?"

"Well," she told me, "I like them a little bigger." She went to the mirror. "Jean hasn't any yet; I have a training bra. Next year I'll get a real one."

Lillian became less defensive in discussion about her family. In a moment of rare candor she said to me, "You know, my mother is the nervous type. She never knows how to help when I have a problem at school—and my father takes so long to explain. I wish *you* would come to my house."

"What would you want me to see?" I asked.

"You would come to my room; I would show you my books . . . my toys, my dolls. You would see everything the way it is—*then* you would understand."

"I know you want me to see what really happens at home, Lillian—all about Mother and Father and how you feel when you're happy or sad—but you know, you really show me a great deal in your plan and in the stories. This is a good way of letting me know what really happens, too."

From that time on, Lillian became even more direct in sessions, expressing her feelings, wishes, and fears openly: "Sometimes I wish I had a mother who was not nervous—and a father who was younger and not tired all the time." She began recalling weekly "dates" that she had had with her father when she was three or four, dressing up and going to dinner or a puppet show. These conversations inevitably led to feelings about neighborhood boys and "crushes" on one or two.

One afternoon Lillian appeared in my office with a small cage containing a six-week-old kitten. "Her name is Kiki. I just got her from the ASPCA and wanted you to see her to make sure she's OK. Please write out a list of instructions I can give to Mother." We discussed her concerns about caring for her kitten and her fears that her mother would let harm come to Kiki when she was at school. "I want her to grow up to be like Coco (my cat, with whom she was very familiar)—frisky and playful." Kiki thrived. Lillian spent many sessions discussing Kiki's progress.

At Christmas time, two years after her first meeting with me, Lillian appeared with a small package and asked to bring out, once again, the doll house, unused for months. "I've brought a present," she announced. Inside the box was a tiny doll's desk and a rocking chair, expensive and beautifully made. "It's for the dolls," she said, "for their play. We can keep it here always."

DISCUSSION

In the beginning of the chapter, the question was raised "What contributes to symptom removal and structural change?" It was implied that the nature of the therapeutic relationship was the critical factor. As mentioned previously, the analyst is a new, need-satisfying object in part, as well as a transference object.

Arlow (1974) has noted that the attitude toward transference distinguishes psychoanalysis from all other forms of psychotherapy. In the traditional view of the positive transference relationship as originally conceived of by Freud (1912, 1917), the patient distorts a realistic patient-analyst relationship by additions from past unconscious and repressed object relations: "There is the overvaluation of [the doctor's] qualities—[an] absorption in his interests—[a] jealousy of everyone close to him in real life" (1917, p. 442).

Greenacre (1966) expanded on this theme when she discussed the universality of the transference phenomenon—the demand for human contact:

> It is probably obvious that the transference relationship in analysis contains by its very nature the seeds for idealization of the analyst in its rootedness in the early omnipotent stage of the mother-child relationship—the child reacts to the *good* parent, the *angry* parent, the *distant*, *unresponsive* parent, the *punishing* parent.

She implies that if early care has not been optimal, ambivalence is covered over with anxious overattachment and overvaluation of the parent.

Besides repetition of past experiences, as Sandler et al. (1965) have noted, "transferences may reflect aspects of *present day* relationships with important objects, in particular the parents." The therapist may represent different aspects of the child's personality (superego introjects, instinctual strivings, self representation). Not only bad experiences are repeated in transference (Gumbel 1974). The happier aspects of earlier relationships may lead to new impressions, while the bad experiences are reworked to show what could or should have been. The child maintains an interest in the therapeutic environment through the relationship with the analyst. This interest can subsequently lead to imitation and thus to identification (Anthony 1966).

In her analysis, Lillian demonstrated many of the qualities inherent in a transference relationship. She accepted me from the onset as a magical helper, the omnipotent "good fairy." She attempted to recapture aspects of the *special* world of childhood, such as she had undoubtedly shared at some point with her mother. In the absence of truly "good-enough" mothering (Winnicott 1965), however, she seemed to have repressed the hostile aspects of her ambivalent feelings. She could not express anger toward her mother, even in play.

The violence of the fantasies—accidents, mutilation, rape—is testimony to the depth of unexpressed rage that she felt toward this often unavailable mother. It is as if Lillian believed that her thoughts could destroy her mother, who in reality had a life-threatening illness and who Lillian imagined might die as a result of her magical wishes. In the presence of a nonjudgmental observer, she was ultimately able to play out her life's drama: the traumatic separations, abandonment, and fear of annihilation.

She eventually grew able to express anger and disappointment without fear of retaliation. The "harsh superego" became less rigid. Projection and denial were given up for more adaptive mechanisms, particularly reaction formation and sublimation. Through her identification with the "healer," jealousy gave way in time to altruism. This shift is exemplified by the Christmas gift of doll furniture, which Lillian knew would be shared with other children.

Little has yet been said here about the nontransference relationship in the psychoanalytic situation. This refers to what is described by Greenson (1969) as the "real" relationship—a necessary component, as it turns out, of any successful therapy. It is often difficult to tease out those aspects of the therapeutic relationship that belong to the transference from those that belong to the real relationship. It is believed, however, that it is the ego-ideal in particular that undergoes changes via identification with a new "real" object. For example, in Lillian's view, women were seen as victims of sexual and aggressive assaults—inadequate and helpless under stress. A new view of herself emerged, as a competent female who took pleasure in her budding sexuality. This change occurred, it is believed, more as a result of her real relationship with the analyst than out of the resolution of any transference distortions.

As Lillian began to regard me as a competent doctor who took care of troubled children, she began to identify with me and to view herself as a competent caretaker for Kiki, her kitten. She learned, through witnessing me in "real-life situations," new ways of coping with anger and jealousy. Laufer (1964) describes the ego ideal "as part of the super-ego which continues to set the ideal standard of behavior for the child." It stems originally from idealization of the parent and leads to idealization of the self. Sandler et al. (1965) expressed the view that "in the well-adapted individual, the content of the ideal self will undergo continuous modification in the light of the person's experiences of reality." Assuredly, identification with (and idealization of) a meaningful "new object"—the therapist—constitutes such an experience of reality.

One must also take into account Lillian's inherent coping mechanisms. In the face of environmental circumstances, these were at first seriously compromised following her mother's mastectomy. It was out of her inability to cope with this additional stress that she developed her phobic and obsessional symptoms.

The moment at which she attached herself to a new object she proceeded to accept, without protest, the rigors of the analytic situation. Lillian was a girl of keen intelligence; her ability to organize her fantasies and to plan her play productions so that her stories had continuity was indicative of her strong will to master the early traumata. With a minimum of analytic interpretation (certainly Oedipal fantasies were never interpreted), Lillian seemed to understand that much of her difficulty was engendered and intensified by her parents' own helplessness in the face of stress. She seemed to be one of those neurotic children whose developmental pull was so strong (Neubauer and Flapan 1976) that relatively little effort was needed to get her back onto the path of normal development.

Would parental counseling or educational intervention have achieved the same result in a two-year period?

The question cannot be answered with certitude. Parents are not always in a position to follow advice, even if analysts wished to give it, often because of their own neurotic conflicts. It is suspected that remedial education would not have enabled Lillian to concentrate on her academic problems, at a time when her own inner world was in such turmoil. It is believed that the dramatic improvement witnessed could have been effected only by means of a treatment technique that emphasized exploration of the child's inner world. What was indicated, in other words, was psychoanalysis. Lillian needed the greater frequency of sessions in order to develop the play themes corresponding to the original conflicts that so tormented her. She needed the neutral atmosphere where she could slowly give vent to pent-up feelings and where she could, with the help of a nonjudgmental but responsive person, work through the early traumata. Therapeutic change took place because of the special nature of the doctor-patient dyad, that is, the transference-plus-real therapeutic relationship.

REFERENCES

Alpert, A. (1954), Observations on the Treatment of Emotionally Disturbed Children in a Therapeutic Center. *PSA Study of the Child* 9:334-343.

Anthony, E.J. in Van Dam, H. (1966), Problems of Transference in Child Analysis. *J. of Am. Psychoan. Assoc.* 14:3, 528-537.

Arlow, J. in Valenstein, AF. (1974), Panel on Transference. *Int. J.* 55, 311-321.

Bornstein, B. (1945), Clinical Notes on Child Analysis. *PSA Study of the Child* 1:151-166.

Brody, S. (1961), Some Aspects of Transference Resistance in Prepuberty. *PSA Study of the Child* 16:251-274.

Dince, P.R. (1966), Maternal Deprivation and Failures of Individuation during Adolescence, in J. Masserman (ed.) *Science and Psychoanalysis.* New York: Grune and Stratten, Inc., 22-37.

Freud, A. (1926), *The Psychoanalytical Treatment of Children.* London: Hogarth Press (1946).

Freud, A. (1965), *Normality and Pathology in Childhood.* New York: International Universities Press.

Freud, S. (1912), The Dynamics of Transference. *Standard Edition.* 12:99–108. London: Hogarth Press (1958).

Freud, S. (1917), Introductory Lectures. *Standard Edition,* 16:431–447. London: Hogarth Press (1963).

Greenacre, P. (1966), Problems of Overidealization of the Analyst and of Analysis: Their Manifestations in the Transference and Countertransference Relationship. *PSA Study of the Child* 21:193–212.

Greenson, R.R. and Wexler, M. (1969), The Non-Transference Relationship in the Psychoanalytic Situation. *Int. J. PSA* 50:27–39.

Gumbel, E. in Valenstein, A.F. (1974), Panel on Transference. *Int. J. PSA 55,* 311–321.

Klein, M. (1932), *The Psychoanalysis of Children.* New York: W. W. Norton.

Laufer, E. (1963), Ego Ideal and Pseudo Ego Ideal in Adolescence. *PSA Study of the Child.* 19:196–221.

Neubauer, P.B. and Flapan, D. (1976), Developmental Groupings in Latency Children. *Amer. Acad. Child Psychiatry,* 15:4 646–664.

Sarnoff, C. (1976), *Latency.* New York: Jason Aronson.

Sandler, J., Kennedy, H., and Tyson, R.L., (1965), Discussions on Transference. *PSA Study of the Child.* 30:409–441.

Settlage, C. in Van Dam, H. (1966), Problems of Transference in Child Analysis. *J. of Am. Psychoanal. Assoc.* 14:3, 528–537.

Stone, M.H. and Kestenbaum, C.J. (1974), Maternal Deprivation of the Wealthy. A Paradox in Socioeconomic Vs. Psychological Class. *History of Childhood Quarterly* 2:1, 79–106.

Winnicott, D.W. (1965), *The Maturational Process and the Facilitating Environment.* New York: International Universities Press.

Part Five

WOMEN

11

THE ENDURING
PSYCHOANALYTIC
CONCEPTS OF FEMALE
PSYCHOLOGY

MARVIN G. DRELLICH, M.D.
New York Medical College

The title of this book, *Changing Concepts in Psychoanalysis*, clearly indicates that we do not regard the psychoanalytic theories with which we
work as final formulations, and that we must periodically re-examine our
hypotheses with an eye to discarding the unsupportable ideas (no matter
how precious we may have regarded them to be in the past) and incorpo-
rating the new ideas that promise to expand our understanding, increase
our insights, and sharpen our tools for therapeutic effectiveness.

FREUD'S THEORY OF FEMALE PSYCHOLOGY

Of all the traditional theories that we have inherited from Freud and his
closest followers, there are probably none that have been more controversial than his theories about female psychology. Especially at this
time, when the role of women in society has been a subject of the most
searching examination and modification, many of Freud's theories of female psychology have been attacked because they are judged to be de-
meaning and derogatory toward women. I submit that this is not a valid
basis for rejecting a scientific theory. We cannot reject a theory because
we find it distasteful or because it conflicts with our political or social
egalitarianism. If Freud's theories are supported by clinical observations,
we have no choice but to accept them, no matter how distasteful we find
them to be. But if some or all of his concepts of feminine psychology are
not affirmed by our clinical observations, then they must be modified or
set aside. These changes must be made not because the theories are de-

meaning to women, but because they are inaccurate; not because they judge women to be inferior, but because they do not stand the test of clinical practice; not because they are unfashionable in a period of social and political activism among women, but because they do not conceptualize the realities of female psychology.

This part of Freud's monumental contribution to human psychology, his theory of female psychology, has been one of the most controversial, even among his closest followers. He himself in 1900 described the psychology of women as "veiled in an impenetrable obscurity" and as late as 1926 he said that the sexual life of adult women was a "dark continent" for psychology.

His first theory of the psychology of women was concerned with the fate of the little girl's Oedipus complex. Between 1900 and 1923, he wrote in at least four different publications that the psychology of women could be taken as analogous to men "mutatis mutandis." In 1923 he wrote that the dissolution of the Oedipus complex is presumed to be "precisely analogous" in girls and boys. As is often the case, this early theory of Freud's may prove to be more serviceable and enduring that the modifications he put forth at a later date. Beginning in 1925 with his paper, "Some Psychological Consequences of the Anatomical Distinction between the Sexes," he offered the idea that there are many differences rather than similarities between the psychosexual development of the male and female. He placed much less emphasis on the Oedipus complex, per se, and much more on the consequences of the little girl's discovery that a little boy has a penis and she does not. This discovery, he judged, invariably leads to narcissistic humiliation and feelings of phallic inferiority. A girl renounces her preoedipal attachment to mother because she judges mother to be responsible for her state of castration and, as a secondary consequence, she moves into the Oedipus phase with father as love object. She develops a life-long penis envy and can only find some partial consolation in her secondary wish to have a child. He also conjectured that, based on the foundation of actual castration and penis envy, the female was fated to be jealous, masochistic, and passive and to develop a weaker super-ego than the male.

This paper and its astonishing theories provoked immediate repercussions in the psychoanalytic community. A few analysts such as Marie Bonaparte (1935) and Helen Deutsch (1930) seemed to support every detail of Freud's theory of female psychology. Many more, including Horney (1926), Fenichel (1930), Melanie Klein (1928), Lampl-deGroot (1928) and Ernest Jones (1927, 1933, 1935), were quick to take issue with one or more elements. As early as 1927, Jones wrote, "There is a healthy suspicion growing that men analysts have been led to adopt an unduly phallocentric view of the problems in question, the importance of the female organs being correspondingly underestimated." Jones's objections were to be repeated by countless psychoanalysts, not only among those who separated themselves from the major Freudian theories, but also among many who remained identified with most of the other classical psychoanalytical concepts.

There was so much opposition to the 1925 paper on anatomical differences that Freud took the theretofore unprecedented step of writing another paper to reiterate his views and specifically to answer his many critics within the psychoanalytic movement. The 1931 paper, entitled "Female Sexuality," repeated his position of 1925, again emphasizing the feelings of castration, inferiority, and penis envy as nuclear determinants of female character and sexuality.

In the 1930s, 1940s, and 1950s, the opposition to these concepts continued unabated both within and outside of classical psychoanalysis. Rado (1933), Greenacre (1950) and Silverberg (1950) were among the most thoughtful and constructive critics.

In 1959 Heinz Kohut wrote, "The obvious biological truth seems to be that the female must have primary female tendencies and that femaleness cannot possibly be explained as a retreat from disappointed maleness."

REVISIONS OF THE CASTRATION THEORY

In 1958 and 1959, Bieber and I undertook to study the psychological consequences of hysterectomy for 23 women. We reexamined the implications of our findings for the psychoanalytic theory of female psychology. Our conclusions are reminiscent of Freud's earliest ideas about the strong similarity, mutatis mutandis, between the psychosexual development of males and females. Our clinical observations supported the following revisions of castration theory.

The psychoanalytic concept of *castration* in the psychology of women should be considered to contain elements that are similar, but not identical, to the traditional psychoanalytic concept of *castration* in the psychology of males. In both sexes, the individual has an idea of what constitutes masculinity or femininity, respectively, and these ideas are derived from the commonly held concepts of the culture, as well as from the privately held notions derived from individual developmental experiences. In both males and females, ideas are related to sexual anatomy. The sexual organs *and their functions* may often be the focus of doubts about one's adequacy as a member of one's own gender. The sexual organs are frequently seen by persons of either sex as peculiarly vulnerable to injury or disease. Both men and women unconsciously fear that the sexual organs will be the site of punishment for guilt-laden activities. (The female superego appears to be every bit as judgmental and punitive as the male superego in this regard.)

In both sexes the sexual organs may be symbolically utilized to express a variety of attitudes, positive and negative, toward oneself and other members of one's own sex.

We suggested that the psychoanalytic concept of castration for either sex includes a real or fantasied mutilation or subtraction of a valued organ (or its symbolic equivalent), which is viewed as necessary for optimal function as a member of one's own sex. Loss or injury to this organ may be conceived of as rendering the individual less effective or totally ineffective in both the sexual and nonsexual activities that are viewed as uniquely male or female, respectively.

In addition to castration fears we found it important to address the question of castration impulses. Castrating impulses, including desires to injure the femininity and sexual attractiveness of other women, were expressed by several women in psychoanalysis. Women who are competitive with other women attempt to minimize and inhibit the femininity and attractiveness of those whom they perceive as rivals. A rivalrous mother may defeminize and interfere with the normal feminine development of her daughter just as a rivalrous father may impair the masculine development and masculine self-confidence of a son.

We further suggested that the female castration complex be divided into two distinct entities. One we called the *feminine component of the female castration complex*. This component includes the recognition that, in normal development, the little girl strives to be feminine and, indeed, to be effectively feminine from earliest childhood, just as the little boy strives to achieve effective masculinity from his earliest years. When a girl experiences real or fantasied interference with her feminine development or when a female perceives injury to the unique sexual organs, her responses can be called the feminine component of the female castration complex.

The second component derives from the recognition that some girls and women do believe that the absence of a penis is a deficiency and, for them, penis envy may be an element in their adult personality organization. This we called the *phallic component of the female castration complex*. We found, however, that significant penis envy was always the consequence of pathological developmental experiences such as emotionally detached mothers, overtly or covertly competitive or destructive mothers, mothers who openly preferred sons, or fathers whose anxiety about their sexual feelings toward their daughters caused them to discourage and derogate the feminine development of the daughters. In all instances, a persistent penis envy is a dependent variable related to specific developmental pathology and not an independent variable related to the mere discovery of the anatomical differences between the sexes.

In order to make these revisions most meaningful, the following clinical material is presented which illustrates the revised concepts of castration and penis envy.

Clinical Examples

I have had two female patients, each of whom dreamed that she had a penis. It was in the manifest content of her dreams that each woman dreamed that she had a penis as a natural part of her anatomy. In each case the patient experienced herself in the dream as being her actual, adult female self with the one additional feature that she had a penis in the general vicinity of her pubic area. Although there was little direct attention to her female genitals in the dream, each woman believed within the dream context that her normal female genitals were intact and that the penis was there in addition to her own genitalia.

It is significant that in both patients the events of the manifest dream were quite similar. In one case the patient dreamed that she was in bed with her mother and the mother was fondling and caressing the patient's penis. This patient experienced conscious sexual arousal during the dream and upon awakening. The second patient also dreamed that she was in bed with her mother and she (the patient) was about to consumate sexual intercourse by inserting her penis in her mother's vagina. This patient had no conscious sexual arousal and awoke with some anxiety.

In the first case the patient was an only child. Her parents had been separated when she was 4 years old, and her young mother related to her in many ways like an older sister or older friend. She often slept with her mother in childhood and early adolescence, and it was not unusual for the mother to hold her close to her and occasionally fondle the daughter's labia and mons veneris. The little girl experienced sexual arousal and remembers engagning in masturbation by handling herself in the manner in which her mother had done. The mother was, in addition, a socially and sexually active woman who brought many boyfriends home and made little or no attempt to conceal from the daughter her sexual relations with these men.

When a man was on the scene, the mother seemed to become oblivious to the child's existence. She expected the daughter to make no demands on her time and to avoid any interference with the mother's and boyfriends' activites: dancing, drinking, and sex.

It is quite clear that the mother's pattern of closeness, intimacy, and sexual stimulation when the two were alone, alternating with rejection and indifference when a sexually active male was around, was traumatically inconsistent and disturbing to the girl.

The dream of having a penis and being fondled by the mother occurred during a phase of her analysis when attention was being focused on the early mother-child relationship. It was clearly an attempt to undo the inconsistent pattern of intimacy alternating with rejection. For her to have a penis was to restore the closeness that she had known and cherished and to eliminate the possibility of rejection by having available the organ to satisfy the mother's highest priority. Here, indeed, is an instance of envy of males and a literal, not symbolic, envy of the penis as a response to the specific mother-daughter relationship of her childhood. The penis envy was real, intense, and needed to be analyzed. It was not the result of the normal developmental discovery of the anatomical differences between the sexes, but rather was the result of her being regularly displaced from closeness with her immature, promiscuous mother. It was a defensive and reparative response, not an inevitable feature of female psychological development.

In her relations with men, the patient herself had been promiscuous before marriage and was consciously aware of great rivalry with men, of envy of their real and imagined advantages over women. She had occasional fantasies of deracinating a man and keeping his uprooted penis as a prize (castration impulse). On one occasion she "accidentally" uprooted a potted plant that she was carrying and immediately had an acute panic reaction because it seemed for a moment to her that she had acted out her deracination fantasy against a man.

The other patient who dreamed of having a penis was clinically very different. She was one of three children, having an older and a younger brother and parents who were hardworking, conventional, and always worried about money. Her father was always tired and detached when he came home from work and her mother was always tired and marginally depressed from her day of cooking, cleaning, and housekeeping. There was little affection between any persons in the household, and the mother clearly conveyed the attitude that special privileges and allowances must be made for the father, because he was the wage earner, and for the brothers who would be wage earners in the future. Needless to say, the brothers were destined to go to college, but the patient did not go on to higher education until long after she had left her parental home, had married, and had received the encouragement and support of a loving and understanding husband.

In one analytic session the patient remembered a childhood experience that was a lasting, though isolated, memory. She remembered being about 7 or 8 years old, sitting in the living room in the evening while her mother was listening to the Lux Radio Theater. It was a highly romantic and sentimental story and, to the patient's surprise, the mother motioned for her to come and sit beside her on the couch. She remembered putting her head *on her mother's lap* and feeling a rush of warm, pleasant feelings. Retrospectively, in analysis, she believed that she may have also felt some anxiety at the time and she volunteered that it was a unique experience, which she had no memory of having had with her mother either before or after that one time.

Very shortly after that session she reported the dream of herself possessing a penis and about to have intercourse with her mother. Her memory of the head-in-lap episode must have included an intuitive awareness that the romantic and probably erotic simulus from the radio program had been responsible for the mother's initiating the episode of affection. She feels that her mother's chronic depression had momentarily lifted and permitted an overt expression of closeness and warmth. There is no doubt that the mother's attitude of male superiority and male preference was another determinant of the dream. In any event, it is clear that for this patient, as for the first patient, the penis was deemed necessary to gain closeness and warmth from the mother, as well as to equalize her status in the family as compared to her brothers. The dreamed-of penis was a means to an end, not an end in itself. This, too, was a powerful, manifest penis envy which made sense as a literal as well as metaphoric deficiency in the context of the patient's developmental experience within her family.

I have also analyzed four women who have all had intense rivalries with men, and active heterosexual lives which were always sparked by active or passive-aggressive acting out of hostility toward the men. All four were highly intelligent women who were successful in their careers. Each was an attractive woman, flirtatious and, indeed, seductive, successful at winning the interest and affection of men, but invariably ruining the relationships because of intense rivalry and hostility. The dreams and waking lives of these women were characterized by envy and hostility toward men and inappropriate feelings of inferiority in comparison to both men and women.

The childhood situations in these four cases were astonishingly similar and their dynamics were also similar and eventually predictable.

Each patient was the older of two daughters and had no brothers. The families were intact, middle-class households. From a very early age the older daughter came to realize that the parents were disappointed in not having a son and that she, the older daughter, was expected to fill the role of substitute son for both parents, but especially for the father.

As a child, the patient was usually praised for being sensible, responsible, and intelligent. The younger sister was considered to be cute, feminine, emotionally changeable and benignly irresponsible. The older daughter was expected to do well in school, to have a serious attitude about money, to be skillful at home repairs, and to participate with the father in going to ball games, fishing, and similar stereotypically masculine activities. The younger daughter was encouraged to help the mother with household duties, to be well behaved rather than academically successful at school, to look sweet and feminine in appearance, and to be mildly coy and flirtatious with the father.

When the younger daughter cried, she was cuddled and comforted. When the older daughter cried, her parents, especially her father, expressed disappointment that she would display such weakness. Generally the family myth was that the older daughter was just like the father—stable, unemotional, realistic, and practical in worldly matters. The younger daughter was just like mother—unstable, emotional, unrealistic, impractical, "beautiful but dumb"—simultaneously loveable and dependent.

The four patients were older daughters and their analyses revealed similar conflicts, particularly in relation to their fathers. The wish for father's respect, admiration, and acceptance was successfully realized when this daughter assumed the stereotypically masculine qualities of the wished-for son. She gained a special oedipal advantage over her mother and younger sister, but she did so by taking on a pseudo-masculine role and suppressing traditionally feminine tendencies and attributes. The older daughter gained father's respect and admiration, while the younger daughter evoked his protective and tender responses. The older was psychologically rewarded for being "one of the boys," while the younger was expressly classified and adored as a "typical little girl."

It is small wonder that these older daughters reached adulthood with considerable conflicts about their relations with men. They entered a male-female relationship with a conviction that winning a man's respect and acceptance as an equal sacrificed his tender responses and sexual interest, and conversely, winning his love and affection sacrificed his respect and admiration. They were convinced that it was a "no-win" situation and a significant unconscious resentment was the continual background affect.

These women felt envy and contempt for those they saw as truly "feminine" women—a transference from their mothers and sisters. They belittled the femininity of such rivals, at the same time as secretly longing to express their own feminity without having to sacrifice the sense of competence and equality with men. Obviously, stereotyped theories of the anatomical differences between the sexes would be of no value in these four cases.

CONCLUSION

I would repeat that revision of the psychoanalytic theory of female psychology continues unabated by virtually all psychoanalysts, including those who are otherwise classically oriented. In 1976 a long supplementary issue of the *Journal of the American Psychoanalytic Association* was devoted exclusively to contemporary psychoanalytic views of female psychology. Among the ideas that were vigorously presented was the realization that vaginal sensations occur normally as early as the first year of life. In that way, a little girl's core gender identity as a female occurs long before there is awareness of the anatomical difference between the sexes. Thus penis envy occurs in a developmental context and persists based on specific pathological experience. Further, the oedipal attachment to father and the wish to have a baby are not the consequences of penis envy or disappointed maleness, but rather the normal consequences of biological and psychological femininity. We even find the emphatic acknowledgment that neither passivity nor masochism is specifically a female characteristic, but that each is rather an adaptational response available to both sexes and occurring in both sexes when developmental experiences are conducive to it.

Indeed, I believe that we would be hard pressed to find any psychoanalyst today who subscribes to all or most of Freud's 1925 formulations. However respectful we can and should be toward the historical value of his original concepts, we owe him the greater respect of retaining only those aspects that meet the test of our fifty years of clinical psychoanalytic observations.

REFERENCES

Bieber, Irving and Drellich, Marvin G. The Female Castration Complex. *Journal of Nervous and Mental Disease,* 129, 1959.

Blum, Harold P., Editor. Female Psychology. *Journal of the American Psychoanalytic Association* Supplement Volume 24 Number 5, 1–350, 1976.

Bonaparte, Marie. Passivity, Masochism, and Frigidity. *International Journal of Psychoanalysis.* 16, 1935.

Deutsch, Helene. The Significance of Masochism in the Mental Life of Women. *International Journal of Psychoanalysis,* 11, 1930.

Drellich, Marvin G. and Bieber, Irving. The Psychological Importance of the Uterus and its Functions. *Journal of Nervous and Mental Disease,* 126, 1958.

Fenichel, Otto (1930). The Pregenital Antecedents of the Oedipus Conflict. In *The Collected Papers of Otto Fenichel,* First Series. New York: Norton, 1953.

Freud, Sigmund (1900). The Interpretation of Dreams. *Standard Edition,* Vol. 5. 4–5. London: Hogarth, 1955.

––––– (1905). Three Essays on the Theory of Sexuality. *Standard Edition,* Vol. 7. London: Hogarth.

––––– (1916–17) Introductory Lectures on Psychoanalysis. *Standard Edition,* Vol. 8. 15–16. London: Hogarth.

––––– (1921) Group Psychology and the Analysis of the Ego. *Standard Edition,* Vol. 18. London: Hogarth.

––––– (1925) The Ego and the Id. *Standard Edition,* Vol. 19. London: Hogarth, 1961.

––––– (1925) Some Psychological Consequences of the Anatomical Distinction between the Sexes. *Standard Edition,* Vol. 19. London: Hogarth, 1961.

––––– (1926) The Question of Lay Analysts. *Standard Edition,* Vol. 20. London: Hogarth, 1961.

––––– (1931) Female Sexuality. *Standard Edition,* Vol. 21. London: Hogarth, 1961.

Greenacre, Phyllis. Special Problems of Early Female Sexual Development. *Psychoanalytic Study of the Child,* 5, 1950.

Horney, Karen. The Flight from Womanhood. *International Journal of Psychoanalysis,* 7, 1926.

Jones, Ernest (1927). The Early Development of Female Sexuality. *Papers on Psychoanalysis.* London: Bailliere, Tindall and Cox, 1950.

––––– (1933). The Phallic Phase. *Papers on Psychoanalysis.* London: Bailliere, Tindall and Cox, 1950.

––––– (1935). Early Female Sexuality. *Papers on Psychoanalysis.* London: Bailliere, Tindall and Cox, 1950.

Klein, Melanie. Early Stages of the Oedipus Conflict. *International Journal of Psychoanalysis,* 9, 1928.

Kohut, Heinz. Introspection, Empathy and Psychoanalysis. *Journal of the American Psychoanalytic Association*, 7, 1959.

Lampl-deGroot, Jeanne. The Evolution of the Oedipus Complex in Women. *International Journal of Psychoanalysis*, 9, 1928.

Rado, Sandor (1933). Fear of Castration in Women. In *Psychoanalysis of Behavior*. New York: Grune and Stratton, 1956.

Silverberg, William V. Discussion of Romm, May E. Unresolved Aggression and Femininity in Feminine Psychology. Department of Psychiatry, Psychoanalytic Division, New York Medical College, Symposium Proceedings. 1950.

12

AGGRESSION IN WOMEN: A REEXAMINATION

JEAN BAKER MILLER, M.D.
Boston University School of Medicine

CAROL C. NADELSON, M.D.
Harvard Medical School

MALKAH T. NOTMAN, M.D.
Harvard Medical School

JOAN ZILBACH, M.D.
Tufts Medical School

The topic of aggression in women has always been a problematic one.[1] According to classical psychoanalytic theory, women's aggression, or at least its sexual aspect, is converted into masochism and its accompanying passivity. Freud (1925), Deutsch (1944), and others have stated that the attempted transformation of women's sexuality and its aggressive components into masochism and passivity constitutes a repeated struggle that is probably never totally accomplished. Inherent in this position is Freud's belief, which few analysts have challenged, that women begin life with the same degree of, or propensity for, aggression as men. Women's life-long effort, then, is the attempt to rid themselves of this direct aggression.

While the struggle to transform aggression into masochism and passivity may not be an easy one, it is also true that the attempt to do so "'succeeds" to a very large degree in the vast majority of women. This observation often becomes more clearly evident today, when many women in treatment consciously seek to change from a masochistic or passive life situation and find that they then encounter severe internal conflict. Precisely because they seek a change from a clearly masochistic situation, these women raise quite pointedly the issues that aggression poses not only for them but for most women.

ILLUSTRATIVE EXAMPLES

The following examples have been chosen because they illustrate the women's difficulties in recognizing and effectively utilizing aggression.

C. S. was the oldest of nine children of an irresponsible father. All of the activity of supplying the material and psychological needs of the family had been done by her typically long-suffering mother. C. S. early assumed the role of her mother's main helper and sympathizer. C. S. was bright at school and had been encouraged by her teachers but never to aspire to a very high level. After high school she began work in a paraprofessional job. She gradually moved to a psychiatrically oriented setting and became increasingly admired for her gifts as a member of a therapeutic team. She was perceived as warm, giving, intelligent, and insightful and was highly regarded and praised by both superiors and colleagues.

Shortly after high school she had married a young man, T., who appeared charming and appealing. C. S. perceived him as more intelligent and attractive than she, and their general plan was that he would pursue college and career while she supported him in these efforts.

Within a short time, it became apparent that T.'s charm hid profound problems. He failed repeatedly at school and at work and became increasingly alcoholic. He became involved with numerous other women. His actions towards C. S. progressed from inattention to extreme derogation and abusiveness. After tolerating his behavior for an inordinate length of time, C. S. began the first of several attempts at separation. On each of these occasions, T. would switch to pleading for her return, and she would rejoin him. C. S. entered treatment during this period and acquired some understanding of her difficulties but had not been able to carry through the separation from T. By this time, she had reached her late 20s.

After good work on many aspects of her problems, it became apparent that the major remaining component of her inability to leave T. was based on her equating leaving with a clear act of aggression. She could not allow herself that aggression. Leaving T. would be a step in her own interest, a step that would increase her own satisfaction and enhance her already impressive effectiveness.

C. S.'s recoil from this step took several forms. One form—one particularly related to self-esteem—emerged around her often-reapeated statement that she "could not imagine herself as a person who could do such a thing." The phrase was interesting and more than a mere colloquial expression. She could not form an image of herself as someone who could stand forth as a person who used her powers in her own interest. The attempt to form such an image led her initially to a blank; there was no way to see herself at all in that light. Later it gave way to an image of "something" very evil. At a still later stage, the attempt to create such an image led instead to repeated fantasies of being viciously condemned. Each time that C. S. came to this point, she was able to talk of the reality that no one would condemn her. She would then cry uncontrollably and insist that she must suffer. At times she would invoke a quasi-religious world view that "life is meant to be suffering."

C. S. was "psychologically minded" and within good reality sense and thus was able to observe the unreality of what she was experiencing. She knew that, in fact, she would not be condemned but would be congratulated by her many friends and colleagues. She knew, too, that her condemnation fantasies contained a projection of the anger she felt toward T. This anger was present and it had been recognized, but it did not seem the critical stumbling block.

A related aspect was her fantasy that T. would be destroyed if she left him. Again, because of her psychological sophistication, C. S. recognized the invalidity of this theme on several grounds. She knew "that T. served some 'sick' purpose for me and I for him." She knew and had dealt with the likelihood that T. stood for her two suffering parents whom she felt she had abandoned and thereby hurt by virtue of growing up and becoming an effective and well-functioning person. The theme persisted for a lengthy period that action in her own clear interest must be destructive and harmful. It signified that her aggression was bad and powerful.

A different but related feature was the theme that T., for all his defects, did love her "for some odd reason" and that no one else could ever love her because she was so inadequate and deficient. What she first labeled as inadequacy, she eventually referred to as her "badness." She was so bad that no one else could or would ever love her. This badness was composed of several components. One of them seemed to derive from her anger at each of her parents for the deprivation she had felt from them. Anger directed toward her suffering and "good" mother was particularly difficult. In addition to these features, there was the linking of this "badness" with her own "sin" of surviving and in fact of "making something of herself and for herself" by emerging from her deprived and depriving family. Her "badness" was indeed the fact that she had somehow been active and now stood as successful, competent, and good for all the world to see. T. had served as a constant shield, detraction, penance, and punishment for this "badness"; he also had served as the constant guarantee that someone would love her even though she had been so "bad" as to actively use herself toward her own survival and functioning.

It was clear that the issue on which C. S.'s course turned was the equation of aggression with powerful evil. That is, direct action in her own self-interest was psychicly equivalent to conceiving of herself as evil, and therefore she was dangerous and worthless at the core. After considerable work on this issue, she definitively ended the relationship.

As a sidelight, it is interesting to note that all of C. S.'s protestations of inadequacy—which stood in gross contradiction of reality—seemed to serve the purpose of obscuring her recognition of her strength and power. These strengths had to be obscured because they were equated with the "evil" of aggression. This point is particularly important because insistence on inadequacy is common in women. In many instances these protestations cover a similar great amount of strength and hide the potential for greater strength.

This point is important to stress in regard to women who may not yet have put their activities into effect, in reality, as clearly as C. S. has done.

Many women can be so convincing in their insistence on their inadequacy; the cultural expectations of women can so readily collude with this perception of women, and the opportunities for effective action can be so limited (or likely to involve women in a conflict with the external realities), that the defensive purpose of this screen of inadequacy can be easily missed. Indeed, many women who have been characterized as passive and helpless may be much more powerful and adequate than they appear. The overt passivity and helplessness, painful as it is, may serve to hide the much more threatening prospect of their aggression and power (Miller 1976).

Example Two: F. W.

Another woman, F. W., also in her late 20s, presented a remarkably similar picture, although her specific situation and early relationships had a different configuration. She was the only child of a successful, competent father to whom she felt close. She had seen him initially as a good man who suffered by his attachment to an incompetent, demanding, hysterical wife who was unable to solve her own problems but unendingly demanded that others, especially her husband and her daughter, supply her needs.

Always bright, F. W. had arrived at a high-level occupation in which she was very competent and which she loved. In contrast to C. S., her work did not involve serving others. She, too, was married to a man, D., who had initially seemed attractive, "strong," and dynamic but who fairly rapidly revealed himself as a weak, demanding person, making excessive use of alcohol and given to boisterous good times and increasingly vociferous demands and attacks on her. His daily demands and attacks were seriously endangering her job performance. F. W., too, had made repeated short-lived attempts at separation but repeatedly rejoined her husband. These separations were fraught with extreme pain. F. W. had worked through many issues, including the fact that D.'s obvious anger allowed her the simultaneous expression and denial of her own anger and that his need for her provided the stage on which to play out her need to serve and to save her incompetent, suffering mother. Despite work on this and other issues, F. W., could not seriously break with D.

She, too, eventually came to face more directly the sheer fact that leaving D. was the equivalent of aggression—the use of herself and her resources for her own survival. She, too, returned repeatedly to the themes that she must serve others, especially others in need. Interestingly, she also resorted to an invocation of religion at one stage and repeatedly tried to proclaim that she—and women in general—were meant to serve others. Anything else was "selfishness and self-indulgence." These proclamations by both C. S. and F. W. would have caused major consternation if known to their colleagues, because they were in such contrast to their external lives as modern, enlightened people.

In a similar, but not identical form to C. S.'s belief that only T. could love her, F. W. eventually arrived at a period in which she dwelt on the belief that she and D. were linked at a very profound level in both their pain and their evil.

Thus, only with D. could she ever feel the kind of "deep sense of true contact" that she felt compensated for all of the overt pain that D. caused. She would not be able to feel this profound sense of connection with anyone else. The rest of the world saw D. as the "weak, bad guy" and F. W. as the good person, but she "needed this sense of linkage with evil." She felt this to be an extremely shameful admission but one that she must make and stick with.

F. W.'s formulation could be passed off easily as the masochistic side of the sadomasochistic relationship, but this "connection" represented many things, including derivatives of her longing for a connection with the mother she had seen as abhorrent for so long and her longing to establish contact with that weak mother and with the weakness she so hated. It was partly an attempt to negate her own strength, the strength that had carried her away from her mother. It was also, however, a desire to express and to ask others to recognize with her the evil that she felt. (In reality, she could never allow herself to appear "bad." She was always the good girl, the one who did the right things and who took care of and served everyone.)

Eventually, as the other components cleared away, the evil stood revealed as her ability and power, or her aggression, the very aggression that had moved her away from her mother's destructive morass and that she had used for survival and success. Furthermore, as she claimed the origins of her own evil for herself, she dropped the need to connect it with D. or to attach it to his "evil," which was, in fact, very different from hers.

F. W., too, repeatedly worked over the theme that D. would be destroyed if she left. As with C. S., this theme seemed to represent the other side of her seeming lack of aggression, that is, that her aggression was so powerful that it could utterly destroy. While this theme might be seen as one of primitive hate and omnipotence, such a categorization is not accurate for these women. It is more likely the lifelong lack of integration of aggression, which will be discussed further. It was not consistent with the much higher level of functioning that was apparent in these women.

After working on these issues, F. W., too, made a final break with D. It is interesting to note that after ending their respective relationships, both of these women continued on a much improved basis. One reason for this outcome was that they had worked through this issue prior to the break in the relationship. Another was that these men had obviously not been contributing to their lives and functioning. They had in reality caused suffering and pain and had in many ways torn away at the women's valid basis for self-esteem. Prior to their psychological work on their fear of aggression, however, even this derogation had seemed preferable to the much greater threat to self-esteem that acknowledgment of their aggression posed.

Example Three: O. R.

A third woman, O. R., came to treatment at a different point. She was depressed, but similar features seemed critical in the resolution of her depression. She, like many other women, came at the point at which her husband left her and her two children. Her husband, a successful professional, had gone into spiraling decline, which included, among other things, utter destructiveness to home and family, financial ruin, numerous affairs with women, and the eventual revelation of a mounting drug addiction. In contrast to the first two women described, O. R. had not dealt with her aggression prior to the separation. It eventually became apparent that this same factor—the necessity to recognize her own aggression—led to the threat to her self-esteem that contributed to her depression. That is, in addition to the other reasons for depression—her reality problems, her husband's abandonment, her anger at her husband, and her anger at his leaving, all of which contributed to her pervasive sense of failure and unworthiness—there was the additional threat to her self-esteem that the recognition of her aggression posed.

At the point at which this material emerged, it became clear that O. R. had a store of ability and aggression that she could no longer put to the service of her husband and that she could now put to use in her own self-interest. She repeatedly attempted to retreat from this recognition. When she eventually did deal with it, she said, "I never felt like the person I feel like today. I never believed I could have felt like this."

Many of O. R.'s attempts to retreat from this recognition were essentially similar to those of the women in the two previous examples. The disruption of the relationship with her husband led to the necessity to face her own aggression. There were many repetitions of her feeling that she must have been wrong and bad for her husband to have left. Her constant reiteration of the question "What did I do wrong?" in the face of her husband's grossly bizarre and destructive behavior indicated another hidden issue. Eventually, the issue that emerged as critical was the avoidance of her own good abilities to act in her own self-interest. When this issue was clarified and worked on, she went on to a better life plan and to satisfaction in the pursuit of her own talents. Here, again, there were the particularities of her history, but they did not link to the critical turning point in her remobilization until she dealt with her aggression.

It is suggested that in depression, which is very much more common in women (Weissman and Klerman 1977) and which often, but not always, follows a loss of a relationship, one important and overlooked feature may be that the woman's own aggression is now "free" and available for use. It is no longer bound in the relationship and in service to the needs of others (Miller 1976). The woman may be highly prone to misconstrue the experience of her aggression and to interpret it as one or another form of anger or hostility. It is most important that the therapist not collude in this misconception by seeing this aggression as solely the hostile part of the ambivalence toward the lost person or the anger at the abandonment. While these features may be present, there may well be the additional factor of the aggression itself. This aggression is a potentially positive and constructive force, but the woman is very likely to experience it as a destructive and dangerous force.

Another woman typified this point. After the ending of a destructive and negative relationship with a husband, she felt a sense of liberation.

However, she could only begin to put her resources into action if she first invoked the fantasy that she was now doing this for her father. She had still to call on this fantasy of serving another—a man—to allow herself the use of her own aggression.

DISCUSSION

These brief histories are cited to suggest one pathway to the study of the hidden field of women's aggression and to illustrate one form in which aggression poses a threat to a woman's sense of self-esteem.

It seems clear that women incorporate early in life the conviction that their own direct, self-generated, self-directed, and self-interested aggression is intolerable. From its beginning, this proposition is elaborated with each stage of development. The ego ideal, which is projected for most women, is one that depicts a figure almost devoid of aggression. Being forced to acknowledge the existence of aggression becomes, by definition, the threat that one is a failure, inadequate, and inferior. Hence, self-esteem plummets. (It is important to note that these all are feelings experienced commonly in depression.)

In a recent paper, for example, Blum (1978) stresses the effect of the early maternal ego ideal on the development of the pre-Oedipal girl's sense of femininity. The maternal ego ideal does not usually include, however, the explicit use of aggression; rather, the lack of aggression, and the care and nurturance of others, are included in the ideal.

Guilt follows the sense of having committed the forbidden, having done a serious wrong, and it is apparent that many girls would experience the presence of their own aggression as evidence of a major wrongdoing. The women in the previous examples experienced their life activity itself as forbidden and wrong. They had used their activity in the service of their survival and growth. This "aggression" made it possible for them to escape from the handicaps of their deprived families. They had exerted their aggression in their own self-interest but without acknowledging it. They needed a masochistic relationship to ensure that they would not have to recognize their aggression and certainly to guarantee that its results would not clearly and directly serve their own satisfaction and needs. By this distortion, they had felt the need of a masochistic relationship to maintain their self-esteem. That is, their aggression and its derivative activity were experienced not as a basis for self-esteem but rather as a major threat to it. In their cases, precisely because they had put forward a large measure of effort and activity to escape a more destructive family background—that is, they had acted out a healthy self-interest and self-preservation—they seemed to need an especially masochisic relationship as insurance against their acknowledgement of their own aggression. Put another way, they needed and used much of their aggression in a basically healthy way to solve their life situation, but they simultaneously had to find a solution for the dilemma of their use of this aggression.

It is suggested that the same basic factor operates in most women. In the paper cited, Blum (1978) has stated the probably generally agreed upon formulation that the woman could not, for example, carry out the function of "good enough" mothering if she had come to a totally masochistic resolution of all of her aggression. The implication is that inevitably all women possess and use a large element of aggression and activity. The further implication is, however, that similarly to the women described here, most women can allow aggression to exist and can make it available for use so long as they are using it in the service of another—in this regard, in the service of a child.

In this discussion, one facet of the problem of feminine aggression and its relationship to self-esteem has been suggested. Further, the part that the interdiction of feminine aggression may play in the character of shame and guilt in the woman has been touched on only briefly. There is reason to believe that the effects of the interdiction of feminine aggression begin even earlier in life; this point is discussed further in a subsequent paper (Zilbach, Notman, Nadelson, and Miller 1979).

One other large portion of this topic can be suggested here: aggression in girls and women is not as it is with boys and men, subject to numerous and repeated attempts at working through and channeling. That is, because aggression is not supposed to exist at all, girls do not go through the constant practice and refinement of the use of their aggression. The aggression then remains more untempered and untested. It is as if it were lurking, suppressed, in a more unorganized state. While used in the service of others, it can seem to the woman herself and to others as nonexistent. This is one reason that the term *denial*, or nonrecognition has been used in this preliminary attempt at reassessing feminine aggression. On the other hand, that women can use their aggression to function so well in serving others and to gain such genuine satisfaction from fostering the growth and development of others in a way that is foreign to most men and then shift so rapidly into massive feelings of worthlessness if the serving relationship is altered suggests that denial may not be the appropriate word. It may not describe accurately the state of abeyance in which women's aggression can often be held for so long a period in a generally well-functioning person.

Evidence for this state in which aggression is held in abeyance—and seeming absence—comes from many sources. To cite merely one example, a paper by Kaplan (1974) describes the girls in a center for delinquents. She notes that these extremely deprived girls do not often strike out in anger in the way in which the deprived boys do. Instead, they tend to be passive and inhibited. When they do become involved in fights, the fights are notably different from those of the boys. The girls do not seem to size up their opponents or to fight with any degree of calculation. Instead, they strike out recklessly, without regard for the very real dangers of injury from bigger, stronger opponents. In addition, in the midst of such fury the girls may dissolve in tears. Further, when they strike out at others, they usually follow immediately with acts of rage against themselves.

The unorganized quality of aggression relates importantly to the basic question of whether aggression in the sense of activity and assertion can be, in truth, separated from aggression in the sense of action aimed at the resistance, harm, or destruction of others (Zilbach, Notman, Nadelson, and Miller 1979). This remains a difficult and unsettled question. For women, however, it seems clear that these components have their special particularities. On the one hand, aggression in the former sense is experienced totally almost as if it were the latter, that is, a destructive force. Thus, when women begin to experience their own aggression, it is most likely to be experienced as both unorganized and destructive and therefore more likely to be disorganizing and overwhelming to the personality as a whole. This feature adds to the fear and self-condemnation, making it extremely difficult for the woman to deal with the aggression.

On the other hand, further attention to the fact that aggression exists in women may lead to a greater comprehension of aggression generally. Until now, our understanding of aggression has been so linked to its manifestations in men that it has not been thoroughly explored as it indeed exists in the sex that comprises the major caretakers and servers.

Women's aggression has been an extremely difficult topic for our culture (and many cultures) to approach. Our inherited mythology and cultural history offer much evidence that it is shrouded in extreme horror and dread. It reaches roots deep in our psychic life. Indeed, it has had implications of the destruction of all of life and all of culture as we have known it, as well as fear of the powerful life-sustaining and potentiallly life-destroying woman. No doubt related to that fear is our general cultural tendency to ignore and deny it. It is believed that this massive cultural interdiction begins to affect the female infant at a stage probably earlier than that of shame and guilt, as has been suggested by many recent studies in the differential treatment of girl and boy infants (Zilbach, Notman, Nadelson, and Miller 1979).

From this possibility it follows that early in life the female infant begins to develop the intrapsychic fear and condemnation of her own vital life activity. Her most basic healthy, active stirrings become simultaneously a source of conflict. It is as if she were carrying within—or were composed of—a large powerful evil. At this early stage, her own physicality can be diverted to a path of constriction and inhibition. This physical inhibition, combined with its mental representations, can lay a base for further inhibition of higher and more complex functions.

On the other side of the picture, despite the massive denial and interdiction of women's aggression, there have come down through history major accounts of the strength and value of women's aggression. These cases have often been observed by men with a sense of wonderment, which reflects the culturally unintegrated nature of their view of this aggression. One recent statement by Milovan Djilas (Ihlau 1976), the Yugoslav anti-Nazi partisan leader and former national leader, typifies these many accounts (and sounds, in tone, oddly reminiscent of some of Freud's own queries at certain points, such as "What do women want?"): "I saw with my own eyes during our partisan struggle that women are braver in war than men. But what happened to them afterwards? They got married, became housewives, and vanished from the scene..." Women have always been brave—and active—even as housewives and mothers, but then they have seemingly vanished; the activity is all hidden. It is important to note that even in the Djilas example, the women were not acting only in self-interest but could believe that they were doing it for others.

It was Freud who clearly stated that aggression exists and is as powerful, at least initially, in women as it is in men. It has been the highly courageous, but equally dangerous, task of psychoanalysis to reveal that which the culture keeps hidden. It is important that psychoanalysis not collude with the cultural denial of feminine aggression and the problems that this denial creates for women—and ultimately, in turn, for men. This chapter pointed to only one small segment of these problems.

It is hoped that subsequent writings will develop further the precise configurations that the early and lifelong suppression of aggression takes in the development of girls. Here, it will merely be suggested in summary that the girl very early in life takes in the sense that the direct use of her physical self is a form of destructive aggression. She thus develops a basis for a pervasive and underlying sense that her own body contains—or is composed of—a basic force that is evil and wrong. This early basis for a sense of evil persists through all of life's stages, although there may be countervailing forces. The ready solution for this early conflict is the belief that her bodily processes and other powers can be put to use not in and of themselves but in the service of others, either for a man's pleasure or in the service of children. This large topic, however, requires subsequent further delineation.

NOTE

[1] Indeed, the topic of aggression is problematic in regard to men. So much is this the case that a definition of the word requires an extensive digression into the psychoanalytic and psychological literature. This discussion is provided in another paper (Zilbach, Notman, Nadelson, Miller 1979). The "working definition" used here will be obvious, and brief comment on it is made in the discussion section.

REFERENCES

Blum, H. P., "Feminine Masochism, The Ego Ideal and the Psychology of Women," in Blum, H. P., ed., *Female Psychology*. New York: International Universities Press, 1978.

Deutsch, H., *The Psychology of Women*. New York: Grune and Stratton, 1944.

Freud, S., "Some Psychic Consequences of the Anatomical Distinction between the Sexes," (1925), *Standard Edition*, 19:248–260. London: Hogarth Press, 1961.

Ihlau, O., "A Walk with Milovan Djilas," *Encounter* 47:54–57, Oct. 1976.

Kaplan, E. B., "Some Manifestations of Aggression in the Psychology of Latency and Prepuberty Girls," presented at the American Psychoanalytic Association, Dec. 14–15, 1974.

Miller, J. B., *Toward a New Psychology of Women*. Boston: Beacon Press, 1976.

Weissman, M., and Klerman, G., "Sex Differences and the Epidemiology of Depression," *Arch Gen Psychiatry*, 34: 98–111, 1977.

Zilbach, J., Notman, M. T., Nadelson, C. C., and Miller, J. B., "Aggression and Self-Esteem in Women," in Notman, M. T. and Nadelson, C. C., eds., *The Woman Patient, Vol. II*. New York: Plenum, 1979 (Forthcoming).

13

MASOCHISM IN WOMEN
A PSYCHODYNAMIC ANALYSIS[1]

DOREEN E. SCHECTER, M.D.
Albert Einstein College of Medicine, Bronx, New York

One of the earliest portrayals of masochism differentiated along gender lines occurs in Genesis. Genesis tells us that the price to be paid for knowledge, for daring to separate and function autonomously as well as to grasp the psychical consequences of the anatomical distinction between the sexes, is a life of masochistic submission for both man and woman. When, after the Fall, "the eyes of both of them were opened and they realized that they were naked" (Gen. 3:7), their gender roles become differentiated, and God punishes them according to gender. For listening to the voice of his wife, man is told by God: "Acursed be the soil because of you. With suffering shall you get your food from it every day of your life.... With sweat on your brow shall you eat your bread..." (Gen. 3:17).

Woman fares far worse, for she is subjugated not only to nature but also to man: "I will multiply your pains in childbearing, you shall give birth to your children in pain. Your yearning shall be for your husband, yet he will lord it over you" (Gen. 3:16). Daring to separate and to feel entitled to the same privileges and prerogatives as the Creator is a greater sin for woman than for man. Man himself is punished, yet he is commanded to punish, to "lord it over" his wife. Woman is denied any autonomy.

THE CONCEPT OF FEMININE MASOCHISM

Although a review of the psychoanalytic literature on masochism is beyond the scope of this chapter, the concept of feminine masochism needs a brief revisit. The term *feminine masochism*, as used in psychoanalytic literature, is a misnomer. The term first appears in Frued's "The Economic

Problem of Masochism" (1924) as one of the three forms in which masochism surfaces: erotogenic, feminine, and moral. Freud limits the term feminine masochism to men who view themselves as castrated and unconsciously identify with women whom they perceive as masochistic, passive, degraded, and inferior. Thus, feminine masochism refers to masochistic fantasies about women, deriving from neurotic conflicts in male patients. Paradoxically, in psychoanalytic history, this concept of feminine masochism becomes the yardstick of femininity, as set forth by Freud and the architects of the theory of feminine masochism (for example, Bonaparte 1935 and Deutsch 1944).

Masochism in some women may reflect a cultural disease, so to speak, in which case masochism may be unlearned as well as learned. The model of masochism as a product of social learning, however, does not apply when masochism is rooted in unconscious neurotic conflicts. Insofar as the cultural ego ideal for women prohibits the healthy expression of aggression and fosters passivity, dependency, submissiveness, helplessness, or childlike behavior, masochism in women will be reinforced and rewarded as a feminine character trait by the "facilitating environment."

Over the past 10 years, though, there has been a significant shift in cultural attitudes toward masochism in women. Whereas, traditionally, masochistic character traits have been elevated to the status of a prescriptive aspect of the cultural ego ideal for women, they have been dethroned for some time now, relegated to the status of a prohibitive aspect of the cultural ego ideal for the successful woman. Thus, it is more difficult for women to get as much mileage or secondary gain from masochistic character traits as compared with 10 years ago. As reflected in clinical practice, such traits in the current cultural milieu appear to be experienced by many women in a more ego-dystonic, symptomatic manner rather than as an acceptable norm for behavior. It is this very perception that motivates some women to seek out therapy.

With the changing status of women in recent years, women have increasingly sought therapy for problems relating to achievement and success. In a previous paper on the fear of success in women (Schecter 1979), it was noted that masochistic defenses appear as a central dynamic in this syndrome: they may surface as the precondition for successful performance; they may function in the service of prohibiting the attainment of success: or they may appear as a necessary sequel of success. This chapter will focus on this syndrome because, as opposed to masochism that appears as a secondary consequence of neurotic behavior, masochism relating to fear of success can be studied in terms of function, purpose, or intentionality.

The term *masochism* is used here in the descriptive sense in which Freud (1924, p.169) refers to it in a discussion of the "unconscious sense of guilt" giving rise to a need for punishment. In moral masochism

> ... the masochist must do what is inexpedient, must act against his own interests, must ruin the prospects which open out to him in the real world and must, perhaps, destroy his own real existence.

Masochistic behavior is consciously or unconsciously oriented toward the achievement of injurious, self-defeating results. Masochism is viewed here as a pathological defense mechanism of the ego subserving a protective function—a response to signal anxiety aimed at warding off a situation perceived as dangerous. What, then, is the ultimate danger for the woman who fears success?

In many women with this syndrome, the key to the nuclear conflict is that success is unconsciously perceived as causing a breach in the primary dyadic bond with the pre-Oedipal mother. The ultimate fear is that success threatens the woman's very survival by anticipation of retaliation from the omnipotent mother in the form of total abandonment, a severance of the mother-daughter bond. Masochistic defenses serve, therefore, to undo the threat of object loss (of the pre-Oedipal mother), and thereby ensure survival for the daughter. They are reparations to the mother or to a symbolic substitute; they are a token submission to ward off retaliation for the taboo success. As Bieber (1953, p. 436) points out, masochistic acts and attitudes are

> oriented to protecting the individual from greater and more painful injury, no matter how realistically injurious the masochistic act itself may be. It is the choice of the lesser evil. It is an unrealistic choice since the masochist brings upon himself real injury to protect himself from a danger that is illusory.

Before elaborating on the psychodynamics that give rise to an illusory danger for the woman and that elicit masochistic defenses as an adaptive coping mechanism, the "success phobia" syndrome requires a brief description.

THE FEAR OF SUCCESS SYNDROME

The conflicts, inhibitions, and anxieties in this syndrome encompass many areas of behavior—vocational, academic, sexual, marital, and maternal. Achievement and success reflect the realization of a long-cherished, deeply rooted wish. Clinically, the presenting manifestations may include the following symptoms: intense anxiety, which may reach panic proportions; marked ambivalence; inhibition of assertion; phobic avoidance of the conflictual area; personalization; detachment; isolation; and emergence of psychosomatic symptoms. The patient may express fears of failing as well as fears of being the object of criticism, humiliation, ridicule, shame, or rejection. Above all, she is often unable to experience any joy or pleasure in success other than transient highs. She may be aware of self-defeating masochistic behavior such as sabotaging her own success or destructively acting out in other spheres or relationships. Attendant upon success, an incapacitating depression may set in. She presents the portrait of a person in mourning, and the message she communicates may be some version of the following: "Now that I have everything I always wanted, I have nothing."

The literature on this syndrome in both men and women has focused primarily on the assumption that fear of success derives from conflicts rooted in the Oedipal phase of development (Freud 1916, Lorand 1931, Bieber 1951, Schuster 1955, Szekely 1960, and Ovesey 1962). Success is perceived as taboo or forbidden because it is equated, unconsciously, with murderous aggression towards the Oedipal rival, and for this hostile intent the patient fears retaliation. The guilt and fear associated with the wish for success lead to an inhibition of assertion; success becomes one's undoing when it is perceived as the instrument that threatens one's very survival. This in turn may lead to phobic behavior. If success is achieved, the need to undo the guilt, via suffering or paying penance, may result in a variety of masochistic adaptations (Engel 1962). Thus, according to this view, masochistic defenses are rooted in Oedipal guilt. Chasseguet-Smirgel (1970) stresses the woman's Oedipal guilt in relation to the father.

It is often pre-Oedipal guilt, however, that underlies masochistic defenses in women with the fear of success syndrome. In the analyses of these women, the rapprochement crisis of the separation-individuation phase is frequently recapitulated as the taboo success is approached. Mahler et al. (1975 p.292) characterizes the rapprochement crisis as:

> A period during the rapprochement subphase [ages fourteen to twenty-four months or beyond] . . . during which the realization of separateness is acute. The toddler's belief in his omnipotence is severely threatened and the environment is coerced as he tries to restore the status quo, which is impossible. Ambitendency, which develops into ambivalence, is often intense; the toddler wants to be united with, and at the same time separate from, mother. Temper tantrums, whining, sad moods, and intense separation reactions are at their height.

At this crossroad, basic anxieties of childhood often coincide: fear of loss of the object's love, fear of loss of the object, and fear of bodily injury, mutilation, or castration. What gives rise to these primitive anxieties? Most consistently, the underlying psychodynamics seem to be that the woman experiences intense envy of the mother's endowed omnipotence; she feels impotent by contrast and believes she cannot achieve success without recourse to some magical reparative maneuver. She wants to be endowed with omnipotence, the magical quality she imagines she requires; she wants to possess both what her mother has and what her mother has denied her (unconscious fantasy). In short, she wishes to exchange places with her mother, to render her mother impotent, to emerge as the undisputed victor in a battle in which she originally felt defeated. The guilt associated with her success frequently has its origins in the unconscious fantasy that she has achieved success at the expense of her mother by robbing her mother of her power, without which her mother cannot survive (mechanism of projective identification). It is as though the woman is unconsciously living in a state of "twinship" with her mother. Every success of hers is equated with a failure for her mother.

Success is achieved via the fantasied "borrowed strength" of the mother in a process designed to destroy the mother. "Success" belongs to the usurper or survivor, and thus the very wish to succeed becomes unconsciously equated with intended, murderous aggression toward the mother. As revealed repeatedly in dreams, the talion law demands "a life for a life." The irrational aspects associated with the fear of retaliation from the mother are a projection of the woman's archaic superego demands. This is the guilt that kills. It is this pre-Oedipal guilt, rooted in the envy of the mother's endowed omnipotence, that gives rise to the most primitive anxieties of childhood, to the recapitulation during analysis of the rapprochement crisis. When this unconscious guilt is tapped in the course of analysis, its reverbations can be shattering for the woman. Frequently, she feels driven to undo the guilt via desperate, impulsive acts aimed at making reparations to the mother. It is at this point that the need for masochistic submission to the mother erupts in full force, in an effort to reinstate the primary dyadic bond.

The woman may signal submission by renouncing her success or its pursuits. She may reenact her submission using an updated symbolic substitute for the mother. For example, when a woman presents her options as "I have to decide between my career and my marriage," frequently the unconscious meaning is "I have to decide between my career and my mother." The woman may also signal submission by entering into "triangulated" bargains to preserve her success. Her submission may be a form of compromise, a kind of peace offering, where she shares her husband (the forbidden success) with her mother or mother-in-law in a triangulated marriage. In a triangulated career, a precondition for the woman's success may that she function in a subordinate position, always deferring to a higher authority. She shares her career (the forbidden success) with her mother by maintaining this submissive position. She may, in time, rebel against this form of self-imposed bondage by reversing the dominant-subordinate roles. In this maneuver, the masochistic adaptation frequently gives way to a dramatic breakthrough of latent sadism in a wish to retaliate against the "oppressor," formerly viewed as the "benefactor."

When the woman assumes a position of authority or power, she may also identify with the aggressor, whom she perceives as the sadistic, malevolent, omnipotent mother. She may "rule the household" (department, committee, institution, and so forth) in an autocratic manner, demanding obeisance. (The pre-Oedipal model precludes the concept of egalitarian co-functioning). She may attempt to vanquish her mother, forcing her subordinates or peers to cringe and bend to her authority. She may "kill off" opponents with biting words (a verbal "breast dentata") or savage criticism intended to reduce her opponents to "nothing," the state of impotency from which she is struggling to emerge. The particular modality is usually a reenactment of the original childhood trauma with a reversal of roles.

Alternatively, the woman may seek out the protection of an idealized, omnipotent husband in order to ward off the intrusive, devouring mother. The intensity, quality, and duration of the woman's Oedipal romance with her thusly idealized father often is directly proportionate to the intensity of her need to escape proportionate clutches of the overpowering and destructive mother whom she feels "possessed" by—the dybbuk, in short. This is the irrational, pathological element. Even if the childhood mother fits this description in reality, it is the adult woman's persecutory anxiety, her own need to perpetuate the "dybbuk-bondage" dyad in her current life, that imprisons her. (A bad breast is still more powerful than no breast.) The intensity of her prolonged, unrealistic, primitive idealization of the father (and via displacement onto any man) is also often a reflection of her persistent envy of the pre-Oedipal mother's omnipotence.

DEVELOPMENTAL ORIGINS OF MASOCHISTIC DEFENSES

The developmental origins of the need for masochistic submission to the mother and its relationship to pre-Oedipal guilt will now be explored. In the analyses of women who evidence this need, it becomes clear, by reconstruction, that masochistic submission is a learned response maintained because it has survival value. A previous study (Schecter 1979) found that two types of family constellations predominate in the history of women with success phobias.

In one group, the daughter is "reserved" for the mother. She is the mother's favorite, the chosen one, lavished upon by the mother, and given special privileges. The daughter, however, always receives the unconscious message from the mother that total loyalty and allegiance are demanded in return. The daughter's relationship with the father is interfered with; he usually is kept at a distance. If the daughter shows any serious interest in marriage or a career, it is taken as a symbol of betrayal of the mother. The mother tends to reestablish with the daughter the original symbiotic unit with her own mother. It is the daughter's function to provide succor for her mother. For some women, this evolves into a psychological marriage with the mother; the mother's relationship with the father appears to be secondary to her primary relationship with the daughter.

The most consistent developmental dynamic underlying masochistic defenses in this group of women is that the mother cannot "take" the daughter's expression of ambivalence, of aggression, or of movement away from the mother. The daughter's separation from her mother becomes a guilt-ridden process, an act of hostile aggression. She experiences the penalty as abandonment by her mother, a severance of the mother-daughter bond. Later in life, with every new step in independent functioning, there remains for her the threat of object loss. What is frequently revived is this pre-Oedipal guilt, that is, the unconscious perception that success is achieved at the expense of her mother. Via symbolic elaboration, goal-oriented endeavor becomes equated with destroying a hostile rival. Just as in childhood, she feels it is safer to inhibit her aggression in order to avoid retaliation from an enraged competitor. This inhibition of aggression is itself a masochistic maneuver since it prevents the attainment of the desired success. For the daughter, any autonomous achievement represents a severance of the symbiotic bond with the mother.

Case Illustration

One patient from this type of family constellation exhibited the following masochistic behavior: After an offer of $5,000 for an artistic commission (the patient had never asked for more than $100 for her work prior to this offer), she almost severed the third and fourth fingers of her left hand (she is left-handed) by closing a car door on her hand. Fortunately, she suffered only minimal nerve damage to one finger. Before she knew the extent of her injury, her first thought was that she would be unable to undertake the commission, at which she felt relieved. After learning the diagnosis, she nevertheless told her mother that she had sustained a hairline fracture of one finger. She claimed that she was angry at her mother and wanted to give her something to worry about. Thus, the hidden wish was to inflict suffering on her mother via her own suffering. Furthermore, she not only was indifferent to the seriousness of her accident but seemed to derive considerable satisfaction from her injury; perhaps because it was also the vehicle for the covert expression of sadistic wishes toward her mother, rendered innocuous via self-suffering.

She was also angry at me for implicitly encouraging her to undertake the commission. It was as if I were creating a wedge between her and her mother, on whom she was partially dependent financially. Although her parents were living together, it was her mother who would surreptitiously slip her money. This secret alliance had existed since childhood. The threat of financial independence overwhelmed the patient with anxiety as it represented a severance of the psychological marriage with her mother.

Prior to analysis, while writing her master's thesis, the patient had sustained three self-inflicted mutilations. She tore away the nail of her right thumb, which required surgical removal after becoming gangrenous (permanent loss); she "accidentally" cut her left foot, allowing it to become seriously infected, and ended up with toxemia; and she fractured a finger in the garage door. Writing her thesis meant the end of student days and the beginning of a professional career. It represented the final step in achieving professional and economic autonomy, a step away from her mother, which filled her with terror. She was phobic about working, and only worked two months during the year following her graduation. Getting her master's degree also represented a taboo success since it symbolized a daring to compete with her mother, who had a master's degree in a related field. Although of superior intelligence, the patient would sometimes have her mother write her essays when she felt too anxious or inadequate.

This patient also had a peptic ulcer, which was symptomatic basically whenever she experienced separation anxiety. Analysis revealed enormous rage toward her mother, usually erupting when the patient felt "betrayed" by her mother, that is, when her mother did not give her precedence over her father and two younger sisters. It was as though her mother were not keeping her part of the bargain, namely, that she permit the patient to share in her endowed omnipotence. This rage was literally reflected in the patient's mouth. She underwent about 10 operations on her teeth and gums. She was finally diagnosed as having Costen's syndrome, which is psychosomatic in origin; gnashing and grinding of her teeth led to splinting, causing pain of the temporomandibular joint, which led to further splinting. This symptom gradually disappeared as the patient's dependency on her mother diminished. With the gradual development of confidence in her own ability to function autonomously, she no longer needed to envy (and therefore to feel guilty toward) her idealized mother. She could give up her mother as the omnipotent introject and view her in a more realistic light.

It is the adult woman's need to perepetuate a hostile, pathological dependency on the mother that imprisons her in a masochistic state of bondage to the omnipotent mother or symbolic substitute. Frequently, the fantasy is to find this magical quality in a husband. The idealized husband becomes heir to the primitive maternal image. The woman may experience masochism as a small price to pay for the benefits derived from living a magically protected life. From this vantage point, masochism may be viewed as a magical reparative maneuver, a vicissitude of infantile omnipotence, perhaps an attempt to restore paradise lost. Masochistic submission to the needs of another person may, indeed, be enjoyed when this maneuver is perceived as the vehicle for achieving power—that is, by sharing in, or fusing with, the endowed omnipotence of the other person.

The underlying fantasy may be that of ultimately controlling, or exerting power over, the all-powerful person. Silverberg (1949) draws attention to this mechanism in his discussion of the "magical maneuver" as a technique for evading the sense of helplessness by the reestablishment of omnipotence through someone else. The person attempts to control external reality by an act of faith (p.390):

> ... somewhere there is someone that is omnipotent, that possesses all power over all things... "I will somehow influence this omnipotent being to exert his, or her, power in my favour"

Bieber (1953) underscores the important role masochistic defenses play in dependent adaptations. He states (p. 445):

> ... the masochistic mechanism is built into the dependency constellation as an integral part of it. Because of this pathological dependency, defenses instead of repairing ego injury add materially in furthering both injury and symptoms ... So long as the need exists to perceive humans with superhuman power so long will there co-exist the need for self-depreciatory and self-destructive masochistic attitudes and behavior.

In the second type of family constellation of women with success phobias, the mother is experienced as cold, critical, and rejecting. The daughter never feels valued by the mother and views the mother as a devalued, inferior person. Unconsciously, however, the daughter is competitive with and envious of the mother, who is perceived as omnipotent. The mother's power lies in what she has withheld from the daughter—her love, nurturing, and support. The daughter's primary relationship is usually with the father, who is experienced as more tender, nurturing, and supportive. The daughter is frequently guilt-ridden over her relationship with her father, since she perceives it as existing at the expense of her mother.

A central dynamic underlying masochistic defenses in this group of women revolves around the issue of premature separation from the mother. In consequence, the daughter develops a "false self," as reflected in a facade of self-sufficiency and a pseudoindependence. It is the daughter's burden to be the "good enough" child for the mother, to meet the needs of the mother by prematurely detaching from her. Some women report that they felt they had to be "mute," "out of the way." Thus, we see the inhibition of assertion in status nascendi. This inhibition has survival value as long as the child is realistically helpless and dependent on the mother. What erupts later on in life, as the woman is attempting to achieve the desired success, is an excessive dependency on the mother or substitute, a feeling that she cannot rely on her own abilities to achieve her goals. She feels cheated in life, as though her mother deprived her of the basic goods of life. The daughter tends to blame herself for the mother's emotional unavailability. Problems of low self-esteem and a basic depressive mood are common sequelae of this type of maternal deprivation. The daughter frequently identifies with the mother's perceived attitude toward her; that is, she treats herself as an object of hatred, as a contemptuous object, to be dealt with brutally. Aggression toward the mother is turned against the self, laying the basis for masochistic character traits.

Mahler (1966, p.162) describes some of the developmental issues during the rapprochement subphase that set the stage for the dynamics underlying masochistic submission:

> ... the collapse of the child's belief in his own omnipotence, with his uncertainty about the emotional availability of the parents, creates the so-called "hostile dependency" upon and ambivalence toward the parents. This ambivalence seems to call for the early pathological defense mechanisms of splitting the good and bad mother images and of turning aggression against the self; these result in a feeling of helplessness, which, as Bibring (1953) has emphasized, creates the basic depressive affect.

If the mother is, in reality, emotionally unavailable and cannot respond adequately to the daughter's active approach behavior, the daughter may experience a depletion of "confident expectation" and "basic trust," accompanied by an acute loss of self-esteem. This may lead to "a masochistic surrender of the child's own indidviduality, precocious over-identification, pseudo self-sufficiency, and flattened affective reactivity" (Mahler 1966, p.167). Menaker (1953) also emphasizes the crucial role of the pre-Oedipal mother-daughter relationship in the subsequent evolution of masochistic defenses in women.

In "Female Sexuality" (1931, p. 230–231) Freud stresses the importance of the pre-Oedipal phase for the girl, stating that both the intensity and duration of the girl's pre-Oedipal attachment to the mother merit special consideration:

> We see, then, that the phase of exclusive attachment to the mother, which may be called the *pre-Oedipus* phase, possesses a far greater importance in women than it can have in men. Many phenomena of female sexual life which were not properly understood before can be fully explained by reference to this phase. Long ago, for instance, we noticed that many women who have chosen their husband on the model of their father, or have put him in their father's place, nevertheless repeat towards him, in their married life, their bad relations with their mother.

The husband of such a woman was meant to be the inheritor of her relation to her father, but in reality he became the inheritor of her relation to her mother. This is easily explained as an obvious case of regression. Her relation to her mother was the original one, and her attachment to her father was built up on it, and now, in marriage, the original relation emerges from repression. For the main content of her development to womanhood lay in the carrying over of her affective object attachments from her mother to her father.

With many women we have the impression that their years of maturity are occupied by a struggle with their husband, just as their youth was spent in a struggle with their mother. In the light of the previous discussions we shall conclude that their hostile attitude to their mother is not a consequence of the rivalry implicit in the Oedipus complex, but originates from the preceding phase and has merely been reinforced and exploited in the Oedipus situation. And actual analytic examination confirms this view.

A woman may be more vulnerable than a man to reexperiencing guilt and retaliation on a pre-Oedipal level because the woman's Oedipal rival is also her pre-Oedipal protector. This is not the case for men. Moreover, the mother continues to be the girl's primary source of identification, on the basis of gender, whereas the boy normally disidentifies with the mother during the separation-individuation phase (Greenson 1968). In view of this, the task of separating and individuating may be more problematic for the girl. However, in terms of consolidation of gender identity, the boy's psychosexual development may be more so.

SUMMARY

Loewenstein (1957, p. 230) has referred to masochism as "the weapon of the weak—i.e., of every child—faced with danger of human aggression." From the child's attempt to preserve parental love in the face of aggression, Loewenstein postulates "seduction of the aggressor" as a forerunner of a masochistic mechanism. This mechanism appears as a central dynamic in women with success phobias. For these women, success is unconsciously perceived as an act of hostile aggression toward the mother, for which they fear retaliation. Masochistic submission to the mother or substitute serves to ward off retaliation from the pre-Oedipal mother in the form of total abandonment, a severance of the mother-daughter bond. Thus, masochistic defenses serve to undo the threat of object loss, thereby ensuring survival for the woman. They are an invariable aspect of the success phobia syndrome when an unconscious sense of guilt is a central dynamic.

In contrast to the predominant focus in the literature on this syndrome, which highlights the theoretical assumption that masochistic defenses are rooted in Oedipal guilt, it is suggested that pre-Oedipal guilt underlies masochistic defenses to a greater extent than is generally assumed. It is believed that this psychodynamic analysis of masochism in success phobias can be illustrated in other masochistic constellations as well.

Perhaps what a woman truly wants is her mother's blessing and permission (in girlhood) to be a separate, autonomous woman, to have the "rites of passage" at a future point in her life. To the extent that a woman remains in bondage to the imago of an all-powerful mother on whom she still feels dependent for survival, she is vulnerable to falling back on masochistic defenses. Contrary to Genesis, which may be regarded perhaps as a phylogenetic fable reflecting on ontogenetic formulation, it might be suggested that for both man and woman, to the extent that one has freed oneself from living a life in bondage to any higher authority, and to the extent that one has truly separated from one's own mother and father, one is protected from imprisonment in a life devoted to masochism, as portrayed in Genesis.

NOTE

[1]A portion of this chapter is reprinted with permission of John Wiley & Sons, Inc., from "Fear of Success in Women: A Psychodynamic Reconstruction," *Journal of the American Academy of Psychoanalysis*, 7:33–43, 1979, by Doreen Schecter. Copyright 1979 by John Wiley & Sons, Inc.

REFERENCES

Bibring, E. (1953), The mechanism of depression, in *Affective Disorders*, P. Greenacre, ed., International Universities Press, New York, 13–48.

Bieber, I. (1951), Pathological boredom and inertia, *Am. J. Psychother.*, 5:714–722.

Bieber, I. (1953), The meaning of masochism, *Am. J. Psychother.*, 7:433–448.

Bonaparte, M. (1935), Passivity, masochism and femininity, in *Female Sexuality*, International Universities Press, New York, 169–178.

Chasseguet-Smirgel, J., ed. (1970), Feminine guilt and the Oedipus complex, in *Female Sexuality: New Psychoanalytic Views*, University of Michigan Press, Ann Arbor, 94–134.

Deutsch, H. (1944), Feminine masochism, in *The Psychology of Women*, Vol. 1, Grune & Stratton, New York, 239–278.

Engel, G. (1962), Guilt, pain, and success, *Psychosom. Med.*, 24:37–48.

Freud, S. (1916), Some character types met with in psychoanalytic work: II. Those wrecked by success, *Standard Edition*, Vol. 14, Hogarth Press, London, 1957, 316–331.

Freud, S. (1924), The economic problem of masochism, *Standard Edition*, Vol. 19, Hogarth Press, London, 1961, 159–170.

Freud, S. (1931), Female sexuality, *Standard Edition*, Vol. 21, Hogarth Press, London, 1961, 225–243.

Greenson, R. (1968), Dis-identifying from mother: Its special importance for the boy, *Int. J. Psychoanal.*, 49:370–374.

Loewenstein, R. (1957), A contribution to the psychoanalytic theory of masochism, *J. Amer. Psychoanal. Assn.*, 5:197–234.

Lorand, S. (1931), "Success" neuroses, in *Clinical Studies in Psychoanalysis*, International Universities Press, New York, 1950, 245–254.

Mahler, M. (1966), Notes on the development of basic moods: The depressive affect, in *Psychoanalysis—A General Psychology*, R. Loewenstein et al., eds., International Universities Press, New York, 152–168.

Mahler, M. et al., (1975), *The Psychological Birth of the Human Infant*, Basic Books, New York.

Menaker, E. (1953), Masochism—A defense reaction of the ego, *Psychoanal. Quart.*, 22:205–220.

Ovesey, L. (1962), Fear of vocational success, *Arch. Gen. Psychiat.*, 7:82–92.

Schecter, D. (1979), Fear of success in women: A psychodynamic reconstruction, *J. Am. Acad. Psychoanal.*, 7:33–43.

Schuster, D. (1955), On the fear of success, *Psychiat. Q.*, 29:412–420.

Silverberg, W. (1949), The factor of omnipotence in neurosis, *Psychiatry*, 12:387–398.

Szekely, L. (1960), Success, success neurosis and the self, *Br. J. Med. Psychol.*, 33:45–51.

14

AN ASPECT OF MASOCHISM
IN WOMEN—FEAR OF SUCCESS:
SOME INTRAPSYCHIC
DIMENSIONS AND
THERAPEUTIC IMPLICATIONS

ESTHER GREENBAUM, M.D.
New York Medical College and
New York University School of Medicine

It is in the area of feminine psychology that most exciting work is going on, and it is in this area that new knowledge and new formulations have occurred. This fact coincides with the generally made observation that also in our society at large the changes made in the condition of women is the most revolutionary happening of our times.

Research on brain physiology, on sex hormonal influences on the brain centers, and on early determinants of core gender identity have greatly contributed to our understanding of biological givens of female sexuality and gender identity (Money 1972 and Stoller 1968). Direct clinical observation and research on early child development and, particularly, the study of pre-Oedipal relationships have enriched our insights into the early formation of gender identity in the little girl. Moreover, our detailed knowledge of ego psychology and of interpersonal dyadic and traingulated relationships as well as our refined observations of family interactions have all made it possible to gain better insights into and to make better formulations about psychology and individuality of women.

Most analysts from different schools of thought have now accepted that femininity is primary and positive and that it is not secondary to a male phase in the little girl and not a compensation for feeling injured and deprived of the penis. The same acceptance has been given to the idea that motherhood is normally a primary feminine desire and not a substitute for a missing penis. Equally, all of us, it seems, have finally arrived at the conclusion, which some of us knew all along, that women have a superego that is as important and strong as the superego of the man. The concepts of masochism and passivity are also being discussed and revised, and one talks now about masochism in women and not feminine masochism (Blum 1976).

All of this has happened because of changes in our knowledge of biology, genetics, endocrinology, psychology, and psychoanalysis but also, to a great extent, because of changes in our society, including struggles for equality, opportunity for underprivileged groups, and, most important, the women's movement is expressing some of the aspirations and struggles of women.

It is necessary, however, to recognize that new ideas do not suddenly arise on the scene. Just as maturation of an individual proceeds quietly at times and then by spurts, so does the development of certain new concepts. There are quiescent times, when slow, painstaking work is going on; there are intense searching, experimenting, observing, and debating occurring in many related fields, and then there is a confluence of findings from different sources, leading to new insights and formulations.

Sometimes these new insights are arrived at by some people much earlier than others, while the majority still stick to old ideas. So it was with the concepts on the psychology of women. Freud made many important observations on the psychology of his women patients and then drew conclusions that were subject to much controversy. He felt that women's psychology was a "dark mysterious continent," and he did not know "what woman wants." He awaited the answers from more biological knowledge and from women analysts who could throw light on this dark continent.

When Freud wrote his papers on feminine psychology (1925, 1931, and 1933), there was great ferment in the psychoanalytic circles on the theme. Some analysts completely agreed with his ideas (Deutsch 1944 and Bonaparte 1953). Some agreed but contributed some important new observations (Lampl-deGroot 1928). Some definitely disagreed and formulated those ideas that are precursors of our ideas of today. Among them were Jones (1927), Klein (1928), and Horney (1926), the latter of whom—very early was able to formulate the primacy of femininity, the defensive meaning of penis envy, and the cultural determinants of feminine characteristics of personality.

The vigorous discussion of that time continued in some countries and in some circles, but in the ranks of the American Psychoanalytic Association, the controversy, except on the part of a few analysts (Greenacre 1950 and Zilboorg 1944), died down. It has resumed within the association only in the last ten years.

The vigorous discussions of the early times in the psychoanalytic movement continued, however, in the ranks of other psychoanalytic groups: the American Institute of Psychoanalysis (Horney), the William Alanson White Institute, and the Psychoanalytic Division of the New York Medical College. The latter organized a symposium on feminine psychology as early as March 1950 and invited members of other psychoanalytic societies, including members of the New York Psychoanalytic Institute, who came and debated before a filled auditorium the ideas on female psychology.

One cannot, once and for all, define women's psychology. It is a constantly changing concept with developmental and historical dimensions to it. Only the biological part of it is "eternally feminine," remaining more or less the same. The rest changes according to the times and the roles predominant in a specific society and according to the family in which a particular child is growing up.

MASOCHISM IN WOMEN

The topic of masochism, so frequently mentioned in regard to women, has always had a fascination for many people. Writers, philosophers, psychiatrists, and psychoanalysts have pondered about its origins, meanings, and ramifications.

It is indeed an intriguing question why one should choose or accept suffering as a response to life's problems. Pain and suffering are existentially part of life. The ways of coping with them are numerous, depending on developmental factors of the individual, on family relationships, on social factors, and on historical times, with the varying ideals of accepting suffering—the martyr ideal—or of fighting and overcoming it—the heroic ideal. The question still remains why some people—and more so women—would accept being defeated, being punished, and suffering as a response to life's vicissitudes.

In the psychoanalytic literature, various answers can be found: Freud saw in masochism the expression of an instinctual force—the workings of the death instinct. Later he recognized the role of aggression in the genesis of masochism. He considered that female sexuality and psychology were masochistic and talked about feminine masochism. His disciple Deutch (1944) expanded on this idea. Other psychoanalysts, such as Horney (1926), Jones (1927), and Zilboorg (1944), ascribed masochism in women to societal factors.

Psychoanalysts working in the theoretical framework of ego psychology or adaptational theories thought of masochism as a defense against a greater evil or a mechanism of adaptation to preserve a bond to a "needed" person or to placate an enemy. Menaker (1953) and Schecter

(1978) have described masochism in women from a point of view of pathological defense. Bieber (1953) saw in it a neurotic adaptation or an adaptation to an illusory threat. Blum (1976) described masochism in women as originating from heightened aggression due to a defective early mother-child relationship. The manifestations of masochism in the form of self-defeat, chronic unhappiness, somatizations, and depression bring untold suffering to women and impede the movement toward productivity, individuation and equality.

The influence of masochism has its impact not only on the current life of women but also on the generation of children brought up by masochistic mothers. In our present-day society, one of the manifestations of masochism is fear of success.

THE FEAR OF SUCCESS

Since today success is more attainable for women, more is also heard about the complications on the way to this goal. The fear of success has become a topic that one reads about in the psychiatric and psychoanalytic literature as well as in sociological and psychological publications.

First, one needs some consensus about the definition of success. One could say that it is the attainment of one's aspirations in the professional and private areas of one's life. One could use a more restricted definition and consider *success* the realization of one's goals in work and the recognition of this realization by some of one's peers.

Whatever definition one chooses, whether it is of a professional work or a life fulfillment, whether it is according to societal norms or according to subjective norms, it must be recognized that there is much more talk lately about success and the fear of success *in women*. This, of course, should not surprise us in view of the changes that have occurred in the status of women, in their aspirations and in the possibilities for fulfillment.

Women have always worked and some have engaged in professional work against great odds. Many women were capable and wanted to engage in professional work but gave up because of societal difficulties. Those societal taboos, even if lifted to some degree in our time and in some countries, still exercise a great influence because they remain like a scar in the psyche of women for a long time, interfering with success.

No wonder, then, that the interest in the psychoanalytic literature has been on those factors that present obstacles to the achievement of success in spite of societal and economic changes. In other words, inspite of the greater permissiveness of society to the women's entry into the world of success, obstacles arise within the woman from the deep layers of her unconscious.

To elucidate those factors that lead to success or to fear of it, studies have been conducted on:

• Economic and social factors, role models, and support systems.

• Familial constellations supporting or interfering with success

• Developmental factors promoting or inhibiting success

• Clarifying the factors promoting or interfering with success (Tressemer 1977)

The focus of this chapter will be on:

• The developmental stage of separation-individuation and its contribution to the establishment of the autonomy so necessary in the pursuit of success

• The formation of the ego ideal and self-esteem and its importance for work and success

• Some therapeutic implications in patients who suffer from fear of success

Success phobias take various forms and have a multitude of origins. In clinical practice, patients have been seen who were not able to achieve success because of societal taboos, because of unresolved Oedipal conflicts, or because of pre-Oedipal conflicts. Some were able to achieve success but paid a high price in anxiety, depression, or somatic symptoms, as can be seen in the following clinical example:

A 32-year-old married woman was very competent and successful in her profession. She suffered from severe anxiety, phobias, and somatizations. Inspite of almost crippling episodes of those various manifestations of her anxiety, she was able to pursue her studies, her work, and her family life, being successful in all areas but paying an enormous price in suffering.
One of the interesting aspects of her life history was the fact that her mother as well as her father had high achievement ideals for her. She had the unlimited admiration of her father and the capacity from a very early age to expand the boundaries of her environment by seeking out significant people in the outside world to become her models, friends, and protectors.

Other patients were on the way to achieving success but for short periods only, defeating themselves again and again:

A young, talented, intelligent women had aspirations to become a musician and achieved some success in it before her children were born. As soon as it became possible for her, she tried to re-enter the field of music and make a career of it. In spite of some successes and very diligent work, she was plagued by guilt, by doubts, and by suffering. She would do well for a while and then be convinced that punishment was due and would fall back into inactivity and pessimism.

One of the predisposing elements in her fear of success was the guilt toward her mother, who never succeeded in her aspirations for herself. Another element was the conflicting identifications with the parental ideals. On one hand, she identified with the ideal of excellence and creativity, and on the other hand, with the fear of being a failure and needing the protection of a strong man. The conflict, until resolved, interfered with her aspirations.

Then there were those patients who had dreams of success but settled for failure because the fear of punishment, the price to pay in suffering, seemed too high:

A 40-year-old woman, in spite of her good intelligence, excellent education, and artistic ability, could not achieve success in work. She started several times and showed great promise but gave up, burdened by anxiety guilt originating from an early conflict in the mother-daughter relationship.

She was, she believed, destined to redress her mother's miseries. She gave up her own aspirations in her private and professional life, pursuing an illusory fantasy of making her depressed, masochistic mother happy.

Succeeding in work was, in her mind, abandoning the chance to have for once, a good relationship with her mother. She kept herself ready for it. In reality, this was a fantasy that was never to be achieved and meanwhile was ruining the life of this talented woman.

The dynamics in each preceding case were different, and the origins were to be found in all phases of the developmental process and also in the social and cultural environment in which this process evolved.

The Significance of the Rapprochement Phase

In some patients, the rapprochement phase experience is of great importance. Mahler (1968) described subphases of the separation-individuation and particularly focused on the significance of the rapprochement crisis for healthy as well as for pathological states such as borderline conditions and narcissistic personality disturbances.

Why is this period so important for the future health of the woman and why, particularly, is her achieving a sense of autonomy so important for her later motivation for success? What happens to the little girl during this period?

According to current research done by Galenson and Roiphe (1976), Stoller (1968), and so forth this phase is considered a nodal point in the development of gender identity as well as of the sense of self and of autonomy.

After a period of normal autism symbiosis and of differentiation of practicing, the little girl (18-24 months) becomes aware of her difference from boys and of her separateness from others, particularly her mother. Her mood changes from one of exuberance and grandiosity—"my mother is all powerful and I am all powerful"—to a more subdued, hesitant mood. She may become fearful of loss of mother or of her love.

At this time, she needs reassurance, affection, and empathy. She may turn to the mother, cling to her, become infantile again, and demand a great deal of attention. Because of her cognitive and her maturational development, she becomes aware of her separateness. If the mother is not available, she may experience rage and envy, particularly if this desired attention is available for someone else. This rage and envy may produce fear of retaliation. There is a real fear of being destroyed or abandoned.

This is the rapprochement crisis when traversed normally, when the mother's availability leads to a healthy outcome. The little girl's belief in her omnipotence should not be suddenly defeated but should lead to an enjoyment of the growing strides towards autonomy. The little girl at this time needs the closeness of the mother for an affirmation of her growing sense of self and of her identity, including her gender identity. It is important that the mother be tolerant of the child's growing ambivalence, anger, defiance, and rage outbursts. All that becomes very important later when the adult woman is afraid to experience or express her aggression—a very important factor in fear of success. If the little girl has the acceptance and empathy availability of the mother at this time, she can gain a sense of separateness, autonomy, individuality, and self-esteem. If everything goes well, she affirms her basic trust and gives up her grandiosity for a more realistic sense of self.

At this particular time she may turn away from mother and temporarily turn to father and then come back for tenderness, closeness, and affirmation. Again it must be asked why this period is so very important for the woman's future capacity to be successful in work and in love.

It is becoming clear that some of the characteristics that help women to achieve success are a clear sense of reality, a sense of autonomy, a reliance on one's own judgment, and a capacity to bear adversity without being swayed away from one's goal. When the lives of successful women are examined, all those characteristics are found to be present.

Two of the psychological characteristics found in those who succeed have been described as (Kundsin 1974):

- The ability to function and not react badly to the view of being regarded as deviant

- The ability to function autonomously, not to give up, to carry on independently (Some successful women do not collapse when meeting disagreement or adversity.)

Other factors in successful women were described as:

- The favorable facilitating environment establishing trust, encouraging autonomy, significant people available for identification
- fathers' and mothers' positive attitudes toward professionalism
- Order of siblings—first-born were more successful
- Successful fathers and mothers; successful and supportive fathers who are not insecure about their gender and not threatened by successful wives

The outcome of the rapprochement period, being very important in the establishment of separation-individuation, promotes autonomy, without which it is impossible to be a well-functioning, successful, individual.

Various possibilities can occur. Some mothers, because of their own need to prolong the symbiotic relationship, do not allow any separation to occur. Some mothers can accept the separation and like the freedom that the child has acquired to move away from them, but when the little girl moves back in the rapprochement phase and becomes clinging and infantile again, cranky, and angry, the mother is not able to tolerate it, as in the following clinical example:

A 28-year-old competent, empathic mother enjoyed her little girl very much when she entered the developmental stage of differentiation and practicing. She loved her independence and admired her daring, her ability, her enthusiasm, and also her capacity to do so well at a distance from mother. When the little girl entered the rapprochement phase and became, again, clinging, needing the mother's presence, cranky, and whiny, the mother could not stand it, particularly that this period of the little girl's life also coincided with the birth of a little sister. Between the mother and daughter, a battle started of rages, tears, and temper tantrums that lasted for a long time and had some deep effects on the personality of the little girl.

Sometimes the mother cannot tolerate this phase because of her own unconscious conflicts, and sometimes she is not available because of a mixture of her intrapsychic conflicts and reality factors such as a new pregnancy, the birth of a new child, illness, marital discord, or lack of family support. The mother who is herself harassed, angry, and impatient reacts to her daughter's renewed clinging with rejection. Under those circumstances, the little girl may become prematurely independent but also angry, with a shattered self-esteem and a feeling of being pseudoindependent (developing, later, the so-called as-if personality).

The resolution of the rapprochement phase depends also on the availability of the father, on his personality, and on his relationship to the mother and to his daughter. The questions that should be asked about the father are as follows: Is he there? Is he ready to have his little daughter turn to him? Can he give her acceptance, support, and care without becoming too seductive and without becoming neglectful and competitive with mother? In some cases, the father is not successful in this, as in the following clinical example:

> The father in this family of three was not able to give the necessary support to his wife when she was pregnant with her little daughter. He felt aloof and abandoned and neglected his wife.
> When his little girl grew into an intelligent, lovely little charmer, he gave her all his attention, siding with her in her disputes with her mother and stating openly that she was the one to give him pleasure in life and, were it not for her, he would leave the family. He not only put her up as a rival to her mother but also competed with his wife for the little girl's love.

Thus, a situation was created for the little girl in which she could not love her father without guilt, and she felt guilty to feel resentment against her mother. She already felt that she was doing better with her father than was her mother. It is this kind of constellation that may later create trouble for the little girl when she is trying to achieve success in love and work.

Does the father triumph in his possession of his little girl and consider her better, prettier, and more precious than her mother? Or is he able together with the mother, to share and delight in caring for her? Sometimes the father is too weak and the mother too overpowering. There is no possibility of turning to father; the little girl has to suppress her anger and submit to mother.

After having gone through the separation-individuation phase, the little girl can embark on her journey as a separate independent person. She can start to be what she can eventually become, and what she can become is dependent on herself, on her parents and their relationship, on their conscious and unconscious values for her, and also on the society and the time in which the little girl grows up to be a woman who is going to be faced with the task to achieve her aspirations.

This leads to another point that will be discussed: the ego ideal and its importance to succeeding in one's life's wish.

The Ego Ideal in Women

There has been a lot of controversy in psychoanalytic literature on the superego and ego ideal in women and whether they are weaker than and inferior to that in men. Lately, this controversy has been laid to rest with the recognition that the superego and ego ideal of women are perhaps different but not inferior. However, the question still remains how the ego ideal of women is formed and what bearing it has on achieving success later.

Again, the histories of successful women must be examined, and it must be recognized that very early in their lives they had aspirations for achievement and were determined to realize their goals (Yallow 1978).

How, then, does this ego ideal get formed?

In her earliest years, it is from the mother mostly that the little girl forms her ego ideal. She endows her with powers and ideal qualities. This is what she feels that she is part of, and later, when she starts to feel separate, this is what she admires or envies and longs to become. As a girl gets older, the ego ideal is influenced by the father, whose importance for the girl's later success in life is more and more recognized by other family members, by admired people (by mother's or father's admired people), by neighbors, and by societal models and values. (Names of children very often reflect the valued and admired literary or political figures.)

The ego ideal contains part of the identity theme that the parents had set for their child. The ego ideal is the conglomerate of one's image of the ideal child, ideal wife, ideal mother, and ideal member of society. It contains one's aspirations in love and in work. It is no wonder that the ego ideal is so important in what one is going to become in the private and professional sphere of life.

In our times, the ego ideal has undergone many changes. It is no more the helpless, suffering, submissive, self-sacrificing, and charming woman; the roles and models have changed.

What seems to be of crucial importance is to ask the following: Did the particular woman form her ego ideal in identification with a mother who was empathic, independent, and resourceful, or did she identify with a weak, devalued, or depressed mother? Does the woman, while trying to free herself from old identification, get involved in guilt, self-punishment, and defeat which interfere with the realization of success? It also has to be asked if the aspirations for success were acquired in identification with the father's work and his values, does that identification involve the woman in conflict and confusion? Is the little girl or the older girl or the adolescent permitted to use her environment, which in every way she feels, to promote her growth? Is she permitted, without having to feel guilty, to admire members outside her family and to identify with them? Or does she do it and feel so guilty that she is forever enmeshed in a conflict of loyalties?

It is also important to inquire whether the woman's goal is along traditional lines in accordance with societal values or whether she dares to be autonomous, even if it is not in conformity with present-day norms. The life histories of successful women in science, art, and literature indicate that those women were able to go against the traditional trend and did not need conformity as much as others.

To know the influences, the identifications, and the counteridentifications that have led to a certain outcome, the very specific constellation of the family must be kept in mind. It must be known that nothing exists in isolation, not even the most intimate of relationships, the dyadic mother-child relationship. The mother's feelings and attitudes depend on her own mothering experience, on her husband, and on society. It is assumed that a mother who is herself confident, trusting, empathic, and accepting of her own identity and femaleness can also promote autonomy and achievement in her daughter without too much guilt and fear. The attitude of the father is also a very important part of the growth and development of self-esteem and the ability of women to succeed. Very often it is from the father that she acquires her inspirations, her ideals, and her drive to achieve in the work world. If he is interested in her intelligence, her studies, her competence, and her femaleness, she can grow into a competent woman sure of her identity. Often, if he only admires her mind and her performance but is indifferent to her gender identity, she may feel conflicted and unable to reconcile the different aspects of herself.

Therapeutic Implications

In conclusion, a few remarks will be made on therapy with patients who suffer from fear of success.

It is very important to clarify what the factors are that stand in the way of success. Is it societal pressures with which the patient is unable to cope and why? Are there intrapsychic obstacles such as dealing with one's aggression, one's narcissistic needs, or one's conflicting identifications? Are the intrapsychic conflicts conscious or are they unconscious? Do they stem from pre-Oedipal, Oedipal, or later strata of development? Do the conflicts go back to unresolved rage and envy at the pre-Oedipal mother? Are they conflicts that are never acknowledged and never solved but re-enacted again and again with people at work, to the detriment of the patient's success?

In all those cases, proper assessment is important, and according to the assessment, appropriate therapeutic work can be done.

In cases of fear of success where it can be traced to pre-Oedipal conflicts with mother and a pathologic separation-individuation phase, these patients often regress in their analysis and, in a transferential manner, re-enact the rapprochement crisis with their analyst. From being strong, effective, capable women they suddenly may feel helpless, clinging, demanding a lot of closeness, and frightened, as if afraid to lose us. The crux of analysis with such patients is how much regression, how much clinging, and how much rapprochement to tolerate without infantilizing the patient, and how quickly one can promote separation.

All such patients infringe on our own feelings and old conflicts with success as well as our feelings with separation and individuation. Analysts could become very intense in promoting rapprochement in empathy with the patient, playing the role of the all-giving good mother, either the mother we wished we had or a mother in competition with the patient's mother. Sometimes we could become frightened by the patient's need to regress and could attempt to skip over that need of the patient and hurry the patient towards premature self-assertion. We may also be caught in the general struggle of women for equality and the right to succeed and so may unwittingly fight the women's struggle through our patients. Similarly, we may act out our own traumatic experiences with success and may try to redress our own feelings of vicitmization. All that is unavoidable, but what is important is that we be aware of our countertransference feelings and use them to the benefit of the patient.

As in all therapy, besides insight and the working through process, there is identification with the analyst going on. The patient identifies with some aspects of the analyst's attitudes and values and with those functions where the analyst is an autonomous human being, works, and does not seem to be afraid of success. For some women patients who have lacked the model of a successful woman, to work with one is in itself very important.

To quote Adrienne Rich, writing about mothers and daughters (1976): "The most notable fact that our culture imprints on woman is the sense of our limits. The most important thing one woman can do for another is to illuminate and expand her sense of actual possibilities." To paraphrase those quotations, even though the analytic relationship is not the same as a mother-daughter relationship, the example of an analyst who is not superhuman but simply human and vulnerable who accepts adversities and victories and has had to struggle to be where she is now is a good model for a woman patient who suffers from success phobias.

REFERENCES

Bonaparte, M. (1953) *Female Sexuality.* New York: International Universities Press.

Bieber, I. (1966) Sadism and Masochism In: *American Handbook of Psychiatry*, ed. S Arieti, New York: Basic Books, 256–272.

Blum, H. (1976) Masochism and Ego Ideal and the Psychology of Women, *J. Amer. Psychoanal. Ass.*, Vol. 24, 157–191.

Deutch, H. (1944) *The Psychology of Women*, New York: Grune & Stratton.

Freud, S. (1925) Some Psychical Consequences of the Anatomical Distinction between Two Sexes, *Standard Edition* 19. London: Hogarth Press, 1961.

Freud, S. (1931) Female Sexuality, *Standard Edition* 21. London: Hogarth Press, 1961.

Freud, S. (1933) Femininity, *Standard Edition* 22. London: Hogarth Press, 1964.

Galenson, E. and Roiphe, H. (1976) Some Suggested Revisions concerning Early Female Development, *J. Amer. Psychoanal. Ass.*, Vol. 24, 29–57.

Greenacre, P. (1950) Special Problems of Early Female Sexual Development, in *Trauma Growth and Personality*. New York: International Universities Press, 1969.

Horney, K. (1926) The Flight from Womanhood, in *Feminine Psychology*, H. Kelman, Ed. New York: Norton, 1967.

Jones, E. (1927) The Early Development of Female Sexuality, *International J. Psychoanal.*, N.8, 459–472.

Klein, M. (1928) Early Stages of the Oedipal Complex, in *Psychoanalysis of Children*. New York: Grove, 1960.

Kundsin, R. P. (1974) *Women and Success*. New York: William Morrow.

Lampl-deGroot (1928) The Evolution of the Oedipus Conflict in Women. *Internat. J. Psychoanal.*, 332–345.

Mahler, M. (1968) *On Human Symbiosis and the Vicissitudes of Individuation*. New York: International Universities Press.

Money, J. (1972) *Man and Woman Boy and Girl*. Baltimore: The Johns Hopkins University Press.

Menaker, (1953) Masochism a Defense Reaction of the Ego, *Psychoanal. Quart.*, Vol. 22, 205–220.

Tressemer, D. (1977) *Fear of Success*. New York: W. W. Norton and Co.

Stoller, R. J. (1968) *Sex and Gender*. New York: Science House.

Schecter, D. (1978) Success Phobias. Presented at the Society of Medical Psychoanalysts, January 18, 1978.

Zilboorg, G. (1944) Masculaine and Feminine, *Psychiatry*, No. 7, 257–296.

Yallow, R. (1978) A Mme. Curie from the Bronx, *New York Times Magazine*, April 9, 1978.

INDEX